SAVED

SAVED

A War Reporter's Mission
to Make It Home

BENJAMIN HALL

HARPER

An Imprint of HarperCollins*Publishers*

HB 02.06.2023 0936

SAVED. Copyright © 2023 by Benjamin Hall. All rights reserved.
Printed in the United States of America. No part of this book
may be used or reproduced in any manner whatsoever without
written permission except in the case of brief quotations
embodied in critical articles and reviews. For information, address
HarperCollins Publishers, 195 Broadway, New York, NY 10007.

HarperCollins books may be purchased for educational, business,
or sales promotional use. For information, please email the
Special Markets Department at SPsales@harpercollins.com.

FIRST EDITION

Designed by Nancy Singer

Library of Congress Cataloging-in-Publication
Data has been applied for.

ISBN 978-0-06-330966-1

23 24 25 26 27 LBC 8 7 6 5 4

To my wife, Alicia, and my daughters, Honor, Iris, and Hero. You are the reasons I am here today, and I love you more than I can hope to convey.

And to the casualties of wars everywhere—the people who have given so much and shown such extraordinary courage, all in the fight to make this world a better place. Your losses and sacrifices will never be forgotten.

CONTENTS

SAVED

PROLOGUE

The first explosion tore through a stand of pine-birch trees twenty feet in front of us, and we'd barely turned to look before the second bomb whistled overhead and landed right next to us and everything went dark.

Not just dark—black. Deep, infinite blackness. A void in which no thought or awareness seemed possible. If I had the slightest hint of consciousness, it was a distant sense of shock waves, and the feeling that every part of my body—bones, organs, sinew, my soul—had been knocked out of me, leaving behind a useless husk.

I was all but dead.

But then—

—improbably, out of this crippling nothingness, a figure came through and I heard a familiar voice, as real as anything I'd ever known:

Daddy, you've got to get out of the car.

• • •

Twenty days before these bombs exploded in the abandoned ruins of a village near Kyiv, I buried my father who died at the age of eighty-nine, in a lovely cemetery at the foot of San Francisco's San Bruno Mountains.

His six children gathered in a chapel of carved white granite, stood in front of a coffin draped in the Stars and Stripes, and took turns telling stories about him. There were many stories to tell. After all, my father had, as one obituary put it, "stayed with tribes in Venezuela, fished in the Amazon, climbed volcanoes in Ethiopia, went birding in the Galapagos and rode a hot-air balloon through Burma."

He had lived a big, long life.

The story that best defined my father, however, was the story of the Battle of Manila—perhaps the bloodiest, deadliest, most savage engagement in all of World War II. The battle that fulfilled General Douglas MacArthur's historic promise to return to the Philippines. The battle that ended a hellish three-year Japanese occupation during which at least one hundred thousand Filipinos were killed in godless acts of mass murder. The battle that left more than six thousand U.S. soldiers dead or wounded.

My father, Roderick Hall, was there for all of it. He was twelve.

Rod was born in Manila to a Scottish father and a Filipino mother and lived there happily until December 1941, when Japan's Fourteenth Army landed on Batan Island and opened its merciless campaign to conquer the country.

The Japanese held his father—my grandfather—as a noncombatant prisoner at the harsh Santo Tomas Internment Camp for three years. Rod's mother, grandmother, aunt, and uncle were rounded up and, it was presumed, eventually killed—he never saw or heard from them again.

Left in charge of his three younger siblings, my father managed to survive and keep his siblings safe for nearly four years, long enough for American forces, under the command of General MacArthur, to storm the shores and liberate Manila in early 1945 (my great-uncle Colonel Joseph McMicking was on MacArthur's staff, walked ashore with him on a Leyte beach, and stood with him as he gave his "I have returned" speech). In the chaos of the American offensive my father led his young siblings into the still-besieged streets in search of American GIs—the only ones who could save him. "There were Japanese snipers everywhere as we carried a few belongings and walked in single file among the ruined houses," he later wrote. "Suddenly a sniper shot rang out and a little boy about fifteen feet ahead of me fell."

Desperate, my father and his siblings ran for their lives toward the American lines, bullets whizzing past their ears. When they got close, GIs from the 37th infantry, the Buckeye division, reached out for them and pulled them to safety. From that day forward, to the end of his life seventy-seven years later, my father felt a profound sense of gratitude to the U.S. (he and his family moved to America) and the U.S. military, and he never forgot how the GIs had reached out and saved him and given his life to him.

I never forgot that story, either—nor did I realize how it would reverberate through the years and finally be replayed, in a way, in my own life.

My father felt so indebted to the American military that after graduating from Stanford in 1954 he enlisted to serve for two years in Korea as a private during the Korean War. He wanted to earn his U.S. citizenship and pay back what he'd been given. He shared his pride in the United States and its military with his children, and I grew up feeling that pride (I am a dual citizen of the U.S. and the U.K.). My fate, however, would not be to fight in wars but to be a war correspondent, traveling to the world's most dangerous places and reporting on its most violent conflicts. I went wherever civilization was collapsing under the assault of factions and ideologies—to Aleppo in Syria, Mosul in Iraq, Kabul in Afghanistan, Mogadishu in Somalia—always maneuvering as close to the front lines as I could. I felt the earth shudder beneath me with the force of Hamas missiles, huddled with Syrian snipers on hilltops, interviewed bloodied jihadists, and sat with mothers weeping for their murdered children. I filed urgent satellite dispatches to the *Times*, the *Guardian*, the BBC, and many others, breaking news and painting portraits of humans under extreme duress. I saw a lot of death, had guns pressed against my head, dreamed horrific dreams—all of it an echo of what my father endured in Manila.

Still, back then, from 2007 to 2015, when I was a war-hopping freelance journalist, I did not dwell on, or even think too much about, what might happen to me in those dangerous places. I knew the risks, and I understood what I needed to do to stay alive. I never acted rashly or thoughtlessly, but I must admit that there were likely times when I sought out the danger, drawn ever closer to the fighting by a relentless desire to go where no one else had gone. I suppose that, like many younger people, I felt a sense of invincibility. And anyway, my unambiguous mission as a battlefield correspondent did not allow for much wiggle room: it was my job to give voice to the voiceless, and to show the world the brutal reality of war, up close and at whatever cost.

I was, to say the least, extremely lucky to survive it all.

Then things changed. In 2011 I met a smart, beautiful, caring woman named Alicia, and we got married, and we had three angelically lovely girls: Honor, Iris, and Hero. No longer was there an entity known as Benjamin Hall, journalist, existing independently of any place or anyone. Now I was part of something much bigger than myself—my family—and there was no separating me from them or them from me. We were the same thing. We were one single entity.

I understood that, or at least I believed I did.

After the birth of our first child, Alicia and I discussed plans for me to move away from the front lines and keep a safer distance from the worst of the fighting. Still, there were always conflicts I wanted to cover and stories I wanted to tell, and they inevitably drew me back into combat zones. In 2015 I took a full-time job with Fox News, serving first in their London bureau and continuing my coverage of wars. It was only in 2021, when I became Fox's U.S. State Department correspondent and moved to Washington, DC, that I made that final decision to pull back from the front lines.

It was much harder than I imagined it would be to make this professional change in my life; the pull of distant wars never weakened or went away. But I understood new paths were opening for me, and as I began to fill in as a TV anchor I understood this was the right decision to make, and in this way I slowly brought my risky wanderings to a close.

Then, at the break of dawn on February 24, 2022, Russian T-90 tanks streamed across the border from Crimea's Chongar region into southern Ukraine. Columns of Russian troops moved in across the northern border with Belarus. Kh-55 cruise missiles and ground-launched Iskander missiles rained down from the sky.

Russia's invasion of Ukraine had begun.

That morning, while I was in the Fox media booth at the State Department in DC, I got an urgent call from a Fox News executive: I was being assigned to go to Ukraine to report on the war from the western city of Lviv, more than three hundred miles away from what promised to be the heaviest fighting in the east. Technically, it was not an especially risky assignment: Lviv was not the front line. Of course, there would prove to be no such thing as a stationary front line in Ukraine—Russian troops and tanks could turn any city into a battle zone at any time. Hundreds of Ukrainian citizens had already been killed in just the first twenty-four hours of fighting.

Are you ready to go overseas and cover the war? the executive asked.

This would be the single biggest military invasion of a sovereign country since World War II. A conflict with historical, global consequences, perhaps even the beginning of a third world war. It was going to be the biggest news story of the year, if not the decade. *Of course* I wanted to go to Ukraine and do what I'd always done—*tell the story.*

But there was also a part of me that did *not* want to go. I had made a promise to my wife and children, who had all agreed to move across an ocean and live in Washington, DC. And I had agreed I'd begin to steer clear of combat zones. How could I now just pick up, pack a bag, and fly across the world straight into a war? Didn't I already know the right thing to do?

There wasn't much time to decide: an Air France plane was leaving from Reagan National Airport in just a few hours on the way to Warsaw, Poland, near the border with Ukraine. Would I be on that plane?

. . .

The reason I wanted to write this book is because the decision I made that day, February 24, 2022, and the events that followed, tell what I think is a universal story about self-discovery, and about how we learn what matters most in our lives.

Nothing about self-discovery is simple or obvious—the journeys we take to truly understand ourselves are long and complex and often wrenching. We are products of what we inherit: in my case, my father's strict moral code and his reverence for soldiers and nations battling against aggression, and my mother's beautiful curiosity about the world and her restless desire to experience it all. We are also shaped by how and where we are raised (watching John Wayne and Gary Cooper war movies as a youngster and wrestling with the meaning of my very Catholic upbringing). Our decisions are born of countless influences, yet also the simple calculus of our identities—this is who we are, and this is what we do.

Somewhere along the journey, if you are immensely fortunate, as I have been, you might discover that the true blessings of life are even deeper and richer and more astounding—as well as more *available* to us—than we ever imagined they could be. Because, as I have learned in the past year of my life, even amid the very worst displays of human nature, the extremes of depravity and brutality, the harshest sorrows and suffering and turns of fate, there exists something impossibly beautiful and indefatigably good, some spark of light and joy that cannot be extinguished.

Believe me, I have seen it, and I would not be here without it.

And so, my wish for this book is that as you read it you recognize something of your own journeys and setbacks and hard decisions, and take heart in an appreciation of your own strength and resiliency and goodness.

Back in my Washington, DC, office, down in the bowels of the State Department, I got off the phone with the executive and called my wife, Alicia, in London. She is a brilliant partner and entrepreneur with talents far beyond mine, as well as a deeply loving and caring person, and I wanted to run the decision by her, as I had so many times in our years together. In some of those phone calls, I had soft-pedaled the risks of my assignment, and even exaggerated how far I would be from the front line. Back then I believed I was sparing her a lot of unnecessary anxiety by not sharing every detail of the assignment with her. In all that time, Alicia never once told me not to go to a danger zone, and I knew that she wouldn't tell me that now. She understood that the invasion was important, and that it was important for me to cover it, and that covering wars was what I loved to do.

But I also knew, and have always known, that she would have preferred it if I did not go.

The day the invasion of Ukraine began, Alicia and I spoke on the phone for just a few minutes. Time was short, and there really wasn't all that much to say.

By nightfall I was on that plane, bound for Ukraine.

• • •

Daddy, you've got to get out of the car.

Immediately, I knew who the voice belonged to and who the figure was. It was my daughter Honor, come to see me. Six years old, a tangle of brown hair and skinny limbs, my endlessly happy and silly and chatty daughter, my world, my heart, coming through the blackness in this abandoned far-off corner of nowhere, just to tell me these important words.

Daddy, you've got to get out of the car!

I heard my child's voice, truly I did, and I saw her face and felt her presence, and the blackness began to lift, and I realized that my daughter was right and I *was* in a car, or what remained of a car, a fire raging around me, the acrid smell of smoke, a pounding in my ears, the feeling of being pinned down, and an awareness—no, a certainty—that I *had to get out of that car* or else I would die. The decision was mine. I had to find some way to move.

Seconds later, the third bomb hit.

ONE

SOMETHING'S HAPPENED

THE PENTAGON
ARLINGTON, VIRGINIA
MARCH 14, 2022

Jennifer Griffin looked down Corridor 9 on the second floor of the Pentagon's D ring and saw a woman running straight at her. Jen knew the woman—Sylvie Lanteaume, longtime national correspondent for the global news agency Agence France-Presse (AFP)—but didn't know why she seemed in such a rush. Not that it was all that unusual; Jen had hurried down more than her share of Pentagon corridors, driven by tight deadlines and breaking news.

"Is your team okay?" Lanteaume asked when she finally reached her.

Jen Griffin, the chief national security correspondent for Fox News Channel, was in the middle of preparing a report about the war in Ukraine, based on pointed questions she had just finished putting to John Kirby, the Pentagon spokesperson. It had been a stressful morning, as all the mornings and afternoons and nights had been since Russia invaded Ukraine eighteen days earlier. Fox News had several employees on the ground in Ukraine, and there was a constant swirl of concern and activity around them, but Jen had heard nothing about anything happening to anyone. The look on Lanteaume's face, however, told her that something was wrong.

"Ben and Pierre may have been hit," Lanteaume said.

Pierre Zakrzewski was one of the cameramen working for Fox News in Ukraine. Ben, of course, was me.

Immediately, Jen slipped into an operational mindset. "My brain goes a mile a minute and I'm spinning up all these moves, who do I know, who do I call, what can I do," she explains. "I'd handled traumatic situations before."

Since joining Fox News in 1999, Jen had been fired on in Gaza while covering the 2006 Israel-Hezbollah War, reported on the killing of Osama bin Laden and the attack on the Benghazi consulate in Libya, and questioned senior military leaders in hazardous war zones around the world. She was known to be as effective a leader and crisis manager as there is in journalism. "Jennifer is the kind of person who walks into a room," says someone who has worked with her, "and within five minutes everyone is asking her, 'What should we do?'"

Outside the Fox News media booth at the Pentagon, Jen was on her cell phone within two or three seconds of Lanteaume's question about her team. She had to find out what had happened, how bad it was, and what she could do to fix it. The first person she called was Jay Wallace.

Shortly before noon that day, Nicole Knee, executive assistant to Fox News Media's president Jay Wallace, picked up the phone in her office in the News Corp Building, Fox News' skyscraper headquarters in midtown Manhattan. It was Greg Headen calling. Greg, head of the Fox News International desk and vice president of News Coverage, asked to speak to Jay.

Nicole told him Jay was in a meeting and would be out in about ten minutes.

Two minutes later, Greg called again.

"I need you to get Jay, it's urgent," he said. "I believe our team has been hit in Ukraine."

Nicole wrote a message on a Post-it and hustled to the second floor conference room, where Jay and Suzanne Scott, the CEO of Fox News, were in a talent meeting. In the conference room she handed Jay the note.

Headen called—it's urgent, it read.

Jay excused himself and hurried to his office. He was a hardened veteran journalist—he ran Fox News' New York bureau when the planes hit the World Trade Center towers on September 11, 2001—and he steeled himself to handle this new crisis. He called Greg Headen to his office, and Greg passed along the little he knew at that point—a Fox News Team in Ukraine may have been hit.

Greg left to work the phones and get confirmation of the attack. By then the talent meeting had let out and Suzanne Scott had just returned to her office, not far from Jay's. He asked her to come by and told her about the possible hit on a Fox team in Ukraine. While they waited to hear more, they went to the third floor for a previously scheduled noon lunch with Steve Harrigan, the seasoned Fox News correspondent who had covered stories in more countries than any other Fox reporter, and who had just returned from Ukraine.

During the lunch, Nicole Knee came in with another note for Jay.

Greg Headen has confirmed it was the Fox News team that was hit.

Not much later, Jay took the call from Jennifer Griffin, who had just spoken with Sylvie Lanteaume at the Pentagon. Jen and Jay were close; they'd known each other since working together during the 2006 war in Israel, and they shared a deep mutual trust and admiration. They weren't just colleagues; they were friends.

"Jay, what's going on? Has Ben been hit?" Jen asked.

Jay responded in a hushed tone with his own question.

"Do you know who Ben was with today?"

Jen knew what that meant. It was confirmation that something bad had happened. And she knew who I had gone out on assignment with that day—my usual cameraman, Pierre Zakrzewski. She knew Pierre as well as I did; they had been on many dangerous assignments together over the years, and, like anyone who has ever spent a day around Pierre, she was incredibly fond of him. Jay's question made her feel physically ill.

"Pierre was with Ben," she answered.

"Ben and Pierre are both missing," Jay said. "We don't know where they are."

• • •

Suzanne Scott had known Jay Wallace for twenty-six years and had never seen him as somber as he was in the moment he told her about the attack in Ukraine. They'd both steered the company through the difficult days of the pandemic, and that experience had brought everyone at Fox News closer together. But now, Suzanne quickly understood, "we would have to face the worst thing we had ever experienced by far."

Suzanne spent the next thirty minutes with Jay, digging up whatever news there was about the attack. Before long they learned that I'd been located and was in a Ukrainian hospital in bad shape. As the company's CEO, Suzanne knew what she had to do next—let my family know that something had happened.

Across the Atlantic, in a town house in West London, Alicia was upstairs in our bedroom, getting ready for dinner with the girls. It was late on a Monday afternoon and the children had just returned from school. The day had been a strange one for Alicia. It was ordinary in most ways—she saw the girls off in the morning; walked our brown Lab, Bosco, down to the river; handled her many calls and tasks; prepped spaghetti and meatballs for dinner—but something felt different.

"The whole day I just had this unusual sense of calm," she remembers. "Plenty of days I'd just throw on some leggings and sweats, but that morning I thought, *You know what, I'm going to get properly dressed today.* I don't even know why."

She was used to not hearing from me most mornings I was in Ukraine. I tried to call her at least once a day, usually twice, and certainly around the middle of the day if it was at all possible. But that day, she still hadn't heard from me by 5 p.m. "I tried him a few times and he didn't pick up, but I wasn't worried," she says. "I remember I left him an email about Easter. I told him I needed to know if he was going to be home for the Easter holidays, which were a week away."

Alicia was sitting on the edge of the bed and about to go downstairs and round up the girls for dinner when her cell phone sounded. She looked down at the screen and saw the number 1 ahead of the full phone number—a call from the United States.

Instantly, she knew.

"It was chilling," Alicia says of that moment. "I thought, *Oh my God, oh no.* I was shocked and my heart just fell, but I also realized why the day had felt so calm—it was because I had a sense that *change is coming.* Like I already knew that something was about to change."

"My name is Suzanne Scott," the woman on the phone told Alicia, identifying herself as the CEO of Fox News. "Ben has been in an accident."

"What kind of accident?" Alicia asked.

"His car was hit."

"How is he?"

"He is critical."

"How critical?" Alicia asked.

"Just pray. Keep praying."

Alicia glanced to her right and saw her reflection in the bedroom mirror. She was still on the phone with Suzanne, still in the middle of this terrible moment of learning, and she froze the moment in her mind. It was, she knew, the before-and-after moment.

"I will call you as soon as I know anything," Suzanne promised. Then the call was over.

Alicia sifted through the thoughts racing in her head. "I said to myself, 'I knew it, I just knew it. Ben had been there too long,'" she remembers. "There was no way he wasn't going to go to Ukraine, and I gave him my blessing to go. But he had stayed there too long. We talked a lot about the balance he tried to achieve between his work and his life. And my thought was *He had lost that balance.*"

Alicia knew she had to go downstairs and have dinner with the girls, betraying nothing, keeping it in. There was no need for them to know anything, especially since she knew so little herself. But before she could go, she had to make a call. She had to find out *more.*

So she called Rick Findler. He picked up in half a ring.

"Something's happened," Alicia said.

Rick had already heard.

• • •

The cabin lights in the Boeing cut off and the airplane's nose dropped suddenly, and it seemed we were plummeting out of the night sky over northern Iraq. Some passengers wept; others prayed aloud from the Koran as we plunged. We had not lost control—the pilot knew what he was doing. We'd gone dark and cut speed and were gliding sharply earthward to make ourselves less of a target for any surface-to-air missiles fired at us by insurgents. Down below, the lights of a runway came into view and at the last moment the pilot pulled up the nose and the plane rattled to a landing on an airstrip in the Kurdistan Region city of Erbil.

Finally, I thought—a war zone.

This was the fall of 2007, and I'd booked my seat on the Air Arabia flight just three weeks earlier. I was twenty-five years old, and I wasn't quite a journalist yet. I wasn't much of anything, really. I was class of 2004 at Duke University in North Carolina, where I spent far too much time at parties and meandered around obscure interests like the films of Stanley Kubrick, Russian revolutionary cinema, history, and writing. At twenty-two, I took an internship at Columbia Pictures in Los Angeles, and after sitting around in meeting after meeting about demographic scores I realized I didn't want to earn my living in Hollywood. I moved back to London, where I was born, took a look around the world, and decided that what I really wanted to do was experience, and record, extreme events in far-flung places—life at its very edges. More specifically, I wanted to know what it was like to live in a place of war. I'd read about some young Iraqi rappers who were embracing U.S. culture and whose concerts were being attacked, and I decided to start with them. I would make a documentary about the rappers.

Of course I had no idea how to make a documentary, or even what step to take first, but just the idea of *trying* to do it excited me like nothing else ever had before.

The choice of Iraq as a destination in 2007 was, for an inexperienced nonjournalist, either audacious or dumb. That year, Iraq remained firmly in the grasp of war following the U.S.'s shock-and-awe invasion in 2003 and the surge of twenty thousand American troops in January 2007. Roadside bombs and other improvised explosive devices (IEDs) routinely killed U.S. troops across Iraq, while insurgents waged fierce battles in Mosul and Kirkuk, Al Anbar and Fallujah, in the capital of Baghdad and smaller cities like Latifiya and Hilla. In fact, 2007 would turn out to be the single deadliest year of the war for American soldiers, with 904 lives lost.

None of this frightened me from going, and I got to work planning out the trip. The problem was I didn't know where to go or who to meet. As luck would have it, I went to a party one night at the School of Oriental and African Studies in an old Edwardian home in London, on the same street as the Russian Federation Embassy. I mentioned my Iraqi plans to someone at the party, and they told me the Iraqi president's nephew was at the party, too.

My reaction was something like panic. What was I supposed to say to the nephew of Jalal Talabani, the first non-Arab president of Iraq and head of the joint Sunni-Shiite-Kurdish administration? Who was I to seek assistance from such a high-level source? In my mind the nephew was a swashbuckling figure and likely a war hero, while I was just some random Brit with oversized ambitions. But never mind that. Three or four drinks into the evening, I took a deep breath and set out to find this exalted nephew.

When I found him, he was, it turned out, just about the complete opposite of what I'd pictured. He was a fully Westernized young man of twenty or so, skinny and polished, in tight white pants and crisp blue blazer, a pocket square perfectly in place and a flute of pricy champagne in hand. He was *not* the unapproachably dashing rogue I'd imagined. He was a lovely guy and he graciously spoke with me about the situation in Iraq, and he even promised me a letter of introduction from his aunt, Hero Ibrahim Ahmed, the wife of President Talabani and one of the most powerful Kurdish women in Iraq. With that letter in hand, my passage to Iraq was off to a great start. I would draw an important lesson from that party and that encounter—you never know who might be the one to open a crucial door for you or give you a key lead. So go ahead and ask everyone, talk to everyone. This is the very basis of journalism—if you don't know, go find out.

Two weeks before my departure to Iraq, I went for a drink at the Champion, my local Notting Hill pub. I ordered a pint and sat at a table and began reading a book about the history of Iraq, savoring the anticipation of the trip and, I suppose, enjoying my little Ernest Hemingway moment—the studious young reporter on his way to the front. A few minutes in, the barkeep, a cheerful ginger-haired fellow about my age, wandered over.

"I see you're reading a book about Iraq," he said. "I might be working here but what I really want is to be a war photographer."

"That's funny," I replied. "Me, too. I'm off to Iraq in two weeks. Want to come?"

Rick Findler paused for perhaps a second and said, "Absolutely."

Two weeks later we were both on that plummeting plane.

● ● ●

We landed near midnight in the run-down international airport in Erbil, an ancient city in the northern Kurdistan region of Iraq. Rick and I had flown out of the intensely lavish Dubai Airport, home to Louis Vuitton shops and a Ferrari showroom and countless emporiums of glitz, the exact opposite of the dismally unkempt terminal in Erbil. But that was okay—we were not there to shop. In fact, the grimness of it all excited me. This *was* what I imagined a war zone would look like.

But something was wrong. Rick and I grabbed our bags and walked to the parking lot expecting to see a driver with our names on a sign and our Iraqi visas in his hand. But there were no private drivers there, just sputtering taxis buzzing around and shouting people picking up relatives, and after about an hour Rick and I were the only travelers left in the lot. We sat on a curb and waited for our prearranged car to show up. Another hour passed. Finally, I called the number of our nameless Iraqi connection and luckily got through to him and asked him where he was.

"Where am I?" he responded. "Where are *you*?"

"We're at the airport," I said.

"*I* am at the airport," he said. "Wait, which airport are you in?"

I told him we were in Erbil. He asked me what the hell I was doing in

Erbil, except he used an expletive for emphasis. Then he hung up. Rick and I were in the wrong place. Our proper destination, Sulaymaniyah International Airport, was *six hours away*. We had no choice but to wait for a ride, so we lay atop our duffel bags and tried to doze off on the sidewalk, in an empty airport in the middle of the night, with two Kurdish soldiers standing nearby and smoking and watching us the whole time and likely wondering, *What is up with these two guys?*

Our trip only got worse from there.

The next day someone did finally pick us up and drive us to Sulaymaniyah. But we soon learned that northern Iraq was not the scene of rampant fighting at that time, and thus was a relatively safe place to be—good news, I suppose, but not for someone seeking the authentic experience of war. In Sulaymaniyah we managed to track down the Iraqi rappers, but it turned out they were just a bunch of kids in a music class with, to put it politely, rudimentary rapping skills (to put it honestly, they were *terrible*). The reporter who wrote them up had obviously embellished reality in order to have a story to file. As for Rick and me, our would-be documentary suddenly had no subject.

"Mate, we've got nothing," Rick said a few days into the trip. "We've got to find a story somewhere."

We decided to walk around the city and look for leads. One morning two Kurdish soldiers stopped us and screamed questions at us, none of which we understood. Fortunately, I had the letter the president's dapper nephew had arranged for us from his aunt, and that defused the situation. Another time Rick and I saw a plume of dark smoke some ten blocks away and, excited by the prospect of a skirmish or any incident at all, ran madly toward it, only to find a pile of burning rubbish.

On one of our last evenings we took to the streets again and happened upon a fancy Kurdish wedding—women in gowns, men in formalwear, a line of Mercedes parked in front. Rick and I looked at each other, shrugged, and crashed the wedding. It was fairly easy, even for a couple of Westerners who didn't exactly blend in. We sampled the *tepsi baytinijan* casserole and hung out with the band and even danced a few dances, until someone clocked Rick taking pictures and several men grabbed us by the arms and escorted us roughly out the front door. We had crashed a wedding that featured a member of Iraq's ruling party.

In truth Rick and I were thrilled to be so unceremoniously booted from the house. Not only was it an actual bit of excitement after so many uneventful days, but what mattered most was that we'd got in at all. Here was a lesson I could draw from a decidedly clumsy attempt at journalism: *find a way through the door.* Get yourself on the inside of whatever is happening. Don't wait for an invitation: just go on in and act as if you've got a right to be there. *Tell* people you belong there. You might get tossed, but you might also get a hell of a story.

Not that Rick and I got anything that night, or on any night of our trip, and we flew back to London with nothing to show for our troubles.

By all rights I should have been discouraged, but I wasn't. The most impactful part of this first war zone journey for me, the event that changed everything and sealed my fate, happened before I ever set foot in Iraq.

It happened in the dark cabin of that Air Arabia plane as it swooped nearly vertically down to earth. Those long moments of descent, of perceived danger and possible catastrophe, all the way to the lurching, last-second nose-up maneuver that landed us safely, were the first time in my life I felt the special, powerful, adrenalized thrill of *taking a risk.* Even during the descent, I wasn't praying or crying or paralyzed with fear. Instead, strange as it may sound, I felt *alive*—more alive than ever before.

It was a monumental, life-changing feeling, and I was instantly addicted to it. My future began to unfurl before me—I would travel the world witnessing history and telling meaningful stories. I would be a journalist—a war journalist. I would go where no one else wanted to go, I would push through my natural instincts to avoid great risk, and I'd learn to adapt to being in situations over which I had no control.

Of all the lessons I learned from my many early missteps, this was by far the most consequential—to tell the true story of war, I had to be able to run toward danger, not away from it.

And I learned that I had it in me to do it.

TWO

WHATEVER IT TAKES

The paradox of covering war is that, while the job exposes you to unimaginable horror, you also have to *love doing it*.

This is not an easy circle to square. How can harboring two such direly conflicting impulses—repulsion at the horror, attraction to the story—be possible? I have learned from experience that it is possible, but achieving this balance comes with a cost—often a very steep cost.

I've also learned it can take a very long time to achieve.

In the end, much of life is paradoxical, bringing us to tears one moment, filling us with joy the next. While there is a sharp divide between good and evil, I also know that these things can coexist in the same space, sometimes even in the same person. Confronted with utter barbarity, it is possible to seek, and to find, absolute goodness.

My mother, Jenny, had an unhappy childhood that she did not like talking about. Her father, an alcoholic, mistreated her mother and shipped Jenny off at the age of six to boarding school. Jenny hated it there and tried to flee often, scaling walls only to find the housemistress on the other side, waiting in the dark with her big hound on a leash. Jenny's father, it turned out, was having an affair with the headmistress, which guaranteed that no matter how urgently my mother wanted to escape, she would always be returned.

Sadly, her mother eventually committed suicide, and at sixteen Jenny ran away from her Yorkshire home, moved to London with no money, and found work as a waitress. She succeeded in creating a new life for herself, this one filled with joy and creativity. Her childhood dream had been to be an actress, and when that didn't happen she found great satisfaction in helping others chase their dreams. Years later, after my father had some success in business, she traveled the world encouraging and nurturing young artists, and she crowded our home with fascinating friends and guests. The life she fashioned for herself and her family was filled with a little bit of magic, and there was wonder in my childhood because of her.

Nevertheless, on my tenth birthday, it was my turn to be shipped off. My father, a strict, old-fashioned disciplinarian, felt that boarding school would be good for me, so off I went to Ampleforth in North Yorkshire, where the winters were devastatingly cold and where an education, led by monks, provided a "Compass for Life." It was, to be sure, a beautiful setting: a series of elegant buildings surrounded by woods and lakes on the grounds of a Benedictine monastery, Ampleforth Abbey. I spent my first night there in a huge, vaulted room at the top of a dark and drafty old building, forty of us boys in creaky old bunk beds, most of us away from home for the first time. I fell asleep to the sound of half the boys crying and whimpering.

But I loved my time at Ampleforth. Parts of it could be seen as harsh, and at first everyone went through the usual bullying; I remember being hung out a second-story window by my feet, bog flushed (head in the toilet), trampled on, and made to do chores for the older boys. The environment broke more than a few students, but bullies, I found, can be disarmed by force of will. I wasn't the best student, but I did well enough and the teachers liked me, and I spent most days as a soloist in the choir or playing sports. Ampleforth is where I discovered that I had a kind of reserve of strength in me, an extra bit of resiliency, that allowed me to remain unfazed by just about anything that happened to me or around me. Years later this quality served me well in war zones, but even at Ampleforth it was a handy trait.

What stayed with me, too, was religion. It was at the very center of the Ampleforth experience, with Mass five times a week, prayers twice a day, benediction twice a week—all of it meant to teach compassion, respect, and forgiveness. Even all these years later those are qualities I value deeply, and they have helped me get through the struggles I've had.

After five years at Ampleforth my mother insisted I'd had enough, and she pulled me out before I completed my time. I don't know if my father approved or not, but I was sad to leave. My mother brought me and my older brother Barnaby back to London and enrolled us at the City of London School. When we could, we joined our mother on her travels. She had grown a bit bored with dinner parties at home and now she wanted to meet people in new countries, and she dove into her wanderlust with abandon.

As a family we traveled wherever and whenever, avoiding anything touristy and comfy beaches. My mother insisted on having the true, authentic experience of wherever she was. So we lived in mud huts in Venezuela and in tents in Botswana. We boated down the Nile and drove around India. When I was fifteen, we went fishing down the Amazon and ate only what we caught, which meant we subsisted for two weeks on piranha soup (the fish itself was too spiny to eat) until we finally caught a large dorado and ate like kings and queens. On my nineteenth birthday my mother took me to Russia, where, one chilly night, we both drank too much and paid some Russian women to borrow their horses. We galloped all over the streets of St. Petersburg through the night.

Then there was the New Year's Eve that began in a hotel in Laos, with us taking in a grand performance of singers and fireworks. Bored of the festivities, my mother whisked us out into the dark jungle at night, where down some tracks we encountered some Laotians locals playing guitar and singing around a fire they had built near their huts. We did not speak their language, nor they ours, yet we spent the next five hours singing and dancing and laughing with them like a bunch of old friends. In that time there were only two things we all understood— soccer and David Beckham—and so we invoked the great player's name whenever we felt the need to share spoken words.

David Beckham! I'd cry out.

David Beckham! they'd merrily reply.

It wasn't nearly as polished as the festivities back at the hotel, but it was far better because it was real. I've since lost count of how many times I've referred to soccer or David Beckham in order to secure interviews, cross borders, and get through checkpoints. It works *anywhere*.

Of course, these travels with my family informed my life and my career. Like my mother, I loved the idea of meeting new people, experiencing new things. I always wanted *more*—more travel, more sights to see, more feelings to feel. My mother had wanted us to see that the world was a much broader, more complex, and indeed more interesting place than we could fathom, and she accomplished this and then some, instilling in us our own wanderlust, our own curiosity about other people and places. Traveling the world was intoxicating and I wanted to see every part of it—particularly the parts few others wanted to see.

• • •

The first man I watched die was a Libyan rebel fighting against government forces in the bloodied streets of Misrata, early in 2011.

He was probably twenty or twenty-one. We were in the parking lot of a makeshift hospital at rebel headquarters, a concrete building in the city district pockmarked with bullets and circled by shattered glass, crumbled walls, and body parts. The hospital had run out of beds and so cots and tables were set up outside. A trail of blood led from the street to the lot.

Two rebels ran in carrying their fellow soldier and hoisted him up on a table. He had taken shrapnel from a blast and was wet with blood. He had huge open wounds and he was coughing and gasping and fighting to breathe. Medics tried desperately to stop the bleeding and pump him with fluids. The soldier did not give up—he fought hard to stay awake, gritting his teeth and muttering and thrashing; his friends tried to keep him from moving so much. A Belgian doctor hunched over him and performed CPR, again and again, pounding harder and harder, refusing to stop. I stood at the dying man's feet, looking straight down at him, my Canon EOS camera in my hands. I was filming his final, painful moments.

And I thought: *What do I do? Am I supposed to record this moment? Is there nothing else I can do but this? Just watch and film his death?*

I had a decision to make, and I made it. I kept filming.

It was, after all, what I'd gone there to do. This was 2011, the time of the Arab Spring, the eruption of feverish anticorruption protests that led to riots and insurgencies across North Africa and the Middle East. It was also four years after my misadventures with Rick Findler in Iraq.

Since then, we'd both upped our games a bit. We understood our goals a bit better—to find dramatic stories, take great photos, and sell them to the top news outlets and magazines in the world: the Associated Press, Reuters, *TIME* magazine, the *New York Times*, the BBC, and so on. With that in mind we returned to Iraq in 2008, and while I was there I wrote an op-ed about the Iraqi elections and sent it in cold to as many newspapers and magazines as I could.

Miraculously, a woman from the *New York Times* phoned me in Iraq and told me they were publishing the story. As I recall, they paid me $150—nothing, really, considering how much it was costing me to travel and live overseas independent of any media outlet or sponsor. But more importantly, as I realized once I was back in London, having an op-ed published in the *Times* right out of the gate was quite a big deal—sort of like my entry pass into journalism. It was my first time being published, and it meant that I was now, officially, a working free-lance journalist.

After that, I took my first solo freelance trip to Haiti following the earthquake in January 2010. I was still somewhat naïve about crisis-zone travel and arrived at the airport in Port-au-Prince with no story to follow, no contact to pick me up, and no idea what to do as I melted into a throng of thousands of Haitians pushing and pulling and searching for people and begging for help—a frenzy of desperation unlike anything I'd ever experienced. Finally, to escape it, I jumped into a random car with a random person and wound up in a beautiful hotel, the Oloffson, an old-world, wood-and-wicker colonial mansion untouched by the earthquake.

I felt somewhat guilty to suddenly be surrounded by such opulence in the face of such devastation and despair, but there was also some-thing exotic about having a drink at the hotel's plush bar, as if I were Graham Greene reporting from French Indochina in the 1950s. I would soon learn that the sudden and jarring contrast between the most dire of human conditions and the splendor of a place or a view was one of the hallmarks of covering a war. Horror and beauty were never too far apart. Spend the day at the front lines, retreat to the swanky hotel.

My month in Haiti led to a few magazine articles, but not about the earthquake. Instead, I went deep into the country, until I found myself in a shabby concrete hut in the coastal commune of Petit-Goâve, where I was to be christened in a late-night, backwoods voodoo ceremony performed by a drunken voodoo shaman. As I sat on the floor in my silk wrap next to a pin-pierced doll in a miniature casket, I remem-ber thinking: *This is not a bit of fun. I shouldn't be messing with this.* Nevertheless, I stuck it out, and when the shaman asked me what I wanted, the desire to which my own voodoo doll would be devoted, I thought first about my job, and I told the shaman that I wanted to reach the top, the very top, of my profession.

"Whatever it takes," I said, "I will do."

Writing this now, I can't help but wonder if my wish that day required me to also give something up. I've certainly never believed in voodoo, but my advice would be to maybe not play around with it anyway.

That night, I was taken to a voodoo ceremony in the middle of the forest, where dozens of women in long robes danced around and around a fire to the incessant beat of large drums, and to many, many cups of rum, until one by one they all collapsed, writhing on the floor and shouting as they offered themselves up to who knows what.

This was not a story I could sell to the *New York Times.*

Despite my failure to come up with a sellable story, it was not a wasted trip. Just by meeting people and following tips and going with the flow, I not only learned a lot about myself but I also had inordinate amounts of fun. One night I got drunk with Jimmy Buffett (who was in Haiti with his charity) and on another I drunkenly crooned Susan Boyle's version of "I Dreamed a Dream" with one of Haiti's biggest drug traffickers as we splashed around in his infinity pool. At other times I was utterly miserable, like when I got dysentery on a bus built for thirty passengers but packed with sixty for an hours-long, dirt-road haul across the mountaintops, and vomited over the side as the other fifty-nine Haitians laughed and pointed and jeered at me. I spent the next week sweating and chugging antibiotics in a tiny bathtub in a cheap hotel. In all those experiences there was some lesson to be drawn, I was sure, and here is the lesson I drew:

Just keep doing it. Just keep going where others haven't.

I learned that no matter where I went, I wanted to get stuck in. I wanted to jump right into the action, to seize every opportunity and not overthink it. Because, as a journalist, you never know where that next car will take you or how that ride will turn out. Back then I was young and unattached, which made it easier to be so spontaneous (or foolish, as some might suggest). But this was the path I wanted to be on. I can't honestly say that in those early years I was motivated by the plight of the downtrodden or driven by some noble cause. If I am being honest, I was in it for me. I wanted to be there. I *liked* being there. It made me feel alive.

• • •

In March 2011, the United States and other NATO countries entered Libya during its civil war to compel a cease-fire, impose a no-fly zone, and stop Muammar Gaddafi's regime from killing citizens. When this happened, I knew I had to get myself to Libya. This was going to be more of a proper war than anything I'd covered, so I made plans with my good mate Rick Findler to go and cover it. In March 2011 I set out for North Africa by myself, and Rick soon joined me there.

By then Rick and I had become a real team. We had the same ambitions and the same energy, and most importantly, we developed a fierce loyalty that made us feel safe around each other in bad situations. Born in Ascot in Berkshire, England, and raised both there and in California, Rick majored in psychology at university but realized he preferred photography after borrowing his sister's camera and shooting sunsets in New Zealand. He earned a master's in photojournalism and, like me, looked for a way into covering wars.

"I was drawn to conflicts," Rick explains. "I was working at the Champion pulling pints and afterwards I'd hang around the pubs in Bristol taking pictures of guys fighting, which they did all the time."

It was while covering violent street protests in Athens in 2008 that he discovered the key to getting "the picture"—the shot that ends up on the front page of newspapers the next morning. "It was something Robert Capa said: 'If your pictures aren't good enough, you're not close enough,'" says Rick, referring to the legendary photojournalist who took his most famous photo—of a soldier being felled by a bullet to the head during the Spanish Civil War—when he was twenty-five. "So that's what I did when I was in Athens. Every night I got closer and closer and closer to the fighting."

I arrived in Libya two weeks before Rick. I'd flown into Cairo, Egypt, and poked around a Facebook page and found a post from a journalist that said Alexandria, the port city northwest of Cairo, was a good starting point to find fighters on their way into Libya. In Alexandria I piled into a minivan for the long drive along the beautiful Mediterranean coastline into Libya, and eventually to Benghazi, where most journalists covering the war were based. We were stopped at the Libyan border, at a checkpoint with a few buildings and a mass of people fighting and pushing to get in or out. I soon learned that I didn't have the proper stamp to permit me entry (who knew that entering Libya during a revolution required a visa?). Some guards detained all of us who were in the minivan, to their great annoyance. As groups of rebels and other travelers pushed and pulled and surged around me, I searched desperately for a quasi-official who might be able to help. Things seemed dire until I finally grabbed someone walking past, slipped a hundred-dollar bill in my passport, and uttered the word *dollars*. Thirty seconds later I had my stamp, and the next day I made it into Benghazi. That was the first of many, many times that a few American dollars opened doors, and after that I almost always kept a hundred-dollar bill in my passport.

What I quickly discovered was that seemingly every other journalist in the world was in Benghazi to cover the fighting, including well-funded teams from all the major networks. How was I going to break any news with this much competition? After a few days I returned to Egypt to meet Rick in Cairo, and we decided our only option was to somehow slip into the coastal Libyan city of Misrata, some five hundred miles west of Benghazi, even though it was entirely surrounded by Gaddafi's army—the savage fighters who, the rebels warned, would kill "half a million" if they weren't stopped.

The only way into Misrata from Benghazi was across three hundred miles of the Mediterranean by boat.

Rick and I heard rumors about weapons shipments going to Misrata, so we went to the harbor in Benghazi and nosed around. The security was intense and we couldn't get anywhere near the boats. We searched for weak points in the fence line around the harbor, sneaking through holes farther up the coast and hoping to double back, but after a few days we had no luck. Finally, we got a tip about a fishing boat that was planning to go to Misrata. We got the name of the captain and talked our way onto the port.

The captain was a gruff and rugged fellow in his fifties who moved slowly and apparently had no interest in anyone or anything other than tending to his forty-foot boat, the *Jelyana*. He spoke a bit of English, and I asked him if we could join him to Misrata.

"Who's going to Misrata?" he said angrily. "We're not going to Misrata."

We went back and forth on this point but the captain didn't budge. The next day we tried again, and again, no luck. Rick and I, however, weren't going to budge, either—we were going to get on the *Jelyana* one way or another. Finally, on day three, the captain, who by then was sick of us, looked me up and down and made an offer.

"Your sunglasses," he said, pointing to my Aviators.

"What?"

"I like your sunglasses. I will take you for the glasses."

Easiest decision ever—I told the captain they were his the minute he picked us up to take us back to Benghazi after our stay. The deal was done and we secured spots on the *Jelyana* for the following day. Destination: Misrata—the very epicenter of a brutally violent war.

THREE

MISRATA

Just before we were set to depart the next day, word circulated in our hotel of a tragedy in Misrata. Two journalists had been killed. The brilliant and veteran war photographers Tim Hetherington and Chris Hondros were traveling with rebel soldiers in Misrata when a mortar shell exploded near them, killing several Libyan rebels and gravely injuring four journalists. Two of them survived; Hetherington, hit by shrapnel that caused massive bleeding, and Hondros, who suffered severe brain trauma, did not.

These were two highly respected and well-traveled journalists known as much for their savvy and preparedness as for their courage and talents. They were the furthest thing from freewheelers as there were in the business. "They realized the risks and tried to minimize them as much as possible," a friend said of them after their deaths. "There are times, unfortunately, when you just don't know which decision is right or wrong. That's the situation Tim and Chris found themselves in."

That night, just before our departure on the *Jelyana*, Rick and I sat down to talk. *Is this the right thing to do?* we asked each other. *Is Misrata where we need to be? Do we go or not go?* It was a serious discussion, but not a long one. We agreed that Misrata was exactly where we needed to be, precisely because it was dangerous and because few people were going there. If we wanted to tell the story, we needed to take the risk. I could tell that Rick was as shaken as I was by the news about Tim and Chris, but it was also clear he wasn't any less determined to make the trip than I was. Perhaps we were both still too young and too inexperienced to make a truly informed and rational decision, but at the time it seemed clear-cut. This was our job.

The next morning we jumped on the *Jelyana* and joined fourteen young Libyans already on board. We pushed out to sea and were off. The boat, we soon noticed, was indeed stuffed with weapons, and the young Libyans were not sailors—they were battle-ready rebels heading to the front. The cabins downstairs were overrun with bombs and rifles and rocket-propelled grenades (RPGs), and even the engine room was packed with crates in every cranny. Under a large tarpaulin on deck was a Russian ZPU antiaircraft gun. There was a NATO blockade in place meant to stop the flow of weapons into Libya, yet here we were, a floating powder keg. Some rebels caught Rick and I snooping around below and shouted at us to get back up on deck. The rebels looked at us quite suspiciously after that.

Eventually they warmed up to us and we all sat on deck in the bright sun and the peaceful seas and belted out songs together. *We're going to Misrata* being the lead line in all of them. It was the calm before the storm. After thirty or so hours on the water, we were bobbing around in the total black of night when suddenly, out of nowhere, a deafening foghorn blasted us all awake and to our feet. Floodlights covered us and allowed us to see a colossal warship just a few short yards behind us on the water, towering ominously over us. The rebels scrambled for their guns while Rick and I held our breaths and tried to make sense of it all. We knew we were part of a highly illegal shipment of weapons, but we had no idea what the consequences of that would be. The captain urged the men to get down, and luckily no guns were pointed in the direction of the massive warship.

"Cut your engine," a voice bellowed on our radio, in what I recognized to be one of the poshest English accents I'd ever heard. This was one of her majesty's warships.

"Identify yourself!" the English voice demanded. "Who are you, what are you carrying?"

The *Jelyana*'s captain froze and we all endured a painfully long silence, until he took the radio microphone and inexplicably smiled and in his terrible English said, "Food! Food for the children!"—which struck me as hilarious, considering our real cargo.

"And we have journalists!" the captain went on.

With that he pitched the mic at me and said, "Go ahead, tell them."

"Hello?" I piped up in the most relaxed tone I could muster. "I'm Benjamin Hall, I'm a journalist, I'm heading to Misrata."

"Well, what on earth are you doing on the boat?" came the reply, followed quickly by, "And what are you carrying?"

I hesitated, but just for an instant.

"Food," I said. "Food for the children. And medicine, too."

By the way, there was certainly some medicine on board, and a few cans of tuna as well, so I wasn't straight-out lying, but in life you have tough decisions to make.

"Very well then," the warship captain said. "Off you go, and be safe. It'll be dangerous."

With that the warship gently drifted out of sight and into the night.

After that the rebels and crew were quite fond of Rick and me and didn't stop giving us cheers and hugs.

We kept going and in another five hours we could see the lights of Misrata up ahead, and that is when we realized we were heading into a war. We stood on deck and watched the shells exploding in the city and we understood Gaddafi was bombing the hell out the place. Rick and I braced for what was coming next, which, at that point, was completely unknown to us. Once again we had no set plans, no real course of action once we landed in Misrata. We were just going to reach shore and start moving inland. You know, get in any car.

The rebels on the ship invited us to join them, and we were driven to a rebel safe house somewhere in the bombed-out center of Misrata. There were about a dozen or so other journalists there, including Marie Colvin, the indefatigable American who'd lost an eye covering the Sri Lankan Civil War and now went into war zones with a black eye patch and even more resolve. To Rick and me she was a hero, one of the top stars of the business. When we finally got the chance, we went over to chat and ask for any advice. Marie was gruff but hugely generous.

"Stick with the rebels, move with them," she told us. "And always have a base to come back to." It was half pep talk, half invaluable tips, and finding Marie there in this perilous battle zone was exhilarating and inspirational. For Rick and me, it was also an affirmation that we were where we needed to be.

Less than a year later, Marie Colvin was in the Baba Amr district of Homs, Syria, covering a battle between the Syrian military and rebel forces when she was killed by Syrian artillery fire. She and other journalists in Homs believed they had been targeted, and were planning an exit strategy just hours before Colvin and photojournalist Rémi Ochlik were killed.

One day not long after we got to Misrata, I met a Belgian freelance photographer. He had just arrived by boat, and he hopped into a pickup truck with us and a team of rebels on their way to find Gaddafi's troops. We pulled around a corner and onto a boulevard, and suddenly bullets whistled over our heads. We moved to the other side of the truck and jumped off, and as we did the Belgian photographer looked at me with a haunted expression. He seemed terrified.

"My wife just had our first child at home," he said. "I can't do this anymore. I have to leave now. This is all wrong for me."

I could not understand his thinking. He was a photojournalist, and here he was, on the front lines of a war, in the middle of the action, right where it mattered most. Why would he want to leave now? I remember feeling angry that he was insisting on going back to the safe house, but of course we took him back, even though it meant missing the story.

Of course, he was older than I was, and he had been at it longer, and he was wise enough to understand that it was his time to go. He just knew it. And so he left the next day.

It would be many more years before I understood his decision.

• • •

Rick and I spent the next few days moving with the rebels and sleeping in the basements of various safe houses, waiting for skirmishes to cover. One day we accompanied the rebels to a detached, two-story residential building where, they had heard, some Gaddafi fighters were holed up. From twenty yards back Rick snapped photos and I rolled video as some fifty rebels fired maniacally into the building, shredding the walls and creating absolute chaos. One rebel hoisted a missile launcher and fired an RPG into a wall of the building. But he was too close to his target and parts of the wall blew straight back at us. Rick and I weren't hit, but one rebel had his throat ripped out by a piece of the wall. More rebels were hurt by their own gunfire than by Gaddafi soldiers. There was a bloodlust to what they were doing, decades of anger being let loose in maniacal ways, a hellish, avenging scrum of humanity where everyone had guns.

Everywhere we went in Misrata we stepped over charred, decomposing bodies, trudged through literal pools of blood, and practically felt the inescapable stench of death. However ready I believed I'd been to see war up close, I'd never imagined it could be as hellish, as utterly bereft of any logic or sanity, as it was. One night I snuck away to the rooftop of our safe house and called my parents back in London on a satellite phone. I felt the need to let them know I was okay. I was speaking to my father when a shell exploded fifty yards away, knocking the phone out of my hand as I hit the ground and ending the call. All my father heard on the other end was the explosion and then silence.

My father knew what it was like to be in the path of bombs. He was a young boy asleep in his bed in Manila in 1944 when an explosion in the middle of the night knocked him to the floor and demolished much of the house. "I woke up with my eyes full of sand," he later recalled. He spent many days during the war listening for the sharp whistle of shells overhead, waiting for the whistling to stop before diving into a shelter. Bombs exploding and shrapnel raining from the sky, my father understood, were the random determinants of who lived and who died in wartime.

It was another hour before I could call my father back from Misrata, and in his voice I recognized a familiar mix of joy that I was alive and a trace of anger that I had chosen to be there at all. Of course, my father also understood why I was there. He grew up in war and served in the military, and he never expressed the slightest wish for me not to venture into dangerous places. Nor did my mother, who may not have known quite as well as my father how perilous a war zone could be, but who was, I was sure, every bit as worried for my safety. I knew what I was putting them through, or at least I thought I did.

Only years later did family friends tell me how utterly terrified my mother was every time I left for another war, and how my father made up stories about me before telling her what he knew.

Yet until I got to Misrata, I hadn't really been in a truly hellish combat zone. The time I spent in the ruins of the Libyan city was an eye-opener for me in every possible way. It was, as I mentioned, the first time I not only saw a man die but chose to film his final moments, to, perhaps, invade the dignity of those moments in order to "get the story." Was it the right thing to do? Or was it wrong and inhumane? I didn't know, because I did not have the time to consider all the moral angles. I could either keep filming or stop filming, and I chose to keep filming.

Still, watching a man take his last breath, and knowing the last thing he felt in life was immense pain, was a staggering experience.

One day Rick and I followed the rebels down a street littered with wreckage and bodies. At the time, all I had by way of protection was tactical body armor—essentially a bulletproof vest. I saw the body of a soldier on the ground, and beside him I saw his helmet. Out of instinct I reached down and picked up his helmet and put it on. It was my helmet now. Later on I picked up a yellow baseball cap with blood on it that belonged to another casualty. I took the cap, too, because I needed it to shield the sun. Had I crossed another line by taking these items from men who had just died? Again, I could not say. The moral quandaries would come later. At the time, all I cared about was surviving.

Toward the end of our first week in Misrata, one of Gaddafi's soldiers was captured alive by rebels. A mob of rebels was set to literally tear the man apart, but someone told them to stop because of the media cameras there. Instead they pushed their prisoner into the back of a van. Quickly, Rick and I followed two rebel soldiers and jumped into the van with the prisoner. He was a tall man from a local tribe, and he'd been badly beaten. I sat directly across from him as the crowd around the van shook it from side to side and bayed for blood, screaming faces pressed against the glass. I asked the prisoner why he was fighting for Gaddafi. Not because he wanted to, he said, but because he'd been forced to. I'd spoken to a number of other fighters and terrorists after they were captured, and they almost all said they had been forced to fight. In this case, as in most of the others, I didn't believe him. But it didn't matter to him in the least if I believed him or not—he knew he was about to be killed. He was resigned to it and almost calm about it.

Within a few minutes another rebel forced open the van door and pulled Rick and me out. He was angry that we'd gone in at all. The van drove off, and later that day we asked someone what had happened to the prisoner.

"He is dead," we were told.

Rick and I understood there was no possibility of anything awaiting this man other than his death. That was just the cruel reality of war.

The hardest day for me was when we traveled to a makeshift hospital set up to treat the injured. We walked in and I saw the bodies of five children laid out on the ground side by side. One of them was an infant. Their bodies were wrapped but their smudged, bluish faces were not. Their mother sat on the dirty floor next to them and screamed with agony at her loss, her head in her hands, her body swaying back and forth. I looked away and noticed that the paint was peeling off the walls of the room. *This filthy place*, I thought. *And here is her entire family, dead on the ground.*

Rick and I had a talk the next day. We had the same thought—that it was time to go. An innate sense that our time was up. We had spent the last seven days running through bombed-out buildings, dashing through shell-blasted holes in the walls from building to building, like mice trapped in a maze, trying not to get hit by snipers but also trying to get closer and closer to the front line. We stole an hour of sleep here and there in basements as bombs landed near us all through the night, rousing us from our stupors. Every day was a surreal and endless mix of adrenaline and exhaustion, wanting to stop but never stopping, and always going against every natural instinct we had to just run away. Every day we had to bury our humanity somewhere deep inside ourselves, so that we could pick up that helmet, or film that dying man, or take whatever step was needed in order to do what we came to do. Nothing interrupted this long blurring of days and nights into a ceaseless, deafening chaos. It just went on, and so did we.

But it took a toll. I have watched videos taken of me when I was on the streets of Misrata, and what I see alarms me. My face is not my face; it is haunted, hollow, blank. I am not me, or even a real person; I am the shadow of a person. There is no humanity to this figure, no evidence of empathy or even concern, just a robotic, inexplicable persistence.

Watching that footage, I knew that this is what it looks like to be part of a war.

Finally, we'd had enough.

"We came to bring the news," Rick said, "not be the news."

We hitched a ride back to the harbor, but Gaddafi's shelling of the area was too intense for us to get to the boats. The land around the harbor, however, was flat and wide open, leaving us nowhere to run or hide except for a small, one-room hut alongside some shipping containers. Rick and I ran to it and huddled inside with four Libyans as the bombs landed around us. Sitting there in the dank and dark, we knew our fate was not in our hands. Either the bombs would hit the hut or they wouldn't. We had entered a lottery in which the only prize was survival and the only strategy was to wait and pray, if you were the praying type. Which I was. I didn't pray often, but I did in that hut, asking God for help. "Keep me alive, I will do better, I'll go to church more often and pray more." When there is nowhere to run, the safest place you can be is in a conversation with God.

Curled up in that hut, as I had in central Misrata, I felt real terror. But just as I had in the basements and streets of Misrata, my reaction to the terror was to box it away and focus fully and completely on surviving. Just sit there and pray and say, *It'll pass.* Stuff your emotions in your pocket. *Endure.*

Rick and I waited in the hut for a long time. When we finally got too restless, we got out and watched the shells fall for a while, until they eventually stopped. We expected to quickly jump on the boat and take off, but it turned out the seas were too rough to push out right then. In the madness of the moment, of waiting to either die or live, Rick and I stripped down to our boxer shorts, ran to the port, and dived into the water. We splashed around and got in and out and did flips. Other people waiting desperately with us to escape on the boat looked at us like we were crazy. Thinking back, it was a highly stupid thing to do. But at the time it made a strange kind of sense. And it was fun.

At last the seas calmed, and we boarded the *Jelyana* and took off. This time we were packed on the boat along with fifty refugees—men, women, and children fleeing the war. The seas got rough again and Rick and I sat on deck and clung to the rails as waves crashed over us and tossed people back and forth. Some of us were nearly swept overboard. Everyone was seasick and vomit covered us all. I squeezed myself into the fetal position and held tight to a soaked-through blanket and wrapped my arm around a steel bollard and kept telling myself, *You're going home, you're going home,* until those words became like their own little prayer.

After a horrid day and a half of stormy seas, we did make it to Benghazi, and two days later Rick and I were back in London. It was the day of Prince William's wedding, and Rick rushed to Buckingham Palace to take pictures. Out of one world, into another.

I understood immediately that I was a changed man. I learned that I could control my fear, even bury it, and keep moving forward into danger. I learned that the hellishness of Misrata was not enough to stop me from going to combat zones. And I learned that my normal, civilized life would never be the same again. No—*this* was who I was now.

When I got back home, my flatmate in London hosted a big party for me in the flat. I showed up but found it nearly impossible to stay. I didn't want the questions—*How was it? What did you see?* Where was I supposed to begin? The dying rebel soldier with his guts blown out? Or the sobbing mother who'd lost all her children? I found I couldn't shift gears back to my old life, or at least not that quickly.

So I left the party thrown in my honor and walked down the street and ducked into a pub, and sat at the bar by myself and had a pint.

FOUR

TELL THE WORLD

In London I waited for something to happen that could even remotely approach the intensity of what I experienced in Libya. I monitored the local news in search of a riot or crime I could cover. A student protest in Covent Garden? Be right there. Someone got stabbed at the Notting Hill carnival? On the way. Most of my time, however, was spent on the balcony of my flat, jotting things in a journal, watching the flow of people outside, waiting for something to happen. Mostly, I waited.

It was frustrating. After Libya I realized that covering wars was what I loved. I was good at it, and when I wasn't doing it, I couldn't shake it. Nothing was as rewarding or vital; nothing matched it in importance.

Without it, suddenly, I was lost.

Two days after returning from Libya I enrolled in a graduate program in broadcast journalism at the London College of Communication. At the least I was hoping that studying for a master's would give my life some much-needed structure. It also gave me a reason to travel back to Egypt to report on the riots and follow a graffiti artist as part of my thesis work. I got shot by Egyptian riot police and was left with twelve shotgun pellets in my leg—but I also completed the graduate course in under a year and earned my master's. Yet the urge to see more, to travel farther, to get closer, remained. It was only a matter of time before a conflict somewhere would whisk me away from London and put me back at the front, where I belonged.

What I didn't yet realize was that the answer to the question that was driving me mad—*who am I when I'm not in a combat zone?*—would not be found in some far-off place, but was rather right there in front of me, in London. It had to do with a bit of magic that happened just before Rick and I had gone off to Libya.

It was 2011, and I was having a night out with some friends in Notting Hill Gate when a beautiful blond woman walked up to me.

"Are you Benji Hall?" she asked.

I told her I was.

"We went to school together, when we were young," she said. "You were my biggest crush in school. Do you remember?"

I *did* remember—her name was Alicia and she'd been with me at Thomas's School in Kensington, which I attended from the ages of four to seven. We spent the next few minutes reminiscing, and then we said goodbye and rejoined our groups. I was smitten. Alicia was lively and friendly and beautiful, with no airs or artifice about her at all, and that night I felt a spark that I still feel today.

Up until then I hadn't really been in what I would call a serious relationship. I dated a fair amount, but not once did I feel the need or desire to make any kind of commitment. The feeling I had when I saw Alicia, however, was unlike any I'd had before, and then and there I knew something special had happened.

Years later, I came across a card Alicia had written for me when I was six. The inscription was simple and to the point.

Benji, I love you, Alicia.

Even so, it took us a while to start seriously dating. I was traveling a lot, chasing stories, following leads, and perhaps I wasn't the best dating material right then. I phoned Alicia from overseas a few times, and when I was back in London we tried to get together. We chatted about a lot of things, but I never went into any detail about what I was seeing in Misrata and elsewhere.

I saw Alicia the day after I got back from Libya and gave her a condensed version of what I'd seen, referring to the brutality but not describing it. As I spoke, Alicia asked me questions that were completely different from the ones I was used to getting about my travels. They were less about what I'd seen and more about what I *felt*. She seemed genuinely concerned about my well-being in such perilous places, about how I was handling everything, and generally how it was all affecting me. Up until then I had exhibited sheer bravado—*don't worry about me, I'm not the story, I'm a tough guy, I'm okay*—but Alicia broke through all that and spoke to the person, not the reporter. It was as if she was able to make that distinction even before I could. As if she saw a man whom no one else saw or even knew was there.

What's more, Alicia asked questions about things I hadn't thought much about. She asked how the war was affecting families and children, how it was changing the people. It was as if she were saying, *Tell me about the people you meet and make them your story. Look for stories that aren't being told and explain how wars are affecting family values.* In this way, over time, Alicia changed the very way I experienced and reported on wars. Her voice and mindset made my work more nuanced and vital and immediate. I knew very quickly that those early dates and dinners with Alicia were the start of something remarkable.

Still, the wars called to me.

• • •

It was two in the morning and we were lying on our bellies, deep in a muddy ditch, our heads to the ground, our breaths held, barely moving at all. This was 2012. In the close distance, the *shabiha*, the most violent of all of Syria's government forces, were slowly walking our way, hunting for us. We'd been stealthily trying to get into Syria and across enemy lines, and as we got closer to the border we must have been spotted.

When their torch beams flashed toward us, we shrank even closer to the ground and wondered what would happen if they caught us. At one point a soldier walked within twenty feet, poking the undergrowth. I was certain his torch beam would land on us at any second.

Just then we heard the rumble of shelling in the distance, and the soldiers ran back to their trucks and drove off. We'd been in the ditch for two hours. The air was cold, but I was covered in sweat. We climbed up and stretched our legs, then just a moment later, out of nowhere, two men carrying AK-47 rifles, and naked except for tight red underpants, leapt from the darkness and ran straight at us. I had no idea what was happening and the only thought I had was *We shouldn't be here.*

"Take off your clothes," one of the men ordered.

We all stripped down to our underpants and stood there in the dark, Rick and I looking at each other in bewilderment.

"Take your clothes, do as we do, do not make a sound," the man said. We followed him a few hundred yards until we finally saw the banks of a river, and then we walked in, first through clammy mounds of mud and then into the freezing water. We formed a bucket brigade and passed our bundles of clothes and bags from man to man until they were on the other side of the river. Then we waded in, the water up to our shoulders, our arms raised above us to keep our balance against the swift currents.

We made it across and got to dry land, and we put our clothes back on, including our Kevlar vests and our helmets. I don't think I'd ever felt as bone-cold as I did right then, but there was no time to think about that. The men were now jogging briskly and we had to follow them. We ran through fields and groves and around olive trees for twenty minutes until we arrived at a small, one-room shepherd's hut.

Exhausted, we went inside, where four Syrian rebel fighters were waiting for Rick and me.

We were now behind the enemy al-Assad lines.

It had not been easy to get there. Back in London a few weeks earlier, Rick and I were closely following the news coming out of Syria,
the Mediterranean country bordered by Turkey, Iraq, and Israel. A
civil war had erupted there in 2011 and worsened a year later when,
according to the United Nations, the Syrian Army, President Bashar
al-Assad's fighting forces, executed 108 people, including thirty-four
women and forty-nine children, in a massacre in the town of Taldou.
The rival rebel forces, led by the Free Syrian Army, escalated their resistance to al-Assad's rule and fierce fighting swept through Damascus
and Aleppo. Few reporters were getting past Syria's rigidly controlled
borders, and Rick and I—still just freelancers—decided we had to find
a way to get in.

Working online chat boards and Facebook pages, I made contact
with a Syrian man who worked as a fixer—the indispensable inside person who helps journalists secure passage, find housing, connect with
soldiers, and do just about everything else. His name was Faraz, and
as far as we could tell he was working with the Syrian rebels, helping
smuggle in weapons, medicine, and other aid from Turkey to Syria.
We made arrangements to meet Faraz in the southernmost province
of Turkey, in the ancient city of Antakya, near the border with western
Syria. Our plans, at best, were sketchy—we didn't know when we'd
meet Faraz, or how he'd get us into Syria, or where we'd go in Syria
if we got in. All we knew was to travel to Antakya and wait for Faraz
there.

I packed light: my laptop, wires, battery and chargers, a shirt, socks,
one extra pair of boxer shorts, and a toothbrush. I packed a handful of
beef jerky, which I took with me everywhere. (Rick packed his mother's
absurdly tasty oatmeal cookies, which saved us both a few times when
we were famished; he also carried a laminated card stating "If I eat the

following, I will die," because he was allergic to everything.) I packed a notebook to write in and I wore a belt with a zipped compartment, where I stashed about six hundred dollars in American currency. I had two more hundred-dollar bills that I hid under the soles of my feet, and another hundred dollars rolled up in a note that read, "We are journalists, please help us escape."

"If you get in trouble, you will need help from someone," Faraz had warned me. "Otherwise, you will not get out alive."

With my life jammed into a small canvas bag, I said goodbye to Alicia and joined Rick at Heathrow Airport, and we set out for Syria.

• • •

We flew down to the city of Gaziantep, on Turkey's southern border, on a flight that had been nicknamed the "jihad express." Over the years we took the flight often, and we noticed how nearly every passenger was a single man, all likely flying down to join ISIS or other rebel groups. We then scored a ride to Antakya, a fertile valley city on the banks of the Orontes River. We were only a few miles from the Syrian border, and about thirty miles from Idlib, where some of the worst fighting in Syria was happening.

We set up camp and waited in a dilapidated but still beautiful old church in the Antakya countryside, home to an elderly German nun named Sister Marie. She opened the church grounds to travelers, and Rick and I stayed in bunk beds in a small adjacent building. It was a slightly unnerving but also strangely serene setup, and Rick and I settled in for what we hoped would be two or three days of waiting for Faraz to appear.

We wound up spending two weeks there.

Those two weeks were, for me, nearly unbearable. They were harder to endure than the days when I was actually *in* a combat zone, because at least then I knew what to expect. Sitting around in the old church, we had far too much time to *anticipate* whatever dangers we might find. That was when the fear would get to me—when I was waiting to go.

"Why are you doing this?" Sister Marie repeatedly asked us in her broken English. "It is too dangerous, do not go."

To pass the time, I had asked her to play church hymns on the dusty upright piano just behind the altar and, because I knew all the Catholic hymns from years of singing choir in church, I'd croon along to her playing, hymn after hymn. We passed some days that way, singing Catholic hymns. It was better than thinking about what awaited us.

In fact, our anxiety about what lay ahead got so bad that we began to worry about ginger-haired Rick and how pale he was—so pale and so redheaded that he truly stood out, especially where we were on the cusp of the Arabian Peninsula. We decided we needed to dye his hair and eyebrows a dark brown to make him less conspicuous, but we made a total mess of it and Rick wound up with streaks of brown dye on his face and brown stains around his eyebrows. He looked like a hugely clumsy Kabuki artist.

Luckily, in Antakya we bumped into the veteran London *Times* photographer Jack Hill, who was far more knowledgeable about what was going on inside Syria than we were. Very graciously he sat with us and unfurled a map and gave us advice on where to go. "Don't call out every day because they can track you by your phone," he told us. "If you go to protests, look out for al-Assad's forces in the crowd." It was invaluable wisdom that initially made us even more apprehensive, but it was also part of a nearly sacred ritual that Rick and I would take part in many times in future years—war reporters passing on their potentially lifesaving insights to the newcomers, often on the border of a combat zone. Jack made us feel like we were a part of this great journalistic continuum of knowledge gathering and passing, and we were grateful for the lessons—and the map—he left us with.

A few years later, Jack Hill and a reporter named Anthony Lloyd were kidnapped in Syria and shot and beaten before escaping captivity.

There were times when we thought we'd never get into Syria. Faraz did text us from time to time, and he let us know we might be embedded with the Seventh Valley Brigade of the rebel Free Syrian Army. But there were also days upon days when we didn't hear from Faraz at all. Rick and I must have packed and repacked our bags a dozen times each.

Finally, we got a text from Faraz that said, It's happening tomorrow. The next day Faraz texted us again: I'm outside. And there he was, slightly overweight and baby-faced, no beard and thinning hair, nice pants and a button-down shirt—not the grizzled, bearded rebel we'd been expecting. He was, like so many other Syrians swept up in the civil war, just an ordinary man, one of the many farmers and teachers and shopkeepers rising up to rally against the brutal al-Assad regime. He was gentle and soft-spoken, not very talkative, and clearly nervous. He got right down to business and pointed to a nearby blue hatchback car.

"We have to keep down low. There are many Assad spies looking for FSA fighters at the crossings," he said.

We got in the beat-up old compact and were relieved to see the driver, who, with his thick beard and camouflage pants, looked considerably more battle-tested than Faraz. Rick and I sat in the back and crouched down below the window lines, and we drove into the night for several hours. We arrived at a small hamlet and scrambled into another vehicle, huddling in the back of the open truck bed. We drove another thirty minutes and arrived near the border between Turkey and Syria.

There we hopped out and were swallowed up by the pitch dark—no moon, no torch, just blackness. We followed Faraz on foot for a half mile until we arrived at a ditch. It was while there, in a ditch right at the border to Syria, that trucks pulled up and Syrian soldiers jumped out and came looking for us.

"Get down in the ditch," Faraz said urgently.

These were soldiers fighting for the al-Assad regime.

"Someone must have seen us and alerted them," Faraz said. "Lie down, don't move, don't breathe."

A couple of hours later, after we had finally crossed the river into Syria, we were in the small shepherd's hut with four Syrian rebels. Once again, not a second was wasted. We got into another car and headed deeper into Syria. For most of the ride our driver hurtled at 90 mph over dirt roads with the headlights switched off. We stopped somewhere and got into a small truck, with Rick and I lying in the back alongside big sacks of vegetables and beneath dark blankets. We sped along more dirt roads and arrived in a little village, where we hopped off and jumped into a darkened little room packed with fifty yellow canaries in fifty cages stacked atop each other. We switched on our cells to look around and realized we were in a bird seller's shop. The canaries chirped noisily at our presence.

Then we were off again, into another car, and we drove until daybreak and finally arrived at a beautiful villa that seemed abandoned and had a magnificent empty swimming pool and was now, apparently, a safe house for the rebels.

As the sun rose, we sat down with the rebels and learned about the operation to smuggle us in. Every move had been planned by a series of forward groups who communicated with each other and steered us clear of army checkpoints. Some rebels were former members of the Syrian Army who defected, and they had knowledge of al-Assad's military techniques. What may have seemed like a helter-skelter dash through darkness to us had actually been a highly organized operation. I've rarely been as grateful for anyone's professionalism as I was that morning in Syria.

Rick and I spoke with a twenty-six-year-old rebel named Abu Ali. With Faraz translating for us, we learned Abu had been a lieutenant in the Fourth Armored Division of al-Assad's army in Homs. There he participated in the incessant bombing of the city, until he came to the terrible realization that he was bombing his fellow Syrians. This was so abhorrent to him that he could no longer follow orders; he deserted the army, took a bus home to the northwestern Syrian village of Taftanaz, and joined the resistance.

"I could not kill my people any longer," he said.

Abu recruited ninety local citizens and started the Seventh Valley Brigade, tasked mainly with protecting the surrounding villages where they all lived. They were ordinary townspeople fighting to save their land and their families. This was also why Abu and the Seventh Valley Brigade went to so much trouble to smuggle us in—they wanted the world to know that they were trying to stop the mass slaughter of citizens.

"Assad is killing us all," one rebel said to us. "Tell this story. Tell the world."

It was a stark reminder of why Rick and I were risking our lives to be in Syria. Beyond the rush of combat reporting that fueled us both, there was the very real and desperate need of people like Abu Ali to *have their stories told*. What hung in the balance was nothing less than the survival of thousands of people and families, and possibly a way of life. We were being entrusted with something precious and fragile and ultimately all-important—*the truth of what was happening*. Truth that others would fight desperately and savagely to keep hidden from the world.

• • •

Soon enough we were off again, this time on the backs of rusty little motorbikes steered by rebels. We drove up winding roads and steep hills until we reached a cave overlooking the Taftanaz valley below.

The cave was the makeshift headquarters of the Seventh Valley Brigade. The opening of their cave was twenty feet high but inside there was far less headroom. When we went in we were hit with a thick, pungent cloud of *shisha* smoke. The rebels loved shisha tobacco, which was flavored with molasses and fired inside hookahs, and they loved drinking tea. One rebel's sole task seemed to be keeping the tea and shisha going all the time.

It was nearly midnight when we arrived at the cave, yet inside the rebels were dancing wildly to Syrian music blaring from a small transistor radio. A tiny TV was on in a corner, broadcasting news of the civil war. Grenades, guns, and RPGs were stashed everywhere against the walls, along with dozens of inch-thick mattresses arranged side by side. A single bulb hung from the center of the cave, providing the only illumination. Some of the rebels were beyond middle-aged, but even they danced with abandon. Most of them still wore their rifles and ammunition belts as they lurched about. One rebel, obviously the joker of the bunch, waited for a song to reach its crescendo before yanking a grenade off his belt, pretending to pull the pin, and tossing it in the middle of the dancing men.

Rick and I looked at each other. All we could do was smile. We were both utterly exhausted and, I would have guessed, not in any mood for dancing. Nevertheless, within a few minutes there we were, dancing our hearts out. After a while the rebels collapsed on their mats and fell asleep within seconds, snoring at a ridiculous pitch. Rick and I, meanwhile, were both too buzzed from the shisha smoke to sleep a wink, so we lay curled up on the ground beside them, waiting for daybreak.

We stayed with the rebels for a week. We went with them in rundown pickup trucks as they toured the hills and monitored an al-Assad army base in the valley below. Rebels on motorbikes always went ahead, checking on which paths were safe and which weren't. One day the rebels arranged a protest against the government in Taftanaz. Rick and I joined the few hundred people crowded together on the main street. It was an old town and every building was cracked and crumbling. The rebels had set speakers on top of a pickup truck and one by one people got up and denounced the regime. *Down with Assad, we want change.* It was a loud but peaceful protest.

About ninety minutes in, Syrian Army soldiers appeared at one end of the crowd and without warning opened fire. There was mass panic as everyone ran for safety. Some were trampled and lifted up by fellow villagers. One child of five or six was separated from his mother and stood stone still as people ran past him. He was neither crying nor screaming—just frozen with fear. Rick and I began filming and ran against the crowd, toward the shooting and the injured. That was just our instinct. Quickly some rebels came over and grabbed us, and one of them said, "Take them away." We were rushed into a truck and back to the cave. When we woke up the next morning, everything was different. We felt an incredible tension in the cave, and we wondered why the rebels were suddenly eyeing us with what seemed like pure contempt.

Soon a car drove up to the cave, and a man stepped out and argued loudly and angrily with the rebels. Faraz explained that Assad's men had spotted us in town and seen us filming the attack. Now they were demanding Rick and I be handed over, and half the rebels wanted to do just that as quickly as possible. They argued there would be brutality against villagers for hiding us. We sat there fraught with worry while the man and the rebels continued the argument for hours. Once in a while, Faraz would tell us not to worry. Then a spotter saw a convoy of military vehicles rushing through the valley and heading our way. Assad's men were leaving their base and once again hunting us.

"Looks like they're going to give you over," Faraz said softly.

Rick and I believed we were doomed. We didn't see a way out. Suddenly Abu Ali jumped up and shouted for everyone to stop talking. Then he pointed at Faraz, Rick, and me and at the mouth of the cave— *go*. "You are brothers to us," he said. "Please go and tell the world what is happening." We ran out and found three rebels waiting for us on motorbikes, and we jumped on and held on tightly as they sped away farther and farther up the mountain. We rode like that for a few hours, not knowing where we were going or whether al-Assad's forces were on our tail.

At last we reached a village and rested in the top room of a two-story building with not a stick of furniture in it. We realized we were on the outskirts of Idlib city, the scene of heavy bombing by the Syrian Army. This was, ostensibly, just the place we had come to find—the front line. But the only way into Idlib, we were told, was to crawl through sewage pipes. Rick and I sat on the floor and had one of our talks. We agreed that the chances of us staying in Idlib and getting a story and somehow getting out of Idlib on our own were impossibly remote. So we made the decision to stick with the rebels, get back across the Turkish border, and go home.

But it wasn't nearly as simple as that. Faraz explained there were no safe paths to the border from where we were. To get out of Syria, our only option was to travel farther *into* Syria. So that's what we did.

• • •

The plan was for the Seventh Valley Brigade to pass us off to other rebel groups who could more safely get us to the border. The risk was that even the rebels couldn't always tell their own soldiers from regime militias. We got back on the motorbikes and zipped around the hills and switched over to a car, and we kept going until we reached a checkpoint. Was it a rebel checkpoint or a government checkpoint? We simply didn't know, but we had to take the chance of finding out.

As soon as we approached the stop, fighters jumped up, raised their rifles, marched on us, and shouted us out of the car. They ordered us down to our knees and fired their weapons over our heads before getting closer and pressing their guns to us. Next to me Faraz was hyperventilating and gasping for breath. Rick was in a bad way, too, saying "Fuck, fuck, fuck" over and over as a soldier's rifle pressed even closer to his head. I assumed we'd run right into the hands of the *shabiha*—the most brutal and mercenary of all Assad's fighting forces.

If that was true, it would mean that we were done.

The shouting and the firing continued. It was madness. Yet, to my own shock, I did not hyperventilate or curse or even feel any fear. In fact, I didn't feel anything at all. It was as if I was able to completely block out the emotions running through me, because I understood they couldn't possibly help me now. Not panic, not dread—nothing at all. I just focused on what was happening and on doing whatever I was told to do. I did not feel like my life was over, because I wasn't thinking that far ahead, or even a few seconds ahead. I was utterly, vitally present in the moment.

Suddenly, after five minutes of impossibly tense shouting and shooting, the soldiers lowered their rifles and went quiet. It turned out they weren't regime forces but rather another squad of rebels from a different group. After a few handshakes and laughs we were back on our way.

That is how quickly your fate can turn in war.

The rest of the checkpoints were all run by rebels, and after many hours we made it to the Turkish border, about two hundred miles from where we'd originally crossed. We took a break in a tiny hut on top of a mountain, the borderline clearly in view down below. Faraz suggested we spend the night and set out for the border further along in the morning. I had another idea.

"Faraz, I can see the border from here," I said. "I am not waiting. We might get discovered here. We don't need your help, we'll go alone."

With that, Rick and I set off for the border. But Faraz didn't want to leave us, and he reluctantly joined Rick and me as we scurried down the side of the mountain in the dark, leaping from one huge rock to another. When we spotted two border towers in a small rural village, we believed we were finally safe. All we had to do was get past a barbed-wire fence and we'd be in Turkey.

We reached the fence and tried our best to hold it up for each other so we could pass, but I got stuck in the deep reams of barbed wire. As I tried to free myself, I heard shouts and saw soldiers rushing toward us with guns. Some of them were only a hundred yards away. Then bullets and shells whizzed over our heads. I kept struggling with the wire and finally freed myself, and Rick and I made a mad dash away from the border, running and running and getting as far from the fence as we could. With bullets still ringing around us, and with shotgun pellets hitting our backs, we leapt over a wall and ran into a farm, and reached a barn there. We wedged ourselves beneath an outer staircase and crouched into a little ball and hugged each other tightly and tried not to make a sound. I remember a single bead of sweat rolling off my forehead, and desperately trying to catch it out of the fear that it would make a noise when it landed.

Rick and I stayed huddled silently for half an hour while the armed men searched the village, shouting back and forth, getting closer to our hiding spot. When they finally moved out of earshot, Rick said, "We can't just stay here," and we sprang up and ran at top speed in the opposite direction. We reached an old rock wall and I jumped over it, and as I did it crumbled beneath me. A farmer, woken by the earlier shouting, was on the other side and grabbed tightly on to me, angry about the rock wall. Rick ran up and gave him a good shove and we kept running for twenty minutes until we knew for sure that we were safely in Turkey, and no one was shooting at us anymore.

We found a place to sit for a while and I turned on my cell and saw several text messages from Faraz.

You have to help me, they read. I've been caught by Turkish soldiers and they think I'm a terrorist. You are westerners and you will be fine. Please help.

Rick and I looked at each other, but we didn't need to talk. We knew what we had to do. Having so narrowly escaped the armed men who were trying to stop us from entering Turkey, we got up, retraced our steps, and walked all the way back to the border. We came upon a group of men who spotted us and began shouting, and we turned ourselves over to them and wound up handcuffed in a windowless Turkish prison cell. Faraz wasn't there; he'd been taken somewhere else. Turkish police, we discovered, were as vigilant about Syrians crossing the border as Syrian forces were about smugglers coming in from Turkey. We convinced the police we were journalists, but we spent the night in the cell anyway. The name that appeared just before ours in the prison log book was Anthony Shadid, the *New York Times* foreign correspondent who died crossing out of Syria that same year.

The next day we were released to Turkish intelligence forces, who took our passports and drove us all the way back to Antakya, the city where our adventure began. To our surprise and great relief, Faraz was already there, waiting for us. He'd been released and pushed back into Syria and found another route to the border. Faraz was happy that we'd gone back for him but not at all pleased by everything we'd put him through.

"You almost got me killed," he said.

It was a fundamental error not to listen to him that night on the mountain. He was, after all, the man who saved our lives in that ditch. I knew right then that I'd made a bad mistake, and I vowed to learn from it.

Two years later, when Rick and I returned to Syria, Faraz politely declined to be our fixer.

FIVE

BOMBS AND BULLETS

The question was the same. It is always the same.

How close do you want to get?

It was late 2014 and I was in the town of Sinjar, in northern Iraq. This was not long after the Islamic State of Iraq and Syria, better known as ISIS, had killed 4,400 Sinjar citizens, abducted twice as many, and exiled 200,000 more in their violent effort to establish a caliphate across the Middle East. After years of chasing stories that no one was paying me to get, I'd been hired as a freelancer by Fox News to file a long-format piece from the Iraqi front lines. Rick wasn't with me; instead, my partner was a freelance photographer named Dominique. We were driving with some Kurdish fighters as they struggled to push ISIS out of Sinjar. Our truck pulled over on a street that was exactly three blocks from the fighting, and I had a decision to make.

Would we go with the rebels as they took on the ISIS troops?

The usual mantra ran through my head: *To get the story, you have to take the risks. Sometimes enormous risks.*

And yet—things were different now.

Back in London, Alicia and I had become a proper couple. Since first circling each other in 2011, we both realized that we clicked on so many levels. It had taken us a while to come together because both of us were independent people off doing our own things. Alicia was the European director of the global shoe company Senso, and she regularly traveled to Italy and Australia. I was always looking for the next plane to a combat zone. Still, as Alicia says, "what we found is that we had very similar backgrounds, mutual friends, the same morals and values. It was a perfect, comforting fit."

We had finally moved in together in 2013. She'd been spending a lot of time in my flat in Knightsbridge, and one day she wondered aloud if she should keep the lease to her own flat. I said, "No, just move in with me," and so she just moved in. It did not seem like a monumental step for either of us, nor did we devote a lot of time to planning a future or anything like that. But we *did* talk about having children. Both of us really wanted to have children. Alicia had a vision of having three children, and she knew that was a nice number for me, too. I wanted the same kind of family she did. And she felt that having a family would be good for me, and I would be good at it. "There was something inside him that I thought would make him a wonderful family man," she says. "The way he was so kind to people and caring and determined to make sure everyone else is okay."

As we'd grown closer, I kept up my freelance work. Rick Findler and I both loved the freedom and open-endedness of freelance reporting, the license we had to go anywhere and cover anything with only ourselves to answer to, but, to be honest, it was a real grind. We'd spend our days chasing stories and dodging bombs and snipers, and in the evenings we'd sit in our rooms or in the hotel bar trying to make a sale. I'd open a beer and read over the scribblings in my Moleskine notebook and type up a story and email it to several media outlets— *Esquire, Playboy, Avaaz, The Independent*, the *Sunday Times*, the *New York Times*, BBC Radio—and hope to get a bite, or even a response, the next day. Once, when we were in Syria and had no internet, Rick and I drove out to a risky border area to try and get reception just so we could email our pitches. The drive to find working internet was just as dangerous as covering the stories we were pitching.

Then, if we were lucky, an editor somewhere would buy our story or photograph (*Playboy* paid the best). Sometimes our material would be published somewhere without any attribution or payment at all. And even the fees we did generate took months and months for us to receive. The work was inspiring, exhilarating, important. The rewards, not so much. In my mind, however, it was all building up to something—ideally, an anchor job at one of the major news networks.

In 2014, Rick and I traveled to Iraq and were there when ISIS made its first big push and overtook Mosul, kicking off their plan to claim a caliphate stretching from Aleppo to Diyala (it was in Diyala that an Iraqi helicopter mistakenly fired on the Kurdish forces we were traveling with, killing some of them a few feet away). We covered some big stories, and I forwarded reporting to my list of usual newspapers, magazines, radio stations, and Fox News—anyone who needed to know about ISIS.

Later in 2014, Rick and I reported from Mogadishu during the vicious and ongoing Somali Civil War. There we witnessed a particularly savage battle in Somalia's parliament building. "Ben and I had seen carnage before in Syria, in Libya, and with ISIS, but Africa was a different ballgame," says Rick. "It was all so grotesque. We were documenting a total lack of respect for human life."

When we returned from Somalia, I had an especially hard time readjusting to life in London. The morning I flew in we went to Alicia's mother's fiftieth birthday lunch and I was utterly vacant, a feeling that got worse. It was the first time that I'd come back from a trip and was noticeably depressed and disturbed, and Alicia noticed, growing concerned about my trouble sleeping and dreaming of war, explosions, death. Over time it passed, and I became my usual jovial self again, but we both saw that something was lingering beneath the surface that I couldn't say out loud.

While Alicia was learning that it wasn't in my nature to divulge too much, for me it was a protective instinct. I did not want to burden her with a lot of unnecessary anxiety about my safety on these trips, nor with any of the grisly details afterward. This is also why, at times, I fell into the pattern of downplaying the danger whenever I told Alicia about an upcoming assignment. I'd tell her I'd only be on the border of a war-torn country, rather than in the heart of it, and then she'd see a photo of me crawling on the ground on my belly with bombs bursting in the background and she'd say, "You told me you weren't going to do that!" I preferred explaining that our plans had changed or we'd been forced to move, rather than frightening her ahead of time with predictions about the kind of danger I might be in. Was that the right decision? I don't know. But in my head, it was the best way to protect Alicia.

Just before I had left for Iraq on the Fox News assignment, in late 2014, Alicia told me she was pregnant. We didn't have very much time to celebrate, since I had to fly out the next day. I felt guilty about leaving her so abruptly after such life-altering news, and when I landed in Erbil I immediately called her.

"I understand we are about to have a baby," I said with unnecessary formality. "With this baby on the way I want you to know that I am looking to change my lifestyle." Meaning—I will stop going to war zones.

When I got to my dingy little hotel room in Erbil, the next person I called was Alicia's father, Kim, in Australia, to ask him for her hand in marriage. "I would love to marry your daughter," I said. "I want you to know that I understand there is danger to the kinds of jobs I am doing, and I won't be doing them anymore."

Yet I *did* keep doing them. Had I been dishonest with Alicia and her father? Or had I believed what I was telling them at the time?

A part of it was my desire to make them both feel more at ease with what I did. I was not a reckless or foolhardy correspondent; I was very serious about my safety, and I didn't always think there was any reason for others to worry. But I knew how frightened my own parents would get any time I ventured into a war zone, and I didn't want Alicia or her family to feel that way. There would come a time when I did stop reporting from the front lines, but until then I simply did not want everyone worrying about me all the time. Whether or not that was the right decision is, again, hard for me to say.

In Iraq, I hadn't expected to share the news of Alicia's pregnancy with anyone, but early on, and for whatever reason, I told Dominique, the camerawoman, about it.

"You just found out and you're here?" she said. "Why?"

I just smiled, but my initial thought was *Why wouldn't I be?* Honestly, it never occurred to me not to go because of the big news.

This was my job. This is who I was. It had to be this way.

Then came the fateful day the Kurdish fighters took Dominique and me within three blocks of where ISIS troops awaited.

The Kurds would park there and go the rest of the way on foot. Would we be coming with them? Normally I wouldn't hesitate to seize an opportunity to capture a conflict up close. Just three more blocks? Of course I'll go. That was, after all, what I'd come all this way to do.

But that day, for the first time, I *did* hesitate.

"We'll stay here," I told the Kurdish fighters, who instead agreed to wear tiny GoPro cameras on their helmets to capture the action.

The irony is that when I say I chose not to go forward, I was already just three streets away from heavily armed ISIS fighters. In the end, even the Kurds only got within one street of ISIS, exchanged some gunfire, and pulled back. So all I did was keep two additional streets—a few hundred yards—away from the very heart of the battle. It was hardly a safe distance.

But it was something. It was the first time I hesitated to get as physically close to the fighting as possible. Did I hesitate because of Alicia and our future child? I would think so. I didn't analyze my decision on the ground in Iraq or even afterward. Describing it now is probably the first time I ever thought this hard about why I didn't go those last two blocks.

It is clear now that that was the moment I began to change.

• • •

There was another way I felt Alicia's influence on that trip to Iraq. At the time the country was utterly overrun by fierce fighting, and there were many combat stories I could have chosen to cover. Instead I got word of a young Iraqi Yazidi girl who'd been kidnapped by ISIS, almost certainly turned into a sex slave, and was finally going to be released to her family for a ransom. I wanted to cover their reunion and tell the girl's story and show that side of the war. That was Alicia's influence—not chasing the bombs and bullets every time.

We traveled to a northern Iraqi town where most of the indigenous Yazidi people had been killed or rounded up by ISIS fighters, who were still active and roaming the area. One of their hostages was the young Iraqi girl. Her family negotiated with ISIS to release her, and they were about to get her back from inside neighboring Syria, at a spot along the banks of the Tigris River. Dominique and I stuck close to the family as they retrieved their daughter, who, it was clear, had endured horrific brutality and trauma at the hands of ISIS. The reunion was deeply raw and emotional and I listened to story after story about the girl and the atrocities that happened to her. The details were unthinkable.

But I was locked in on getting the story and I kept going. I made sure Dominique was in the car with the girl when she was picked up and recorded the intimate reunion, and then again when the women ushered the girl into a little room and surrounded her and wailed and prayed at the top of their voices. I felt as if I was invading a terribly personal moment. But that was the job: to tell this story to the world. To look away now would be pointless, it seemed, so we kept the camera going and we captured their torment up close.

It turned into one of the most powerful stories I've worked on.

When we finally left Iraq and I returned to London, I was happy to be with Alicia again. I was still struggling to find a balance between my work life and the rest of my life, and I was finding it quite hard to do because of how deeply invested I was in my work, and how closely I had tied it up with my identity. But seeing Alicia again made it plain that covering wars no longer meant *everything* to me, as it had just a few years before. The scales were beginning to balance.

I made plans to propose to Alicia. My good friend Cosimo Pandolfini had weekend reservations at Babington House, a beautiful manor hotel in the English countryside, and when his wife went into early labor he asked us if we wanted to go. I didn't have an engagement ring yet, but I didn't want to wait to ask Alicia for her hand, so we drove up for the weekend with me determined to seize the most perfect moment to pop the question. And there were many such moments. We took several lovely walks through the most idyllic gardens and pathways and orchards you can imagine, all perfectly appropriate for any romantic gesture.

Yet, for some reason, none of the moments struck me as perfect. I kept saying, "No, I will find a better place." I put off the proposal so often that the weekend ran out and Alicia and I got back in our car for the glum drive home. Alicia was painfully quiet on the way, and when I asked her something, she responded with one-word answers.

"I was cross," Alicia recalls. "I didn't know he planned to propose but it did occur to me that this would have been a lovely setting for it. And my mother expected him to do it. She said, 'He's going to propose this weekend, you'll see.' So on the drive back, yes, I was angry."

When the levers in my head finally clicked and I realized I'd been an idiot and missed a wonderful chance to propose, I knew I had to do something. Maybe I could pretend that this had been the plan all along, to delay the proposal to the last minute (not a very good plan, had it been true). On the drive up to the countryside, we had passed

Stonehenge, and so I headed there. I drove us to a back entrance gate, which of course was locked. Then I drove up a muddy road until I found a place that at least *overlooked* Stonehenge, and I pulled over and guided Alicia to a spot next to a big barbed-wire fence that wasn't completely covered in mud. It could hardly have been a worse place for a proposal. By then Alicia obviously felt the moment had long passed, but I pushed on anyway.

I bent to one knee in the mud and said something silly about how Stonehenge represented the circle of life, and finally I proposed to the woman I love.

Thankfully, she said yes.

Or perhaps she said, "Get up, it's really muddy."

Right then a car pulled over and a man stepped out and asked us if we'd like him to take a photo of our big moment.

"No thanks!" Alicia cried out.

Honestly, I would give my proposal an F. Only later did I realize how much the place I picked to propose resembled a war zone—dirt road, barbed wire, dark of night, middle of nowhere. Hopefully I made it up to Alicia by more properly proposing in Morocco some months later.

"That time he genuinely surprised me with the ring," Alicia says. "Finally got it right."

• • •

I had spent so much time on the front lines in Iraq and learned so much about ISIS that I decided to write a book about them, based on all my reporting on the ground. *Inside ISIS: The Brutal Rise of a Terrorist Army* was published in March 2015. I was doing some publicity for the book and made some appearances on Fox News to talk about ISIS. Afterward, Fox set up a meeting with me at the company headquarters in New York City.

I had a good feeling about the meeting. Alicia and I, now freshly engaged, were expecting our first child in just a few months. Up until then I had only worked as a freelancer, which meant that, while I was very busy sending out stories to the major news outlets, I wasn't making a lot of money. Rick and I had started our own little news agency, Borderline News, to collect front-line cell phone footage from around the world, which we would then distribute to various outlets. One of our ideas was to attach GoPro cameras to the tops of thirty British military ballistic helmets we bought, then smuggle those cameras into Aleppo, Syria (which, on its own, was not dissimilar to smuggling in weapons). We found thirty rebels willing to wear the cameras, but of the thirty GoPros we sent out, we only got four back. Three of them showed rebels looking curiously at the cameras before shutting them off; the fourth provided very clear point-of-view footage of a rebel sitting in a room waiting around for hours.

After the GoPro failure, we spent the week reporting from the front lines in Aleppo and came across an Al Qaeda affiliate group on a bombed-out city street. Terrified of being captured, we struck up a game of darts with them in their shelter as barrel bombs fell around us, covering us in smoke and peppering the shelter with shrapnel.

Among them was a Canadian fighter, one of the first foreign terrorists who had gone to fight. Immediately I knew this would be our most interesting, salable story, and we followed him for a while. Another character who stood out was our fixer, Rizgar, who had once been the Syrian military sprinting champion. He had dreamed of turning professional, but now he was here, at war. Whenever we came to a road that was known to have snipers perched above it, we agreed to count to three and run madly across the road at three. Rizgar, the sprinter, would always run at the count of one, leaving us flailing behind him as sniper bullets raked the ground at our feet.

The Borderline News agency didn't make a lot of money either, with most of its cash going to rent giant billboards across Afghanistan and Baghdad, advertising good money for footage.

As passionate as I was about being a war correspondent, with a child on the way I had to at least consider finding another line of work. I simply wasn't making enough as a freelancer to support a family. Things had gotten even worse when certain news organizations stopped accepting footage and stories from freelance war correspondents out of Syria, because they didn't want to encourage them to continually endanger their lives. I thought of different professions that I might be suited for, and even wondered if I could make it as a real estate agent, or something like that.

Then I had my meeting at Fox News headquarters. I traded some small talk with a few producers and was whisked upstairs.

"Roger wants to see you," one of them told me.

"Roger who?" I asked, revealing how very little I knew about the broadcast news business.

I was shown into a big boardroom and sat through an entire long board meeting, during which Roger—as in the late Roger Ailes, the man who essentially turned Fox News into the industry leader—asked me a couple of questions. *What do you think of waterboarding?* was one of them. It went well, and after the meeting Roger invited me to his office.

"How do you get your stories?" he asked.

"I knock on doors and I just keeping knocking," I said.

"Do you ever make any money from these projects?"

"Actually, no, I've lost money," I said.

"Well, great, you're hired," Roger said.

And that was that. After the meeting I asked a Fox producer, "What just happened?" He said, "You got the job." The problem was, I didn't quite know what the job was. Once I was out of the building and on Sixth Avenue, I immediately called Alicia and told her what happened.

"I think they hired me," I said.

"To do what?" she asked.

"I don't know. Be on television?"

The truth was, I didn't really care what the job was. I was elated to be staying in the news-gathering business. Still, when I didn't hear back from anyone at Fox for three months after my interview with Roger, I got a bit worried. "Hey, do I still have a job?" I emailed a Fox executive. "Don't worry, we're looking into it, we'll figure it out," came the response. In a way that made me feel good. Clearly, they weren't hiring me to fill a specific position, but rather because they liked me and they liked my work. Eventually I did hear that I might be stationed in Fox's Rome bureau. Alicia and I talked about moving to Italy, and while she wasn't overly keen on it (neither of us spoke Italian), we were both ready to do it.

The truth is, Alicia would have gone anywhere if it meant I was able to pull back from the front lines. She believed that working at Fox would give me structure and limit the need for me to fly off and chase dangerous stories that weren't under the umbrella of the company.

Finally, we learned that Fox wanted to station me in the London bureau, based in the headquarters of Sky News (which, like Fox News, was founded by Rupert Murdoch) near Heathrow Airport. It was the best outcome and it meant we wouldn't have to move at all.

But first, there was our July wedding. Neither Alicia nor I had any interest in a lavish, over-the-top type of wedding; having kids together was really all that mattered to us. Still, I came from a very Catholic family and it was important to me to have a proper Catholic wedding. One potential obstacle was that Alicia would be demonstrably pregnant at the time of the July ceremony. Fortunately, my father was friends with two priests, Father Rupert, the serious one, and Father Julian, the livelier one, who were very fond of our family and agreed to officiate. "I remember my grandmother worriedly asking me, 'Are you sure the priest knows you're pregnant?'" Alicia says. "I had to assure her that he did."

We all gathered in the Brompton Oratory, a beautifully neoclassical Roman Catholic church in Knightsbridge where I used to sing as a choirboy. Alicia wore a bone silk, floor-length yellow slip dress, and she was stunning. Her father, Kim, walked her down the aisle. The ceremony was perfect, and afterward the reception was at Alicia's family home. Someone told Alicia that they'd never seen a happier bride, and I think they may have been right. We were a couple, having a baby, and there was nothing for her to be nervous about.

Around that time I reported to the Fox News London bureau for the first time. I dressed up in my smartest suit and I was eager to get started. The first person I spoke with was Dragan Petrovic, then the chief of the London bureau. He was Serbian and he cut a dashing figure at six feet five, with a polished bald head, and carrying with him all the renown of thirty years of gritty reporting from the front lines. He still had shrapnel in his leg from a visit to Iraq. He was as respected a producer as there was in the industry, and when he saw me, he had only one question:

"Well, who are you?"

"I'm the new correspondent," I answered happily.

"Well, we've never heard of you. Can you just go home and we'll figure out if you're working here or not?"

At the time, we were among several Fox staffers who all looked at me and cringed at this less-than-stellar beginning to my career at Fox. More weeks passed, until one day I got a call from someone at Fox who said to come into the bureau right away so I could go on the air.

"They found some remnants of Malaysia Airlines Flight 370," they said. "You have to do a live hit in an hour."

My first reaction was surprise that they actually *did* want me to be on the air, and so quickly. That had never been part of the plan in my mind, and though I had appeared in some on-air reports from the field, I assumed that for any big breaking story they would use some more polished on-air presence. Yet suddenly I had precisely one hour to get to the bureau and go live with a story I knew nothing about. I hustled to the office, where I was guided into the TV booth chair and had someone slip a receiver in my ear.

"When they say hi to you, you tell them the story," they said.

What story??? I wanted to yell out.

Before I knew it, I was live on-air. I buried the surge of panic I felt and summoned whatever authority I could and began to relay the precious little information I had about the doomed flight that disappeared a year earlier. Afterward, it seemed to have gone well enough and everyone was pleased. I went home again and waited for the next call. Finally, it was made official that I would start my full-time duties any time after the birth of my first child, who was due in August, about a month after our wedding.

I had gone overseas on assignment twice during Alicia's pregnancy, but I made good and sure I was there for the birth. We did a dry run to Chelsea and Westminster Hospital, and that very night Alicia began her contractions. We stayed up all night, her timing the contractions, me scurrying to do whatever I could to make Alicia feel safe and relaxed. In a way, preparing for the birth was like preparing for one of my forays into a combat zone—the pressure only made me more focused and alert, and everything seemed to slow down. In the morning we drove to the hospital and I held Alicia's hand as she went into labor. I had the option of positioning myself in the delivery room so I could watch the birth or staying away from the action. Naturally I chose to watch. The impulse was almost journalistic: if there was something for me to see, I had to see it.

But I also wanted to experience the emotion of my child's birth as fully and deeply as possible. I had seen death up close, and I'd felt the solemnity and importance of the moment, and I'd been moved by it, and I wanted the birth of my child to feel at least as powerful and moving and monumental as what I witnessed during war.

And it was. Alicia, strong and determined throughout, delivered a healthy, beautiful baby girl we named Honor Scarlett Elizabeth. We both held her in those early moments of her life and we marveled at our blessing, at the wonder of this miracle before us. We were now, the three of us, all at once, cast into new and sacred roles—mother, father, daughter. *Family*. It felt like we were the luckiest people on earth.

But then it was back to work. Fox told me I could start any time after the delivery, so I reported to the London bureau *one day* after Honor's birth. I wanted to get started and get back to being a reporter, because I was so excited about this new chapter in my professional life. But I realize now that it was not at all fair to leave Alicia alone with all the parental duties and ceaseless attentiveness a newborn requires. I know now that this was a bad move on my part. I just didn't know it then.

SIX

TOOTH FOR TOOTH

Our van turned a corner in the northern Syrian countryside and we encountered the very last people we would ever want to see at that moment—an entire brigade of Syrian Army troops. For the first time ever in a combat zone, I had a singular thought:

I'm a goner.

It was 2019, and I was part of a Fox News crew assigned to cover the Turkish aggression against the Kurds in northern Syria. The nearly decade-long violence in Syria had taken a strange and deadly turn, and the lines between allies and enemies had blurred. Turkey was a NATO ally, but they were bombing the Kurdish fighters, whom the U.S. had supported in their successful fight against ISIS. Our crew was with the Kurds as they fled positions in Syria now being bombed by our ostensible ally Turkey. Fleeing the bombing alongside the Kurds were Syrian Army soldiers, who elsewhere in the country were fighting *against* the Kurds in the endless Syrian Civil War.

It was a volatile and potentially lethal mix of friend and foe.

I was in the van with my Fox News producer, Tim Santhouse, and our cameraman, Pierre Zakrzewski. The three of us had all been in precarious battle zone situations before and none of us was prone to panic or overdramatizing, yet I know that all of us felt the same sickening existential dread when we found ourselves face-to-face with Syrian Army soldiers. We had all spent years trying like hell to avoid them. They were known for their brutality and for kidnapping and killing journalists. It was Syrian Army soldiers who killed the revered war correspondent Marie Colvin in Homs in western Syria. It was the Syrian Army that, we believed, kidnapped the ex-Marine, American freelance journalist Austin Tice, in Darayya, Syria, in 2012 (if alive, he has yet to be released). Surely if they discovered that we were Americans working with an American media network, they would take us, too.

The three of us looked at each other in the van, fear in our eyes and an unspoken question hanging in the hot air: *What do we do now?*

"Act normal," I heard Pierre say. "Just get out of the van and start setting up."

We swung open the van doors and confronted the Syrian Army.

• • •

By then the dimensions of my new job as a Fox News foreign correspondent were taking shape and I realized they would include not only a lot of on-air work from London but also just as many, if not more, trips to combat zones as when I was a freelancer. Still, Alicia had been right— there was much more of a structure in place for these trips. There was more security, more clarity about assignments, more backup, more experienced colleagues and producers, more everything. It was no longer just Rick and me wading across a freezing river in the dead of night. Yes, I was still being sent to dangerous places. But generally, it felt like I was far less exposed.

The first big story I worked on Fox News was the Paris attacks in November 2015. I got a call to come into the studio while the coordinated attacks by Islamic terrorists were still unfolding, some in Paris and some in the suburb of Saint-Denis. The terror spree left 130 people dead, including ninety who died in a massacre at the Bataclan theater—the deadliest attacks in France since World War II. I got to the London bureau at 8 p.m. and stayed on the air for about twelve straight hours, talking to contacts on the ground in Paris, absorbing new reports, coordinating the coverage, and going live almost nonstop to tell the story of what was happening.

When it was over it felt like the most exciting, adrenalized, incredible thing I'd ever done as a journalist.

Soon afterward Fox sent me to Brussels, Belgium, to further report on the Paris attacks. Some of the attackers came from Brussels and I would be looking for background on them. This is when I realized I was at the bottom of the list of Fox correspondents, because all the top guys were in Paris, about 190 miles southwest of Brussels. I knew it would be difficult finding a story good enough to compete with the Paris reporting and get on-air, and it was. For five days I dug around for a story, with no success.

Finally I went into Molenbeek, the most Muslim part of Brussels and the Islamic center of Belgium. Terrorists were known to frequent some of the more than twenty mosques there. It could be a dangerous place for Western journalists; I'd heard stories of correspondents getting robbed or threatened with casual regularity. "Mate, we're taking your camera and we're going to beat the shit out of you" was a typical approach.

In Molenbeek my producer Baz and I went into mosque after mosque asking if anyone knew Salah Abdeslam, one of the Paris attackers. We went to a mosque that was down a dark cobblestone street and through two big double doors, and we waited in a small room as worshipers in Taqiyah skullcaps exited past us. I asked everyone if they knew Abdeslam (they all spoke French and so do I). Most of them told us to get out of the mosque. Finally, one man stopped and told us he had a friend who knew Abdeslam. We pushed him for more and he persuaded his friend to meet us in a tiny café nearby.

We sat with this man and his friend in the café, surrounded by chain-smoking Tunisian immigrants, and I asked him about Abdeslam. Many people I approach as a journalist initially refuse to speak so much as a single word to me, but this guy was ready to talk and talk, and an incredible story emerged. He knew precisely how Abdeslam had been radicalized, and why he'd carried out the attacks. I had done many stories about how mosques were radicalizing people across Europe, and Abdeslam's story fit right into this pattern.

But then, as we talked, a man sitting next to us leaned forward and spoke to us, too. "They are killing ours so we kill theirs," he said. "Tooth for tooth." Others chimed in and drilled home the point—in the eyes of these Muslims, the Paris attacks were more than justified; they were righteous. When we showed our footage to Fox, they were stunned to see that ordinary people in a modern country like Belgium could feel the way they did about the attacks, and could have such conviction about the use of terroristic force. The piece we put together to air surprised viewers, too, and the report received special attention around Fox. A week later, they reassigned me to Paris.

At Fox News I learned as I went. As a freelancer I had to fight relentlessly to secure an interview with, say, the third secretary of the environment in some war-torn country. At Fox, presidents, prime ministers, and foreign ministers were happy to talk to us. What I learned, however, was that 90 percent of the time you knew exactly what answer you would get from a top government official, and the answer would be whatever they wanted the public to believe. My job then became to somehow squeeze a single kernel of truth out of these seasoned world leaders. Ironically, I had often scored far deeper and more useful intelligence from people way down the government ladder when I was a freelancer.

I often felt like I didn't know what I was doing, but I was lucky to be around the most professional colleagues anyone could ask for: senior foreign affairs correspondent Greg Palkot, who's covered stories in every part of the world, from Tora Bora to Pyongyang; my producers

Barry-John Davies and Claire Cooney and Tim Santhouse; and my cameramen Pierre Zakrzewski and Mal James. They had been at the front of so many big stories, and when I started at Fox they all encouraged me whenever my frustrations may have shown.

"Don't worry, mate, you'll be totally fine," Mal told me on my first day at Fox. "Just keep talking."

Then there was Pierre. The son of a French mother and Polish father, Irish-born and raised in Leopardstown, County Dublin, he was a free spirit and an idealist who from a young age wanted to be a journalist and "save the world," his mother, Marie-Ange Zakrzewska, once said. Tall, gentle, and known for his exuberantly bushy mustache, Pierre did everything with such passion and sureness of purpose that you felt you were in the very best hands whenever you teamed up with him.

His work ethic was unmatched, and it led him to take on several jobs on every assignment in addition to manning the camera: electrician, expense accountant, therapist, whatever was needed. We called him MacGyver because he was so astonishingly handy. He could go into a hotel and bypass their electrical system without them ever knowing it. "I'll take a little bit out of this outlet and a little out of that cable and it will all work just fine," he'd say. He could take a metal coat hanger and hook it up to a wire and jam a paper clip in it and hold it down with a brick and suddenly the satellite phone would be working again. He approached everything like an adventure that was to be savored and treasured and tackled with passion. He made things happen and he made things fun. For me, Pierre was, more than anything, a teacher. And what he taught me about was life, about the joy and adventure of it, about kindness and hard work, about just how amazing it all was. I'd never known anyone who was so loved by everyone he met, on all corners of the globe.

We worked together on dozens of overseas assignments. We traveled to Singapore for President Donald Trump's meeting with North Korean leader Kim Jong-un, bonding over dim sum at 5 a.m. in a local

dive. We explored ISIS tunnels deep under Mosul, roamed through
royal weddings, sat in on NATO meetings. In 2017 we were sent to
Barcelona, Spain, in the wake of a terrorist attack on hundreds of pe-
destrians on La Rambla. It was a difficult trip for me because I was
struggling with two major events in my life: the birth of my second
child, Iris, a few weeks earlier, and the death of my mother, Jenny,
shortly before that.

My mother had been ill for many years, though we never knew it.
She did not want anyone worrying about her or mourning for her, so
she kept her health issues to herself. She'd even warned us when we
were young that if she ever got cancer or any other illness, she would
never tell us. And she didn't. Late in her life she had enormous trouble
sleeping, and often could only fall asleep in a moving car.

One morning while in Portugal my father took her for a drive.
When she fell asleep in the passenger seat, he parked in the driveway
and sat with her so as not to wake her. Suddenly my mother bolted up,
opened her eyes and gasped, reached out to grab my father, and then
simply slumped down and passed away. My father tried desperately
to save her, but it was no use. It was only a week later that we found a
letter from her doctor saying she had been suffering from pulmonary
hypertension, a type of high blood pressure that affects the lungs and
heart. Some of our relatives were upset that she didn't tell anyone of
her illness; they felt they might have been able to help her or at least
comfort her. But her secrecy did not upset me. I knew she'd devoted
her life to helping others and could not bear the thought of being the
one who needed help. I also knew that she had lived her life fully and
without apology until her very last moments.

Still, losing her was difficult and it wore on me when I was in
Barcelona, as did leaving Alicia and my newborn daughter in London.
To suddenly be reporting on the tragic deaths of so many innocent
people—when I was already contemplating questions of life and birth
and death—was emotionally wrenching. I shared all of this with Pierre,

and in our downtime he sat with me for long talks about just these weighty matters.

What came through was his insuppressible love of life and his belief that there was always something good to be found in even the most tragic moments. He spoke about how lucky we were, and what incredible jobs we had, and how, no matter where we went, we would always find stories of people's goodness and humanity, of the inherent joy of children, of neighbors helping each other survive, of people finding ways to persevere. Pierre was amazed by just how loving and generous people could be. To him the world was far more wonderful than it was frightening.

That night in Barcelona he did not talk to me about my mother's death, but rather helped me celebrate her life. What an impossibly rare and beautiful gift that was to receive just then.

• • •

At Fox I got to cover the world. Every day there was another major event somewhere that demanded attention. An earthquake in Asia; elections in Africa; a bomb attack in the Middle East; landslides in South America. We covered it all and it never stopped. Much of my early time at Fox was consumed by the terrorist attacks across Europe. In 2016 I was sent to Nice, France, after a Tunisian terrorist, Mohamed Lahouaiej-Bouhlel, drove a nineteen-ton cargo truck down the Promenade des Anglais on Bastille Day, killing eighty-six people and injuring nearly five hundred more.

When I arrived, I went straight to work and did live hits around the clock for three days straight. In the middle of it all there was a coup attempt in Turkey and we mixed in hours of coverage about it with everything we were reporting from Nice. Through a contact, I discovered where Lahouaiej-Bouhlel had lived in Nice. We went to his building and someone came out, and we slipped inside and made it up to his apartment. As a freelancer I would have pushed right in, but at Fox there were certain lines we could not cross. Still, we were the first ones to find the apartment and look inside from the threshold and get reporting about how the terrorist had lived.

In 2019 I insisted on being part of the team that was covering the final battles to wipe out ISIS in Syria. Rick Findler and I had been there at the beginning of ISIS's terrible reign, at the front lines in Mosul, when the dream of a multicountry caliphate seemed within ISIS's reach. Now, three years later, U.S. forces were bombing the last remnants of ISIS in Syria. Pierre and I worked together, and we were one of the first teams to find and film the secret ISIS tunnels. Some Kurdish soldiers took us down into the dark catacomb, in which ISIS fighters lived in cramped rooms with flimsy mattresses and hid out from bombing raids. There were multiple entrances and hand-carved turrets and even electricity. Standing in these tunnels—where ISIS fighters had been just days before—gave us an extraordinary view of what the war in Syria was actually like, and how the terror group had held on for so long.

Pierre and I also drove to Sinjar, scene of the bloodiest battle to push out ISIS. We drove to a little forward base out in the desert that was being attacked by ISIS, and we met up with Kurdish soldiers there. The base was nothing more than a few tiny huts with mud walls and metal sheets for roofs. We slept shoulder to shoulder with the soldiers our first night and spent the next twenty-four hours setting up satellite equipment and planning reports, all with active ISIS forces less than a mile away in three directions.

This was the beginning of the end for the ISIS caliphate, and we followed the battle against them all the way to its conclusion in Syria, where we witnessed a truly astounding scene. Along with my cameraman Mal James, I traveled into the bombed-out remains of the final ISIS town and crawled up to a rooftop and looked down on what the Syrian democratic forces had told us were the last scraps of ISIS fighters, the remnants of a brutal terror army now in defeat. We climbed up to a higher perch on a hill and watched as the Kurdish soldiers went into the village to wipe out their enemies, while the soldiers who stayed with us opened fire and picked off the few fighters who emerged to do battle. Later we traveled to the desert just north of Baghouz, which had just been bombed into oblivion by a top-secret U.S. air strike. We watched as thousands of men, women, and children streamed out of the town in surrender to U.S. and Iraqi forces. They had been ISIS members, but now they claimed not to be. For weeks they had slept underground, seeking shelter from the carnage, and they were a terrible sight. Many of them hadn't eaten in days, even weeks, and were starving to death. Hundreds of hungry babies cried out. Girls and boys trudged absently alongside their parents, too young to understand why their childhoods had been stolen by this evil. They looked like nothing so much as an army of zombies following each other into prison camps.

They were the ghosts of people that had once been.

This wretched exodus moved me in a powerful way. Emaciated people who could barely walk, babies sliding toward death in front of us—the sheer inhumanity of it all was staggering. These were the remnants of a once-potent terrorist force, now stripped of everything. An evil that had been defeated, and people who had believed in a cruel and violent caliphate reduced now to dregs in the cruel desert. It was, I understood, a victory for good, and I had no sympathy for the ISIS supporters.

But the children—they were another story. Children who had committed no sins of their own, caught up now in a brutal cycle, destined to be raised in ISIS-filled prison camps and inevitably become terrorists themselves. Watching them trudge through the desert was difficult.

When Pierre, Tim Santhouse, and I returned to those prison camps months later, they had become too dangerous for us to enter. In essence, ISIS controlled them, smuggling in weapons and smuggling out people. Up to sixty thousand people were being held in one of the camps, and they lived under strict Islamic rules. If a woman in the camp broke an ISIS rule, she would almost certainly be killed. The best we could do was to stick close to the guards, stay on the other side of a fence, and talk to anyone who came over. Several women in burkas and their children did come over, and they were openly hostile.

"When we grow up, we will kill you all," the children shouted, some in English, some in French. The remnants of ISIS, waiting to emerge again.

Terrorism was breeding more terrorism. One war was leading to another. Children were being pulled into the pipeline every day. How could this ever be stopped? Or perhaps it never could be. Perhaps it was just the way of the world. For me it was a stark illustration that there will always be evil in the world, waiting patiently to rear up again, and that there must always be someone there ready to keep it down. Wars did not end; they just waned and fired up again someplace else, consuming new generations, destroying new lives.

• • •

In the Syrian town of Tall Tamr we stopped the van as soon as we saw the Syrian Army brigade. Quickly we contacted Dragan Petrovic in London to tell him we were surrounded by Syrian soldiers and to let him know our coordinates. None of that would help us in the moment. I fully believed we were in a situation from which there was no escape, and in my mind I was preparing what to say when the Syrians bound us and hooded us and badgered us with questions. Even our Syrian fixer, Serbest, was seized by panic and said, "I don't know what to do."

Then the strangest thing happened. We got out of the van, as Pierre had advised, and acted normally as we began filming. I'd never felt such suffocating tension, such dread of the inevitable, in my life. But the Syrian soldiers did not ask us who we were. They did not demand to see credentials to prove we were Westerners. The unpredictable calculus of war had suddenly thrust us all together—the Syrian Army, the Kurdish rebels, and us—and created a common enemy: the Turks who were trying to bomb us. The tension melted away.

When I realized we were not in imminent danger of being taken hostage, I approached some of the Syrian fighters and asked them about their experiences. They were happy to talk, and they never asked who we were or where we were from. They allowed us to continue setting up, and later our Fox News team moved forward alongside them and watched the Kurds and the Syrians surge together toward the heavy shelling at the Turkish lines a mile away. It was a truly mind-bending moment—die-hard enemies suddenly fighting together against a U.S. ally—and we captured it all and had what we thought was a vital and unique report about the war.

A day later U.S. special forces killed Abu Bakr al-Baghdadi, the brutal leader who had turned ISIS into a global terror network, in a raid in southwestern Syria (al-Baghdadi detonated a suicide vest when he realized he'd been trapped, killing himself and two children in his below-ground escape tunnel). His death instantly became the biggest story about ISIS, and our report from Tall Tamr never made it onto the air. The night we filmed that piece, we went back to our base and our producer, Tim, got on the phone and called his rabbi. He had until the end of the day to finish his child's school application, and he was on the phone persuading his rabbi to help him get it in.

This was the strange, incongruous reality of reporting on war.

I had issues with my family that needed attention, too. Alicia and I had both figured that working for Fox News would give me more structure and more time to be with her and the children, or at least more quality time. But things didn't work out that way. As a freelancer I might be gone for two weeks, three at most. But now when I went on assignment I could be away longer, and with less notice. I could tell Alicia was surprised I was gone so often, though she never objected or made an issue of it. All she would say is "Well, that was really quite hard, but I know how important it is for you." And that would be that.

Even when I wasn't traveling, I was often absent from our home. My work out of the London bureau always ended late at night, and for many years I was away from Alicia and the children just about every evening. I had a job I absolutely loved, but it entailed missing out on dinners together and putting the children to bed—missing out on a lot of what it means to be a family. I would say it was a steep learning curve for me, and for Alicia as well. Once again, she never complained, not even when I went away to dangerous places. But in our discussions, we both agreed that something needed to change.

In 2021, I began to hear talk of Fox News transferring me to the Washington, DC, bureau. I was on the grounds of Windsor Castle covering the funeral of Prince Philip when I got a call from Kim Rosenberg, the senior vice president of news, and Amy Sohnen, a senior vice president of talent development. They asked if I'd be interested in moving from the London bureau to the U.S. State Department in DC. The timing was perfect; Alicia and I had talked about me pulling back from war zones, and reporting on foreign policy in the U.S. seemed like a good chance to focus more on studio work. I would also be returning to America, a country that I loved. It was a chance for all of us to start a new chapter in our lives.

But, as usual, it was not as simple as all of us packing up and flying to the U.S. By then we had three children—our third daughter, Hero, was born in 2020—and two of them were in school. Uprooting them on a moment's notice seemed ill-advised. This was also one year into the COVID crisis, and transferring young children to a strange environment in the midst of a pandemic and all its protocols and mask requirements made the decision even harder. Alicia had never been to Washington, DC, and didn't have the most positive impression of it;

she knew it was an industry town where getting dolled up and going to embassy parties is what passed for a social life. We sat down for long conversations about what the best move for us as a family was.

In the end we decided I would go to Washington on my own at first, in October 2021. Once the children were done with the school year the following August, and assuming mask mandates had been lifted, my family would join me in the States. It was hardly an ideal situation, and when I left, I felt like I was abandoning Alicia and the children yet again, this time for an even longer period. I went from living with my wife and children to living alone in an apartment in a strange city. It felt wrong to me, and it was a strain on Alicia as well. I tried to fly back every other weekend to catch Honor in a ballet performance or some other family event, but these weekends were often rushed and unsatisfying. Those few months when I was in DC were hard on us all, but I believed it would all work out when we were together.

"I'd always known that covering wars was who Benji was, but what I think he didn't always understand was that there needed to be a balance there," Alicia says. "When he went to DC by himself I think he lost some of that balance, that sense of being in the family and having those responsibilities. I think the decisions he made in DC would have been different had he been at home with us when he made them."

My time in the DC bureau had many bright spots. I was filling in as an anchor for the top Fox News broadcasters, and I believed this was my future. I talked to Alicia about how the network was moving me in that direction. The few times I traveled it was with well-organized delegations. I flew with the U.S. secretary of state, Antony Blinken, to Kenya, Senegal, and Nigeria for his talks with foreign ministers, and we developed a cordial relationship while chatting and joking on his plane or at media events.

In January 2022 I flew with Blinken to Ukraine, which was then seemingly in the crosshairs of the Russians. At that time even the

Ukrainians didn't believe Russia would actually invade, but Blinken was there to assure Ukrainian president Volodymyr Zelenskyy that the U.S. would support the country no matter what. On the same trip we went to Geneva, Switzerland, for a sit-down between Blinken and the Russian minister of foreign affairs, Sergey Lavrov. Blinken and other U.S. officials appeared to already know that Russia was going to invade Ukraine. Even so, the meeting was a chance for some heroic last-minute diplomacy.

Lavrov and Blinken met in a room at the opulent Hotel President Wilson, on Lake Geneva. The room was festooned with flags and other trappings of a high-stakes geopolitical conference, and when I went inside before the meeting, I felt flutters. *This is an incredibly important moment*, I thought—one last chance to prevent a terrible war. I watched as Lavrov and Blinken marched in with their respective teams and took their seats at two long, white-clothed tables about fifteen feet apart. I joined the other reporters in barking out questions, most of them variations of "Will Russia invade?" Then we were ushered out so Lavrov and Blinken could have their private talks for the next ninety minutes.

When it was over Blinken spoke in murky terms. "We didn't expect any major breakthroughs to happen today, but I believe we are now on a clear path in terms of understanding each other's concerns." Eventually I realized that the high-level meeting in Geneva, as exciting as it may have seemed, was pure theater. Russia was going to invade Ukraine all along, and the U.S. already knew it. The important decisions had already been made.

Sure enough, early on the morning of February 24, Russia invaded Ukraine. A bit later that day, I got the phone call asking if I was ready to cover the story on the ground in a country under attack.

SEVEN

THE BLOODLANDS

Ukraine has sat at the center of history for a millennium. It has been called the Gates of Europe, the passage point between civilizations. The historian Timothy Snyder has called it the Bloodlands, one in a stack of ill-fated nations between the Baltic Sea and the Black Sea, between empires to the west and east and, in the middle of the twentieth century, between Adolf Hitler and Joseph Stalin. Some 14 million people died in the Bloodlands between 1933 and 1945, not in wars but because of the killing policies of dictators. In that span, nearly four million Ukraine citizens were exterminated during the German occupation, while the Holodomor, Stalin's engineered Great Famine, killed another four million.

The country's independence has come and gone but what has persisted is a fierce national character. In 1991, when the Soviet Union fell, Ukrainians arose and declared themselves an independent nation intent on democracy. But beginning in 2013, domestic unrest opened the door for Vladimir Putin, the president of Russia and a former KGB officer, who saw the Soviet Union's disintegration as a catastrophe that needed to be rectified. In 2014 Putin sent soldiers into Ukraine's Crimean Peninsula and annexed it without bloodshed. This was the true beginning of its war with Ukraine, which exploded on February 24, 2022, with the largest military mobilization in Europe in eighty years—the invasion of Ukraine.

At Fox News, rumblings about the invasion began months earlier. Russians troops were amassing at the border and shipments of blood and supplies to the area were being tracked. "I had pitched going there in late 2021," says Trey Yingst, my fellow Fox News correspondent. "I finally went there in February a few weeks before the invasion, and I was in Kyiv when the Russians began the attack." Fox had several teams in the country, mostly in Lviv, a western city that was far from the eastern front lines. Greg Palkot, one of Fox's top reporters, was there, and so was Pierre Zakrzewski, Fox's trusted, go-to cameraman, and by then my great friend.

In the early weeks of Fox's deployment of personnel, I did not believe I was going to be sent to Ukraine. I was preoccupied with my father, who had been very ill for the last few months and was being treated for a series of small internal bleeds that became worse and worse. And I was focused on covering the State Department angle of the crisis, and it didn't seem like a good time for me to ship off. But as the drumbeat about a pending invasion intensified, I could not stop thinking about going. If there was going to be a war in Europe, I wanted to cover it. At the same time, I understood my obligations to Alicia and my family, and I knew I had to stop putting myself in dangerous situations.

Still, I wanted to cover the war.

In the days before the invasion, I picked up my phone several times intending to call one of my producers and pitch myself to go to Lviv. Each time, I put the phone down before making the call. I was truly torn, and I went back and forth, unable to settle the conflict between what I wanted to do, what I *had* to do, and what I *should* do. Then, on the morning of the invasion, I got the call.

Fox wanted me in Ukraine, where I would anchor a nightly show.

Up until then I hadn't spoken with Alicia about going, because I didn't know if I would be asked. But suddenly, on February 24, the day the invasion began, I had about an hour to tell her about the request and talk it all through with her. I already knew what I was going to tell her: *I won't be on the front, I'll be on the opposite coast, I'll be okay.*

I also already knew what she would say.

"When the opportunity arose for him to go, I knew he was going to go," Alicia says. "I understood this conflict hit very close to home with him. It was on Europe's doorstep, and there were displaced children and families, and it was always going to be a huge story. Every single news person who had ever reported from a war was going to be there. So, when he told me he was asked to go, I said, 'Well then, you should go.'"

What I hadn't known then was that Alicia had an uneasy feeling about me leaving, different from her usual trepidation about my traveling to a combat zone. "It started the last time Benji left our home in London to go back to DC in January," she says. "He'd flown in for the weekend to see Honor in *The Nutcracker,* and he was leaving late on Sunday night, and I remember thinking, *I don't think you should go. I think we should tell Fox we all need to get back together, that this isn't working.* And perhaps I was even slightly ignoring him a bit as he was getting ready to leave. I just had the oddest feeling that if he walked out the door he wasn't going to come back."

· · ·

In London I had a prepacked war bag: ballistic eyeglasses, body armor, proper boots, my own med pack, the whole kit. But I had no such bag in DC, and I was underequipped as I boarded the plane at Reagan National Airport, on the way to Warsaw through Paris. Fox would have body armor waiting for me once I was there. In Poland we got to sleep for an hour or two at a Warsaw airport hotel before we started driving west to the Ukraine border. It was me, DC cameraman Stephen

Kanicka, a Polish driver, and our security agent out of the U.K. Stephen had something like fifteen cases of photography equipment, so we had to rent a beat-up old station wagon with a trailer hitched behind it. We all squeezed in and angled for room, while Stephen listened to Bible excerpts on his phone.

We drove through the city of Lublin and arrived at a Polish checkpoint at the border. Getting into Ukraine was not that hard. Someone checked our papers and quickly searched our gear, and then we were on our way. What shocked me was how hard it was to get *out* of Ukraine.

On our way in we slowly drove past a line of vehicles exiting the country, and it stretched back for *twenty miles*. On other crossings the line was even longer. None of the lines seemed to be moving at all. Thousands of cars and vans were filled with children and relatives and pets, as well as husbands who would not be able to cross the border—no men of fighting age could leave—and were only accompanying their families so they could say their proper goodbyes. Hundreds more people were walking along the side of the road, pushing their little buggies or dragging their bags on wheels—those whose cars had run out of gas, or thought walking might be faster. These were the people who believed Russia was coming for the whole country, not just parts of it in the east and south. At one point there were so many cars trying to leave, they spilled into both lanes of traffic, and often we couldn't pass through for long stretches.

It was a heartbreaking scene. Babies crying, terrified children clinging to their parents. Fear, disorientation, anger—anger toward Putin and toward the United States and the United Kingdom for not doing more to stop him. When we were blocked from driving, I got out and talked to some of the families, and we learned that many had fled from villages that were already being bombed. "As soon as the first bomb hit, we left everything and just got out," they told us. Most of them had no idea where they would go, or where they would sleep or eat or work. They felt lost and abandoned. I was reminded of the news-reels I'd seen of desperate families fleeing parts of Europe at the start of World War II. About five million people left Ukraine in just the first seven to ten days of the invasion.

Every car carried its own story of disruption and suffering. We filmed a report about the mass exodus, and it aired on Fox the next day. Whenever you cover a conflict, there is a moment when you finally feel like you are *in it*. A moment when you are caught up in the systems of war: the chaos, the fleeing, the panicked crowds, the crying children. Seeing the looks of absolute terror on the faces of the escaping Ukrainians was the moment I knew I was in a place of war.

We finally arrived in Lviv at 6:45 p.m. on February 26, after ten hours of driving. Outside it was snowing and frigid—winter in Eastern Europe. Fox News had rented three floors of a hotel for its teams of producers, cameramen, correspondents, and security guards, and we met up with about twelve Fox personnel at the hotel. Someone had told us to "stock up" on our way to Lviv, so we'd stopped and packed the car and trailer with about thirty bags of food and supplies—cans of tuna, crackers, spiced meats, Spam, anything that wouldn't go off. We set up shop in one of the hotel rooms with access to a balcony. Cameras were already set up facing the balcony, where, against a backdrop of the elegant architecture of Lviv, we would all do our live hits about the war.

The next day we went to file a report from a train station in Lviv. The station was so crowded that we literally could not move in any direction. All the tunnels leading in were clogged with people, everyone trying desperately to get out of the city and out of the country. We inched our way toward a platform and tried to film the scenes of mothers carrying their crying babies and pushing their way through the snow and cold to squeeze onto a train. We filmed a scene of a train pulling away from the station and clusters of men standing by the tracks and waving at the train until it turned a corner and disappeared about a mile on down, and then turning in unison and trudging back to whatever their fates would be.

From the moment we got to Lviv we hardly stopped working. We put together a very good piece from the train station, which aired that night, and at the hotel I anchored a show that Fox broadcast at 11:00 p.m. on the U.S. east coast—7 a.m. my time in Ukraine. It was the first show I'd ever anchored solo. There were a million moving parts to everything we did: technical problems, logistics, evolving stories. No one on our crew slept in anything other than spurts.

Everywhere we went we encountered astonishing resistance to Putin and Russia. We interviewed a Ukrainian woman in her twenties who was setting up an operation to help supply Ukrainian soldiers should the Russians make it to Lviv. "We are not leaving," she told us. "We are going to stay here and fight." Nearly everyone we spoke to told us the same thing. Should Russia succeed, plans for a resistance were already in place.

We kicked off the nightly 11 p.m. show, and our goal was to bring in stories from across Ukraine, looking at the geopolitics but also at the human effect of the war on families. The U.S.'s primary concern was avoiding a third world war, and there was a big push and pull about just how much help the U.S. would provide. We saw a lot of anger among Ukrainians that the U.S. had not sent more weapons and support.

Over in the eastern part of the country, the fighting was underway and intensifying. Russia had taken control of dozens of little villages around Kyiv and had cut off the main road into the capital. A massive convoy of Russian troops and vehicles was poised to enter Ukraine and presumably sweep into Kyiv. Fox News made the decision to pull most of its personnel out of Kyiv, including all its news producers. They left a skeleton crew of two cameramen, one reporter, and two security guards.

At the time of that decision, we were summoned for a Zoom call with Fox executives and all the Fox teams in Lviv. There was a discussion about sending one more correspondent to Kyiv. All of us wanted to go, including me. But it was the executives' decision to make.

Halfway through the call, they asked me if I wanted to go.

I phoned Alicia from the hotel and told her they'd asked me to shift to Kyiv.

"Why do you have to go?" she asked. "Why do they have to send you?"

In other such calls I might have tried to downplay the danger, but I did not want to do that now, nor would she have believed me. The whole world was watching the carnage in Ukraine. The only thing I could tell Alicia by way of assurance was that I wouldn't go anywhere near the front lines, and that Pierre, the veteran cameraman who had traveled the world, was already in Kyiv and would be working with me.

By then Pierre had not only become my close friend but had also come to know Alicia as well. She spent time with him and she knew how thoroughly professional he was, and also how caring and protective. That Pierre would be with me in Kyiv was a big factor, and Alicia—who was never going to tell me *not* to go—gave me her blessing, however tentative, yet again. She trusted Pierre to be as careful as humanly possible in the war zone.

Of course, I knew the reason Alicia agreed to my move to the DC bureau was that she saw it as a trade-off that would keep me away from war zones. And here I was, going into one again. I think we both knew I could not say no to the offer to go to Kyiv and continue anchoring the show from there. It was, in a way, the culmination of all that I had worked on and all the risks I'd taken before. It was the big one, the war that might change the world—change the course of history. This was who I was and what I had prepared to do.

And so, on March 2, I set out from Lviv to Ukraine's besieged capital, Kyiv.

Back in London, Alicia was understandably less than thrilled. One day she took Iris to a birthday party, and a mutual friend, who was a reporter, was there. The talk turned to Ukraine, and our friend asked about how I was doing there. Alicia told him I was going to Kyiv. Then she asked him if he would make the decision to go to Kyiv if he were asked.

"Absolutely not," the man said. "I wouldn't risk it. It's far too dangerous."

Alicia winced and thought, *Oh, God*.

• • •

The passage into Kyiv would not be easy. With the Russians having practically surrounded the city, there was only one relatively safe route into it: from the south on the E-95 highway. I got into a car with a Ukrainian driver and Jock, the Fox security man who'd been heading up our Kyiv team, and we set out for the besieged capital. The drive between Lviv and Kyiv would normally take about seven hours. We were on the road for twenty.

What slowed us down were the dozens of makeshift checkpoints set up by the Ukrainians on the lookout for Russian death squads trying to sneak in. Many of the checkpoints were run by local villagers with no connection to the Ukrainian army, each one acting independently, and each manned by very unnerved people. The checkpoints were crude collections of sandbags, straw bales, tires, slats of sheeting, chunks of concrete, and a series of old hedgehogs—angled metal beams that could not be driven through and were designed to stop tanks. To get to the points, you had to zigzag around obstructions blocking alternate sides of the road, placed there to deliberately slow cars down. Ukrainian militias were housed in structures near the checkpoints, at the ready to confront Russian tanks and troops. We weaved around the bales and concrete for hours, passing through the checkpoints and getting closer to Kyiv. As night approached, we arrived at a small, German-style hotel and former spa in the forest south of the E-95. The hotel was packed with people fleeing the country, but we managed to rent a small room so we could spend the night and try to grab a little sleep, Jock and me on the bed, the driver on the sofa.

Early the next morning we headed to Kyiv. As we got closer, the checkpoints became harder to cross. At each one we had to get out of the van as the Ukrainian soldiers yelled "Who are you?" and "What do you want here?" and waved their guns and demanded to see our press passes. They insisted we put our phones and cameras away and not film the checkpoints, for fear of giving away their locations. There was barbed wire everywhere and guns pointing at everyone. The tension was palpable, and there was a real sense that Kyiv was a city on the verge—of what, no one could say for sure. We passed several military convoys heading out of the city; the Ukrainian army was moving assets around to keep them from being bombed. Kyiv was essentially shutting down.

We knew that if we got into the city and the Russians attacked, we would be trapped.

We kept going and on March 2 arrived at the InterContinental hotel in the heart of ancient Kyiv. It was a luxurious hotel, at least during times of peace, and you could see the elegant spires of three old Orthodox churches from its balconies. The hotel was the headquarters of all the major news outlets in Kyiv: CNN, ABC, NBC, BBC, and others. The reporters there had already scoped out the parking garage beneath the hotel and deemed it a good place for us to shelter if and when the bombing began. They had all scrambled down there a few times already.

Fox News rented eleven rooms at the hotel: eight for us to sleep in, one work room, and two rooms for live shots, each with a balcony overlooking the city, one on either side of the hotel should bombing force us to flee one of them. I noticed with some anxiety that the Ukrainian Police Intelligence Building—certainly a high-value bombing target—was right next door. At that point the Fox team consisted of eight people: two cameramen, two security agents, two correspondents, a driver, and a brave young Ukrainian journalist named Oleksandra Kuvshynova, who had signed on as our fixer. We all knew her as Sasha. I learned Sasha had pushed to be our fixer because, like so many young Ukrainians, she wanted to do something to help defend her country. She had worked in production and been part of Fox teams on other trips. Working with us, she hoped to bring the world's attention to the atrocities happening in Ukraine.

When I got to Kyiv, I was thrilled to see my friend Pierre. Since no news producers were left in Kyiv, he was basically in charge of the Fox team at the hotel. Both the work room and Pierre's room looked like military bunkers; Pierre had stocked them with piles of food and water and other supplies. Wires hung from the ceiling, connecting machines and systems to each other, and boxes and black cases covered every inch of the rooms. Pierre had taken down the heavy double doors leading to the balconies and set up cameras pointing out so we could do our live shots from there.

Pierre was a whirlwind, in charge of everything, even though he'd already been in Kyiv for close to forty days and had to be exhausted. He was constantly looking for more food sources, getting SIM cards, securing medicine. He also put himself in charge of expenses and kept meticulous records of every tiny expenditure. I remember thinking that a receipt for a bottle of water could hardly matter given where we were and the threat we were under, but that was just Pierre. He couldn't stand filing expenses, but he stayed on top of them anyway, working on them night and day.

The other Fox cameraman in Kyiv was David "Dudi" Gamliel. He was also a top-notch cameraman and I'd worked with him many times in Israel and other countries. He was a family man, a hard worker, and a great friend. I trusted him implicitly, the way I trusted Pierre, and I would have worked with him anywhere.

The only other Fox News correspondent left in Kyiv was an amazing reporter named Trey Yingst. Then twenty-eight years old, Trey had started an online news website and reported stories from Ukraine, sub-Saharan Africa, and Gaza all while attending American University in DC. Like me he had a curiosity about the world and a strong desire to tell stories others didn't dare tell. Since joining Fox four years earlier, Trey had reported from Baghdad, Beirut, Kabul, Gaza (which was under rocket fire at the time), and many other hot spots. I suppose I saw a little of myself in Trey, and it did not surprise me that he was the only other Fox correspondent in Kyiv.

I could always tell that, like me, Trey had a fierce drive to cover wars up close. Or, as he puts it, "I was most fulfilled in work and in life when I was on the front lines." When Fox pulled most of its staff out of Kyiv, they told Trey that he could leave, too, and work from Lviv. In a way, they almost urged him to leave. But Trey opted to stay. "I just wanted to be there," he says. "Pierre and I were both that way. Pierre and I talked about it and we agreed we would both stay in Kyiv until the war was over. There was no out date for us, so we stayed."

I understood Trey's approach to his work. But as Trey himself points out, he had no wife or children or family, and he had only himself to answer to, and covering wars was the only thing that truly mattered to him—much as it had been all that mattered for me before I met Alicia and we started our family. Pierre, on the other hand, was fifty-five years old. He had a spectacular wife, Michelle Ross-Stanton, whom we all knew as Mich. He had a slew of nieces and nephews who adored him, a lovely home in his native Ireland, and all the friends around the world. There were things in Pierre's life that could have pulled him away from war.

Yet, as anyone who knew him understood, Pierre was extremely driven, too—he was driven to do good things in the world. He was intent on helping the besieged, speaking up for the underdog, finding the blessings in the worst tragedies, and doing whatever he could to make the world a better place. These were high ideals, and Pierre strove tirelessly to meet them. I was not the least bit surprised that Pierre, too, had chosen to stay in Kyiv, even after what surely had been forty hellish days.

I arrived in Kyiv with the idea that I would continue anchoring an hour-long show from the hotel, delivering news from the city and linking up with other Fox correspondents in Lviv and the U.S. But Pierre was dead set against me going on the air live for an hour at a time. He didn't think we had the proper facilities for that, and he feared that the setup for extended coverage was just too complex and too risky. But when I arrived, we got a call saying we'd be anchoring live for an hour that very day. Pierre was furious, and I had to assure him that we would somehow make it work. "Put me up there for an hour without a script and we'll just do it," I said.

That is how my first several days in Kyiv passed—with me doing an hour-long live show from the hotel balcony at 7 a.m. Ukraine time, or 11 p.m. on the U.S. east coast. I would set the scene and round up the latest news from around the country, cut to some taped interviews and reports I'd done earlier in the day, and sometimes throw the coverage over to Greg Palkot or Lucas Tomlinson in Lviv. We would add in some U.S. politicians and analysts, and at the end of an hour we hoped we'd delivered an informative show.

The hardest part, perhaps, was that I was broadcasting from the balcony, which, without its double doors, was piercingly cold. The rooms weren't any warmer. During broadcasts the sprinkler pipes would freeze and start leaking, and our security guard, Jock, had to hold a blow-dryer up to the pipes during commercial breaks to keep them from shattering. That was a strange little scene. Between live shots I'd dash into the rooms and huddle near any source of heat and rub my frozen hands together, until it was time to go live again. For those first few days I rarely left the hotel, and I called Alicia to let her know I was relatively safe indoors.

"I am not going to the front lines," I told her. "I will just be reporting from the hotel."

• • •

Eventually I did leave the hotel to shoot reports on the streets of Kyiv. We all knew Russian bombs could hit the city at any moment, but you can't cover a war while sitting in a concrete shelter, and Trey and I ventured out carefully when things were quiet. Trey worked the outskirts of Kyiv and moved toward the front lines in the embattled town of Irpin, while I spoke to politicians, doctors, and families inside the city. From our hotel room we could hear air sirens and distant shelling, and we could see smoke on the edges of the city, in the villages Russia was seizing one by one. During one broadcast we heard aircraft roar overhead, an air defense system just 1,500 feet behind us blasted off, and we followed the white streaks of the missiles as they screamed through the air, seeking to bring down a plane. Sometimes the war in Kyiv was noisy and chaotic. But other times, everything was quiet, and that's when we chased our stories.

Trey and I worked out a split schedule where one of us would go out in the morning to work a story while the other stayed behind and did live spots. We worked in a nonstop series of four-hour shifts, which at least gave us tiny bits of time to sleep or plan or think. Pierre and I drove to train stations and hospitals and churches in Kyiv, looking for the human stories behind the immense military maneuvering.

As usual, what affected me the most was the sight of children fleeing with their families. People had piled their cars with as many possessions as they could on the car roofs, and sometimes even fastened a dog or two up there. Almost every family, it seemed, was fleeing with a dog. Others, however, only took what they could carry in one hand. I'd see a boy clutching a small toy, or a girl holding on to a doll. I saw someone carrying a houseplant that had belonged to their mother. Everything else in their lives was, they likely knew, gone forever. I thought about what it must be like to have just a few moments to choose the one single possession you could take with you as you fled your home. The one thing you could keep from a life that was already in the past. What would I choose? What would anyone choose? I recognized the full horror of the war in those singular possessions carried away like sacred relics by those who no longer had homes.

Nothing of what I felt in Kyiv, however, ever made it into my coverage. It was not my job to tell people how I felt. It was my job to give viewers the news they needed to know, and to convey how the Ukrainians felt about what was happening. By then I had learned how to squirrel my emotions safely away in my pocket. That was the only way I could pull together all the elements of the war—military matters, public opinion, economics, politics—and deliver a report to Fox's viewers that had the most meaning and power.

Yet I also had to find ways to switch off the war for a few moments here and there, and that, too, is an acquired skill. The InterContinental hotel was closed to all visitors except for the media, and though the kitchen was shut, the staff put out a daily buffet. If you had a few free minutes, you could slip away to the buffet room and chat with some of your colleagues or security guards you knew from other assignments. Clarissa Ward, Richard Engel, Matthew Chance, and numerous other great reporters were there, along with several security guards I'd worked with before. For just a minute or two I would gather with my colleagues and clear my mind and temporarily step off the nonstop, speedily whirring treadmill that was our coverage.

My favorite respite, however, was taking out my cell phone and making little videos for my daughters back home. For a couple of years, I had taken three tiny hedgehog figures with me, and I traveled to Ukraine with them in tow. We called them Yellow Jumpsuit, Red Shorts, and Blue Pants, for their respective outfits. I kept them in an inside pocket of my coat, beneath my body armor, and I took them with me everywhere. On breaks I would take them out and film little vignettes, mostly of the toy hedgehogs playing hide-and-seek or trying to steal the food off my plate, or going out on great adventures in the city. I'd send them home and Alicia told me the girls just loved them. When I could, I would chat or FaceTime with the girls and listen to them scream and giggle, and I would forget altogether that I was in a war zone half a world away.

On March 13, ten days into my time in Kyiv, Pierre and I left the hotel to film a piece in the Children's Hospital nearby. We knew that during the early parts of the invasion dozens of children had been taken there by their parents and hidden away in the cellars to keep them safe from any bombing. Many of the children were brought there from orphanages. But when we got there, all the children had already been evacuated from Kyiv.

All except for two.

A doctor walked us through the nearly deserted hospital. We stopped and talked with some staffers about the injuries they had seen and the children they'd treated. A nurse told us the story of a twelve-year-old girl who was still there. The girl had lost her leg in a bombing that also killed her mother, and she had watched her mother die. At the hospital she was in hysterics, until she stopped crying, pulled a doll close to her, and just went mute. Her father was there, and, in the depths of his despair, he asked us, "What do I say to my daughter? How do I talk to her about the death of her mother?" The father kindly allowed us to visit his daughter in her room.

When I walked in, I could see how shut away she was. Her face was vacant and pale. I felt a wave of sadness for her and for every child who's had to endure something like what she went through. I thought of my own daughters, and especially of my eldest, Honor, who would be this girl's age in just a few years. Thinking of them made me reach beneath my body armor and into the pocket of my coat and pull out the three little toy hedgehogs. I went over to the girl's bed and handed her Red Shorts.

"These are my daughters' favorite toys," I told her. "They would want you to have one."

For a moment, I noticed the girl's face light up. She took the small stuffed animal from me and held him tight.

"There is one other child here," the doctor told us. "A baby."

Pierre, Sasha, and I followed him down a dark corridor (the lights were off in the hallways and most of the rooms to save electricity). At the end of the hall, we saw a glow coming from one single room. Inside there was the baby, just a few months old, in a bassinet with a tube in his nose, all by himself. The doctor explained that the child had been born to a surrogate Ukrainian mother not long before the Russians invaded. The baby had a slight problem in his bowels and needed an operation. The British parents who intended to take him refused to have anything more to do with him, and the surrogate mother also fled. And so the baby was there, abandoned to the chaos of war, alone in the dark.

The hospital staff called him Prince Charlie because of his British parents. Pierre and I set up and shot a piece about little Charlie, and we aired it on Fox that night.

When we left the hospital, Pierre and I felt totally hopeless. We could not understand how this tiny innocent could be stuck in the middle of hell like he was. The more we talked about Charlie, the more we realized we both wanted to pursue the story further. "What if we could somehow save the boy?" I said. "That could be the one good thing we do here."

"Maybe I will even adopt him," Pierre said.

The thought of helping Charlie buoyed us both, and we went back to the hotel and did our work. The next day, March 14, Pierre and I decided to visit the defensive trenches being dug in Kyiv and find a story there.

EIGHT

HORENKA

On March 14, I anchored the show live from Kyiv at 7 a.m., stole two hours of sleep, and got ready to do some reporting. It was a cloudlessly sunny, typically cold day. On that day, Trey Yingst was scheduled to do the early live shots, while I would go out and film a report. I told Trey we were planning on filming some of the city's defenses and said we'd be back by 2 p.m., when we usually changed shifts.

Our young Ukrainian driver pulled around our big white press van, and the team got in: Pierre, our fixer Sasha, our security man Jock, and me. It was around 11 a.m.

We were almost at the one-month mark of the invasion. Reports of Ukrainian casualties were unreliable, but it was clear that hundreds and hundreds of citizens had already been killed. Millions more had been forced to flee the country, creating Europe's single worst refugee crisis since World War II. There was a great fear that Russian assassins would sneak into Kyiv and kill President Zelenskyy, and there had even been a report that Zelenskyy was dead. The president posted a defiant Twitter video and said, "I'm here. We are not putting down any arms . . . this is our land, our country, our children, and we will protect them. Glory to Ukraine."

Still, the situation was dire. The Ukraine army was vastly

outnumbered and outmanned and barely holding its own in violent street battles around Kyiv. Village after village was falling to the Russians. Whole cities around Ukraine had been reduced to ruins, and just days earlier a Russian air strike had destroyed a children's hospital in the southern city of Mariupol. The hospital was being used as a shelter and had the word for "children" painted broadly on its roof. The Russians bombed it anyway, killing thirty-three Ukrainian citizens. The big prize for Putin was Kyiv, the capital. Russian forces had carved a solid line of attack toward the city, and some Russian troops were in the surrounding villages, battling Ukrainian forces in close quarters. And, as everyone knew, a forty-mile-long convoy of Russian tanks, carriers, and trucks had worked its way down from Belarus, the country north of Ukraine, and was poised to enter Kyiv.

The only question: *Why hadn't Russia stormed Kyiv yet?*

There were reports of tactical mistakes by the Russians, including exposing the convoy to Ukrainian Stinger missile strikes, which indeed stalled the convoy and made resupplying it difficult. We had already seen numerous military errors, as well as a clear lack of tactical coordination by Russian troops. We had also heard voice mails from Russian soldiers who'd been told they were going to Belarus simply for training, and not to invade Ukraine. Morale among Russian soldiers was low.

Even so, most of us believed it was only a matter of time. Kyiv was surrounded, and Russian missiles had already hit civilian targets in the city, and we all expected Putin to tighten his grip at any moment. The feeling in Kyiv was that Russian bombs could soon be dropping from the skies.

On March 14, Pierre and I knew how we would cover the elaborate trench systems the Ukrainians were building within Kyiv as a defense against Russian military units like the Wagner Group, ruthless mercenaries dispatched by Putin to fight his wars across the globe. Our explicit intention was to *avoid* the front lines, stay clear of active fighting, remain within the city's borders, and only report on the trenches inside Kyiv.

Sasha coordinated with a contact in Ukraine's press corps, who confirmed the Ukrainians were okay with us traveling to the trenches. Sasha arranged for us to meet a press liaison officer by a six-story, rectangular concrete building in Kyiv. It looked like a blocky, drab, Stalin-era office, maybe a processing center, but when we saw twenty armed Ukrainian soldiers jog out, we knew it was being used as a military command center. As usual, the liaison asked us not to film inside, and introduced us to two soldiers from the Azov Regiment—Mykola Kravchenko and Serhiy Mashovets—who were tasked with helping us. They hopped into a little red car and we followed in our van.

We tailed them for about twenty minutes. Our windshield had two long cracks in it, and a red air freshener dangled from the rearview mirror. The roads through the city were clogged with concrete stanchions and rows of hedgehogs, some built quickly by Ukrainian metalworkers and some borrowed from a World War II museum. The roadblocks slowed our speed to a crawl. On the sides of the road were tin-roofed one-story structures that could be used by Ukrainian troops to fire on Russian forces if they made it into Kyiv. I realized that if the situation in Ukraine devolved into a full-scale urban war, it was going to be as brutal as wars can become.

On the drive I scribbled notes while Pierre shot footage of tank traps on the highway. We passed an empty checkpoint and saw piles of dirt along the road, as well as two yellow backhoes in the woods—Ukrainian troops building trenches, the story we were after. We pulled over and watched as Ukrainian soldiers did target practice down a makeshift range. One of the Azov soldiers rushed over and told Pierre to put down the camera. The location of the trenches was sensitive information. I tried to negotiate with the soldiers through Sasha, but they were adamant. Our plan to report on the strategic trench system was not going to happen.

The soldiers told us about a nearby village that had been destroyed some weeks before, and was abandoned except for some Ukrainian troops. The Russian forces, we understood, would be at least thirty miles away and not pushing in our direction. The soldiers had gone through the village with a team from the *New York Times* a day earlier, and they offered to take us there as well. They made it sound as if it were only a short drive away. It seemed like a good chance to depict the devastation Russia had caused, and Pierre and I agreed to go, which we later learned was named Horenka.

The soldiers also said that from that point on, it would be better to travel with them in their little red car—the same way they escorted the *Times* reporter a day earlier. Unfortunately, with the two Ukrainians up front, the four of us—Pierre, Sasha, Jock, and me—could not fit in the back seat. Pierre and I both needed to go, and we needed Sasha to translate, and so the three of us squeezed into the small car and we set off for Horenka.

• • •

We took off in the red car, and Pierre kept filming from the back. The soldier drove slowly, 15 mph, and we crept past rows of dead trees and desolate woods. We passed a large billboard for Naftogaz, Ukraine's state-owned energy company, that pictured two infants sitting together and playing with toys. We passed damaged bus shelters and advertisements for housing developments that were no longer feasible. I was getting a bit antsy and wanted to start filming something, so I said, "Right, let's just get out, then," but the soldier kept driving. "A bit farther is better," he told us through Sasha. "Just a bit farther."

We passed one final set of concrete blockades and arrived on the outskirts of a bombed-out village. The roadside church and houses we could see were all but demolished. There was no sign of people anywhere. We asked the driver to stop so we could film there. On the horizon we saw billowing black smoke, and in the distance we heard shelling that sounded at least twenty miles away. Pierre and I knew we had to work fast. Very fast. Just get what we needed and get out.

We saw two large black canisters, each the size of a sofa, that were marked Lockheed Martin and had housed Javelin missiles. Pierre started the camera and we filmed a live spot there. "In all the villages just surrounding Kyiv you can see the signs of battle," I reported. "Russians have tried to push up this far and they were repelled. They attacked churches and homes, and these villages all lie completely empty."

Before we left, Pierre shot footage of the damaged church, its ten-foot-tall statue of Christ, halo and all, untouched. We drove a little farther into the village, past a gas station that had been bombed and the charred ruins of a five-story building. We passed the shells of four destroyed lime-green buses. The streets were empty and brutally quiet.

"You can film here," one of the soldiers said, and we got out to shoot a quick report on what was now an eerie ghost town. We set up behind a row of crumbling one-story structures and filmed as the distant shelling continued—*boom, boom, boom.*

"This town has been shelled repeatedly and heavily by the Russians," I said as Pierre filmed. "Everyone has fled. There is little left of these towns. All that remains is wreckage."

As we kept shooting, the noise of a single shell suddenly landed in an open valley ahead of us and sounded far closer than all the rest. We were startled when we heard it and we ducked and ran for cover. Then the shelling stopped. We jumped straight in the car and started back the way we came. After a while, the soldiers told us that everything was fine and we could stop to shoot another report if we needed. Pierre and I looked around for a location. We passed a side street and saw a two-story stand-alone industrial building that was damaged and had been abandoned. It was an auto service shop and there were two bombed-out white vans in front. Behind it a plume of thick black smoke rose from a fire. The soldiers went ahead of us and made sure it was okay for us to film. They poked around inside the auto shop and met ten or twelve Ukrainian soldiers resting there. We asked if we could interview them and they said yes.

Pierre trained the camera on one young soldier, maybe twenty-five, with a thick torso and a beard and a baby face, and in full gear—AK rifle, ammo clips across the chest, LED headlight, walkie-talkie, and a patch with an ace of spades featuring a skull. The soldier had spiderweb-like patterns tattooed on the backs of his hands. I asked him a question and didn't wait for Sasha to translate his answers before asking him another.

"Are you going to hold off the Russians?"

"How long have you been out here?"

"What do you need most?"

He answered wearily in just a few words but with a quiet authority. I asked, "What is the most dangerous thing about being here?"

"Bombs falling from the sky," he said without hesitation.

I shook the soldier's hand and thanked him, and he gave us the peace sign. We got straight into the little red car and headed back.

• • •

The soldier drove faster now, getting us out of the village and back toward the city. He slowed a bit so we could look down a long road, and he asked if we wanted to film there. We told him we were done for the day and wanted to head home. I remember sitting in the back of the car, Pierre on my right and Sasha on my left, and thinking that what we had shot was going to make a great package. In my mind I was already editing it and choosing which shots to use. We drove past an empty checkpoint and swerved around a concrete barrier and I saw a dead dog on the road. I could tell he was an Alsatian and seeing him limp on the road like that made me sad. *Poor dog*, I thought. *Who killed the bloody dog?*

We kept going and approached another abandoned checkpoint on the main highway. The driver turned right and we went around the first of two long concrete barriers. It pushed us all the way to the right side of the road, beyond which there were some sandbags and a sloping road leading into a village. Before the driver could turn left to go around the next barrier, we heard the shrill, distinctive whir of a missile.

It was loud and close and over our heads and then the whirring stopped, and one second later there was an explosion thirty feet in front of us in a stand of trees. The blast rocked the car and we shuddered to a stop.

"Reverse the car!" Pierre shouted. *"Reverse the car!"*

The car stalled.

"Get out of the car!" Pierre yelled as he opened the right-side passenger door.

And then—*boom.*

Another explosion, this one seemingly right on us. Instantly, everything went black. It was as if someone flipped a switch and shut off my being, my existence. No pain, no agony, no feeling. Nothing. Nothing. Nothing.

Then—something.

A voice.

Daddy, you've got to get out of the car.

And there she was, my beautiful daughter, Honor, and her voice was so pure and simple and innocent and so *real*, and hearing it roused me from my nothingness, and her request became a request from all three of my young daughters, and it became the only and absolute focus of who I was. Suddenly I had awareness: I was in the back of a car. I felt like I was stuck. The world rushed back into me—light, sound, smell. The car door to my right was open, and Pierre wasn't there. He must have gotten out. Now it was my turn. Now I had to get out. But I couldn't move.

But I *had* to move. I turned my head and tried to move, tried desperately to find the *key* to moving, this mad inclination to use every muscle in my body and marshal every ounce of energy and propel myself out of the car, somehow, and I did it. I got my head out of the car first, through the open door, and then somehow the rest of me, and I stumbled forward, one step, two steps, starting down a slope, and then, overhead, the whirring, and the silence, and the third explosion.

And then I was on the ground.

Not in blackness but in a daze, a mad swirl, disoriented. I was on fire. Instinctively I started rolling my body and patting my legs to smother the flames. I looked around and saw where I was. I was lying on the slope about twenty feet from the car. I looked at my legs and I saw that my right leg was gone, just some flesh and bone hanging by a flap of skin, and half a foot dangling there. My shoes were gone and my pants were gone, disintegrated somehow, and of all things I thought, *Where the fuck are my shoes?*

I didn't know where Sasha or the two Ukrainian soldiers were. I didn't see them or hear any crying. But about fifteen feet in front of me I saw Pierre lying prone on the ground. I called out his name. "Pierre. Pierre."

"Don't move," he said quite urgently. "Russian drones."

I lay still again. I was conscious of my breathing and how loud it was, and how quickened it was. My own breaths rang loudly in my head, nonstop. For the next few moments it was like everything I'd ever done had brought me to this point, this moment, and it all condensed into one single thing—survival. Nothing else. Just—*live. Survive. Move.*

I called out Pierre's name again. "Are you all right?" I asked.

"The Russians, the Russians, don't move," he said.

I saw a small piece of blue foam a few feet away and in a haze I thought it would be better for me if I sat on it, so I dragged myself to it and got on it and lay there some more. I searched for my cell phone and found it and turned it on—no reception. I held it up, like we all do, searching for a connection. Then I looked at my legs again. I realized, perhaps for the first time, that I was hurt. Really hurt. Hurt very badly. There was blood coming from my head, around and above my left eye, and the blood had covered my hands. There was no pain, but there were clearly injuries, and that worried me.

I thought, *How am I going to get help? How am I going to save us?*

I felt compelled to take a photo of my legs. The journalist in me, perhaps. But when I took it, I realized I didn't want Alicia and the children to ever see it, and I deleted it. I called out to Pierre again and told him I was badly injured and I said we had to find a way out of there. He just kept saying, "The Russians, the Russians."

It never crossed my mind that Pierre was in danger of dying. He didn't appear to have any injuries or even bleeding I could see, and he wasn't crying out or moaning in pain. Besides, he was Pierre! He was the strongest, most experienced, most resilient war journalist I'd ever worked with. He was larger than life. *No*, I thought, *we will both get out of this somehow.*

I sat there in a kind of stupor, looking at my leg and trying to think, for a while longer. Then I saw a flash on the periphery of my vision. It was a car driving past. I waved madly at it, but it didn't stop.

"A car, a car!" I yelled out.

"They are Russians," Pierre warned again.

"Pierre, it doesn't matter, we have to get out of here, I am badly hurt," I said.

Adrenaline surged through me and I decided I had to pull myself up the slope to the side of the road, where I could be seen. I pulled myself along on my left side, clawing at the dry, orange dirt, moving inch by inch. *Just keep pulling yourself along because you are going home to see your kids.* I dragged myself farther up the slope and had gotten nearly to the side of the road when I saw a car coming from the other direction.

I waved at it and grabbed dirt in my hands and threw the dirt at it and yelled out and did everything I could to make whoever was driving the car see me.

Then the car stopped in front of me. I felt a hand on the back of my coat, and I was dragged along the dirt. Intense pain shot through me.

Everything after that was a blur.

NINE

EMERGENCY POSTURE

A bit after 2 p.m. on March 14, Trey Yingst checked to see if Pierre and I had returned from our morning outing. He was told we weren't anywhere in the InterContinental, nor had we checked in. Trey knew that cell reception around the city was spotty. Communications, or comms, were down all over. Not hearing from us wasn't initially a concern.

Another hour passed, and Trey phoned a Fox News desk producer stationed in Jerusalem. Fox had pulled its producers out of Kyiv, and correspondents in Ukraine were coordinating coverage remotely with the producer in Israel. "Have you heard from Benji?" Trey asked. She had not.

A few minutes later the producer texted Trey: Who is shooting with Ben today? I can't get a hold of Ben.

Trey knocked on the door to my room and then Pierre's room. When no one answered he felt his first pang of concern. He called the desk producer, who told him she had heard that Pierre and I were with Ukrainian soldiers who had taken our phones away. Trey thought that didn't sound right (and it turned out to be wrong). "I know Pierre and I know he would never give up his phone," Trey told Shane, the other Fox News security agent in Kyiv besides Jock. "It didn't make sense."

The desk producer asked Trey to be on standby to do the live report that afternoon.

At 4:43 p.m. on March 14, Trey got a text from Jock, the security agent who'd been separated from Pierre and me and was still waiting in our white press van at our drop-off point.

Have you heard from them? Jock asked. Do you have any idea when they're heading back to the van? Trey said he didn't know.

Meanwhile, Shane phoned around to his contacts in Ukraine and checked in on security-related chats on WhatsApp and Signal, to see if there was any word about three Fox journalists in the field. Every media network uses different security personnel, but it was a small community and many of the agents were close and often traded useful information.

One of the security men Shane contacted had news.

A short while later, Shane summoned Trey and Dudi to the rooms that served as our workspace in the InterContinental.

"I wanted to keep you guys updated," Shane said softly. "Based on preliminary info, and this is not confirmed, I am hearing, the guys I'm talking to, that two Fox journalists were killed outside Kyiv."

Dudi exhaled deeply. He felt like a weight had crashed down on him. Trey uttered a profanity. Trey's thoughts raced: he didn't know which of us, if any of us, had survived. He quickly got on the phone and called Greg Headen, Fox's vice president of news coverage, and Jay Wallace, the president of Fox News. He told them what Shane had shared—preliminary and unconfirmed reports that two Fox journalists were dead.

"No one knew for sure what happened or where it happened or even *if* it happened," Trey says, "but after my call to Jay and Greg, the leadership in New York sprang into action. They understood something was off, and they immediately went into emergency posture."

• • •

Lying on the ground, dragging myself to the road, throwing clumps of dirt at the passing car and waving frantically—I remember the utter desperation of those moments. I knew that if the driver didn't see me, I might not get another chance to be seen. I was in the middle of nowhere, a random stretch of asphalt in an abandoned village outside a desolate city, and I was on a slope that was slightly lower than the level of the road, making it even harder to notice me. What were the chances of anyone finding us at all? They had to be minuscule. It had already been about forty minutes since the attack and there were no villagers, no patrols, no chance of any communication. And then to have a car pass, and pass again, and still not be seen? The thought was too horrifying to bear.

So I gave it all I had, hoisting myself into a sitting position and waving and yelling and hoping that God or an angel would let me be seen.

Then the hand on the back of my jacket, pulling me up the slope and toward the road. For the first time I felt terrible pain as my burned body was dragged along the rough ground. Then I was lifted, and the back doors of a van were opened, and I was heaved inside.

I was in and out of consciousness in the van, mostly out. I remember it felt like I was in the van for a very long time as it rumbled down the road, and I remember thinking, *Stay with it, stay awake.* I remember the van stopping, and someone pulling me out of the van and putting me into the back of an ambulance. I kept mumbling "Benjamin Hall, Fox News, journalist, American citizen" over and over. I thought I was in the hands of the Russians. I saw someone jab a hypodermic needle into my arm.

After that, I was out cold.

• • •

The Ukrainian special forces agent drove down the main highway out of Kyiv and toward the city of Irpin, scene of the worst urban warfare since the Russian invasion began. A stocky, bearded man in his thirties, with a stern look but a warming smile, and tattoos on his thick forearms, he went by the code name Song. Song had spent the last month fighting the Russians at different combat spots in the east, and now he was heading to Irpin, which had been under siege since February 27, when Russian Armed Forces arrived in their bid to surround Kyiv. The Ukrainian ground forces battled fiercely to keep them at bay, but by March 14 a member of the Irpin city council estimated Russia was in control of at least half the city. Some called Irpin the most dangerous place in Ukraine.

Song was well aware of this as he and fellow agents, one in the van with him and others in a separate car ahead, weaved through the long concrete barriers blocking swaths of the highway. Their particular skills—tactical expertise, extraction, intelligence—were sorely needed at the front. They passed the remnants of a bombed-out car and kept going; the whole country had become a junkyard for the shells of burnt cars. A short while later, Song realized they were on the wrong highway. They'd taken a wrong turn. The two vehicles turned around and headed back the way they came.

When they passed the bombed-out car again, Song saw someone waving from the side of the road, down on a slope and behind a damaged power line post.

The two cars stopped. Song jumped out and saw me half-sitting a few yards away down the slope. Russian shells exploded in the distance, and Song knew he had to move quickly. He looked me over and saw I was covered in blood and badly injured. There was no time for a longer exam. I was alive, that was all that mattered. He grabbed me by the back of my jacket and pulled me to his van and lifted me into the back. Song turned around and ran to the spot where he found me.

Just beyond it, he saw Pierre.

Pierre did not appear to be badly injured. Song bent over him and took his pulse.

Pierre was gone.

Song spotted Pierre's camera, marked Fox News, lying beside him. He grabbed it and took it with him. He went over to the smoldering remnants of the car, which had once been red but was no color now, just shards of metal charred white, and he saw body parts in and around the car—arms, legs, a head. He could not tell if it was one person or many, and there was nothing more he could do. "We saved who we could save and got away," he says.

Song headed in the direction of Kyiv, looking for a manned checkpoint. He knew ambulances could usually be found at the block points, waiting on standby. Sure enough, he came upon one about two and a half miles away from where he found me, and he pulled over and helped load me into the back of it. The ambulance took off and headed to Kyiv.

I remember that when I felt Song pulling me by the back of my jacket, I had a single thought: *We've been saved.*

• • •

Jock waited impatiently in our press van, parked at the drop-off checkpoint. It had now been more than two hours and he hadn't heard from us. A Scottish-born military veteran who had been in the security business for more than a decade, Jock grew more and more uneasy in the van and began calling around to his contacts.

He reached out to security agents who he knew were in Kyiv with other media outlets. One of them, a security officer for the *New York Times*, had heard news from another security man at the BBC. It was unconfirmed but somewhat specific—there were rumblings that two journalists had possibly been killed, and a third seriously injured. "No one knew exactly who or what or where," Jock says. "It was something that was in the jungle drums, the media passing information back and forth."

Jock stayed connected to his network of security agents, pushing for confirmation and searching for any details about where the injured journalist might be. There were a dozen hospitals in Kyiv, many of which had been shelled; all told, some thirty-four medical facilities in Ukraine had been damaged, though most remained open, and fourteen doctors, ambulance workers, and medical technicians had already been killed.

Jock heard from his contacts that at least two security agents were on the ground in Kyiv calling and visiting hospitals, checking to see if a journalist had been brought in. They went to the Children's Hospital where Pierre and I had earlier shot a piece, knowing that an injured American journalist had recently been taken there. Then they tried City Clinical Hospital No. 7, a facility that normally treated stroke victims but was now consumed with caring for war casualties. They asked around and learned that I was there. Immediately they called Jock.

It was the first bit of concrete information Jock had received, and now at least he knew what he had to do. He got in the van and sped to Hospital No. 7, about ten miles from where he was. He also returned a call from Dragan Petrovic, the Fox News London bureau chief who was part of the Fox executive team scrambling for information. He told Dragan where I was, then called Shane, the Fox News security agent back at the InterContinental, and shared the news with him. It was the first time the Fox News team looking for us learned that I was alive.

Jock pulled up at Hospital No. 7 and ran in and found my room. I was under sedation and unconscious. Jock spoke with a surgeon and learned that my right leg had been amputated just below the knee. The hospital, in crisis mode because of the invasion, was not equipped to treat all my injuries, and was patching me up so they could move me to a bigger hospital. A doctor called around and received approval to ship me to the National Military Medical Clinical Center on Hospitalna Street in Kyiv, near the Dnipro River and two miles from the InterContinental. Once the doctors had stabilized me, I was bundled up and put in an ambulance, and two Ukrainian military medics drove me the forty minutes across town to the Clinical Center. They didn't allow Jock to accompany me in the ambulance, so he followed in the press van.

When he had a moment, Jock texted Trey Yingst at Fox's Ukrainian bureau at the InterContinental. He let Trey know I was alive and in a hospital, and he provided specific details: Ben is currently undergoing serious operations. Fracture to base of skull. Left eye cut in half. Brain op at 2:30, two pieces of shrapnel from skull. An op to save his left foot. Trey quickly sent that information on to Fox in New York.

"It was such a great relief to hear that he had been found," Trey says. "My first thought was *Okay, he's alive, we've got to get to him. He can't be alone in a hospital. One of us has to get to him.*" Shane was preparing to visit me at the hospital, and Trey insisted on coming along. Shane would not let him. "He said he had orders to not let me leave the building," says Trey. "The next couple of hours were incredibly frustrating, and all I could do was pace around and check in for word. But I understand their decision to keep me there. That morning Fox had five people in Kyiv, and now they only knew two were safe."

Trey worked his laptop, checking message boards and chat rooms, searching for any news about Pierre and Sasha, who were still missing in the field and unaccounted for.

• • •

Jennifer Griffin, Fox News' chief national security correspondent, was outside the Fox media booth at the Pentagon, on the phone with Jay Wallace in New York City. Jay had just delivered bad news: "Ben and Pierre are both missing. We don't know where Ben is." Jen felt her stomach turn and steadied herself. Instantly her focus turned from assembling a report about the war in Ukraine to managing the operation, whatever shape it would take, to find out more about what happened, and to bring her colleagues home.

She had just finished interviewing John Kirby, the Pentagon spokesperson, and Kirby was still sitting behind her in the leather chair in the Fox News media booth. Kirby heard the urgency in Jen's voice and got up to give her privacy. He made it two steps before Jen stopped him.

"John, don't go, please stay," she said.

Jen got off the phone with Wallace and told Kirby the news about her crew in Kyiv. She still had no idea of my condition or where I was, but she couldn't wait to find out. She had to get things moving.

"Can you help us get Ben Hall out of Ukraine?" she asked Kirby.

Jen knew Kirby's hands were tied. The official position of the United States Department of State regarding Ukraine was that the U.S. was not authorized to conduct any kind of operation inside the country. The U.S. fully supported Ukraine's effort to fight off Russia's invasion and committed itself to providing Ukraine with lethal defensive weapons, technical support, and billions of dollars in aid. That kind of assistance would both send a strong signal of support and increase the cost to Russia of any further escalation. But the U.S. did not want to enter a proxy war with Russia, or otherwise intensify the conflict. On February 12, the U.S. embassy in Ukraine issued a Level 4: Do Not Travel alert and warned Americans there to "be aware that the U.S. government will not be able to evacuate U.S. citizens in the event of Russian military action in Ukraine."

In Corridor 9 of the Pentagon, Kirby confirmed as much to Jen.

"We cannot step one foot into Ukraine," he said. "Our troops cannot go in. You would have to get him to the Polish border."

Jen was ready for that response. She knew a U.S. Army lieutenant general named Chris Donahue, then the commanding general of the Eighty-Second Airborne Division. She knew Donohue had handled the evacuation of U.S. soldiers, personnel, and citizens from Afghanistan during the U.S. military pullout in 2021, transporting wounded evacuees to Landstuhl Regional Medical Center in Germany, the largest American military hospital outside the U.S. For many years Jen had volunteered with a variety of relief organizations and veterans' groups, doing everything from raising money for wheelchairs to arranging therapeutic storytelling for wounded soldiers. She understood the military medical system, and she knew that Donahue's team was somewhere in the vicinity of Landstuhl, some 1,200 miles west of Kyiv. Jen believed that getting me to Landstuhl was possible. It could be done. She understood what had to happen.

"I had John Kirby give me a gentleman's agreement that if we could figure out a way to get Ben to the border," says Jen, "he would try and get it to [U.S. secretary of defense] Lloyd Austin and ask for a waiver or permission to have the military transport and treat a civilian injured in combat."

Kirby said he could not help get me to the Polish border. But he could help with Lloyd Austin.

"We can sign off for compassionate care of a journalist," Kirby told Jen. "I think Austin will sign off on that."

That was all Jen needed to hear.

She thanked Kirby and flipped through the Rolodex in her head. She thought of a friend named Sarah Verardo, whose husband lost a leg in a catastrophic IED explosion while serving in Afghanistan and then endured 140 surgeries at the Walter Reed National Military Medical Center in Washington, DC. She had met Sarah at a charity luncheon in Charleston, South Carolina, in 2010. They became friends and later worked together reorganizing the board of the Independence Fund, a group that provided extensive support and aid to wounded veterans, and for which Jen had helped raise millions of dollars. In 2021, Sarah cofounded a remarkable humanitarian group called Save Our Allies, a vast network of military veterans, intelligence operatives, nongovernmental organizations, and other miracle workers devoted to, among other things, extracting people caught in dangerous combat situations.

"Sarah and SOA were part of the effort that rescued twenty thousand Afghans from the airport during the pullout," Jen says. "I knew that after Afghanistan they shifted their focus to Ukraine."

As soon as she finished talking to John Kirby, Jen called Sarah. It was 1:30 p.m. eastern time. Sarah picked up and Jen asked her if Save Our Allies had anyone stationed near Ukraine.

"I have the *best* people near Ukraine," Sarah said.

The operation to get me to Poland had begun.

At that time, however, I don't think anyone could have fully understood the extent of the obstacles that lay in the path between me and the Polish border. Physically, I was in very bad shape. In addition to the damage to my legs, I had a serious eye injury and open head wounds. A large piece of shrapnel was still wedged in the middle of my neck. I was also badly burned. I was in imminent need of several more operations and there were absolutely no guarantees I would survive my time in a Kyiv hospital, much less an arduous journey to the border. There were hundreds of checkpoints between Kyiv and Poland, many controlled by the Russians and all on the highest of alerts. What's more, there was a great fear of Russian special forces sneaking into Kyiv and going after President Zelenskyy, and the city was hours away from enacting a strict, days-long no-movement curfew that authorized Ukrainian forces to shoot anyone seen outside after dark on sight. Getting me to safety was, to say the least, an exceedingly long shot.

"For your rescue to happen, a series of improbable to impossible events would need to not only happen but also align like clockwork," someone involved in the extraction effort later told me. "When I understood what was involved, I said a quiet prayer out of desperation."

• • •

It was Monday evening in London, and my wife, Alicia, had just spoken to Fox News CEO Suzanne Scott, who told her everything she knew at that point: "Ben has been in an accident."

Alicia then called my mate Rick Findler, who had also just found out something had happened. Two hours after the bombings, Iryna Venediktova, a prosecutor general with Ukraine's powerful security agency, the SBU, posted a photo of my U.S. congressional press pass on Facebook (with my eyes and mouth eerily blacked out for privacy reasons) and reported a diagnosis of "the fracture of the two lower limbs . . . given by Ukrainian doctors to an American-British citizen-journalist. He is in intensive care." Venediktova added that my injuries should lead the West to impose a no-fly zone.

The picture of my press pass circulated on a Whatsapp group for journalists, and Rick saw it there. He promised Alicia he would call around and find out whatever else he could. Alicia felt a powerful need to talk to her mother in Australia, but it was the middle of the night there and she had to wait at least two hours to call. She thought of who to phone next and dialed my brother Barnaby. He picked up right away and Alicia told him what she'd heard. "I just need you to know," she said, though there wasn't much she could tell him. Then she called her sister Skye, who was away on a vacation, and filled her in.

"We're coming home," Skye immediately said.

After speaking with her sister Alicia knew she had to go downstairs and see the children. If they didn't see her, they would know something was wrong. She had already decided that she would not tell the girls what happened that night. "I have never lied to them," she says, "but I never wanted them to see anything with Benji that might possibly make them worry or feel upset. There was no reason to tell them anything

yet." Alicia went to the dining room and greeted our daughters, who were bathed and in their pajamas and chirping away at the table. Then she went over to Lor, our housekeeper, and whispered, "Something happened to Benji, can you feed the girls?" Our daughters adore Lor and were delighted to have her handling dinner that night, while Alicia went back upstairs.

In the bedroom she saw that Rick Findler had called. She called him back and he told her all he knew was that a reporter had been injured on the ground in Ukraine. He would keep pushing for more. Alicia also took a call from my friend and agent Olivia Metzger. Olivia was on vacation on March 14 when she got a call from Suzanne Scott, the Fox News CEO in New York. "There was an incident with Benji," Suzanne told her. "The reports are not optimistic." Suzanne said she'd already called Alicia with the news. Olivia got over her shock and pulled up my home number, so she, too, could connect with Alicia. "I had never spoken with her before then," Olivia says. "I didn't know if she even knew who I was. And I thought, *What am I going to tell her? What can I possibly say?* I was afraid to call her."

Finally, she did call and shared what Scott had told her.

"Oh my God," Alicia said. "Is he gone?"

"I don't know," Olivia said. "I don't know."

She couldn't leave it at that, with nothing but uncertainty. She had to tell Alicia *something*. "What I can say," Olivia went on, "is that when an organization like Fox News comes together, they will do anything and everything that is humanly possible to get Benji back. It's what they do. I've seen them do it. He is in the very best hands."

Alicia put the girls to bed and returned to the quiet of the bedroom. She is a problem solver, a hands-on fixer, and as she paced the room she did not know what to do with herself. "I was *all* adrenaline," she says. "Benji and I were a team, and we had always protected each other at every step, and now this whole thing was completely out of my hands. There was no way I was able to sleep at all."

Alicia called her mother in Australia and they talked for a long time. Alicia's hands were shaking and her body was trembling. She had never experienced anything like that before, and she knew it had to be trauma. She told her mother she didn't think she could breathe. Her mother said, "Just keep me on the phone and we'll get through this together."

In the middle of the long night, as Alicia lay on the bed and waited for the sun to rise, she could not shake the feeling that I would die.

TEN

SEASPRAY

Word about what happened to us was beginning to get out.

Two hours after the bombings, Iryna Venediktova posted the photo of my press pass, and not much later, Fox News filed its first on-air report about the incident. "This is news we hate to pass along to you, but . . . a Fox News journalist has been injured while news gathering outside of Kyiv," Fox anchor John Roberts reported. "Very few details, but teams on the ground are working as hard as they can to try and gather more information." Later that evening, March 14, after Alicia and the relatives of Pierre and Sasha had been contacted, Roberts went on-air and read a more specific statement from Suzanne Scott: "Earlier today our correspondent Benjamin Hall was injured while news gathering outside of Kyiv. Ben is hospitalized."

I don't remember much about my stay at the first hospital they took me to, City Clinical Hospital No. 7, except for the sight of doctors hovering over me in headlamps (most of the hospital's electricity had been turned off), the beams of light dancing across my body. I do not remember the discussions that led to the decision to amputate my right leg.

The first thing I remember is waking up in an apparently pristine hospital bed in a large room at the National Military Medical Clinical Center in Kyiv. I saw that I had big metal rods sticking out of my right thigh. There were six other beds in the room, and there was a man in the bed directly opposite mine. I looked around and assumed I was in Russia, and that the man in the bed was Russian. I was certain I'd been captured. I saw nurses outside the room, looking at me and talking and smiling, and I thought, *That doesn't seem right. They are Russian spies pretending to be nurses.*

Then someone came in, presumably another Russian, waving my State Department press pass at me and loudly asking, "Who are you? Who are you?" I saw the man in the opposite bed shift around beneath his bedsheet, and I knew he was pointing a pistol straight at me.

I had awoken in a spy novel.

I thought desperately about what I could do to get out of this mess, but I couldn't move and my mind was racing and I started to feel as if I was trapped in a nightmare with no way out.

Just then an American man walked in and over to my bed.

"Who are you?" he asked softly.

"I'm Ben Hall," I said.

"Well, Ben," the doctor said, "how about we get you out of here?"

"Let's do it," I replied, "but let's be careful. We're in Russia and that man's got a gun."

• • •

Sarah Verardo sat in a chair in her optometrist's office in Charlotte, North Carolina, getting her eyes dilated for an exam. She was also on her cell phone, talking about various work issues with a contact in Poland. Before the exam could begin, her second cell phone went off. "Hold on, I'm getting another call," she told her contact, then picked up and heard her friend Jen Griffin's voice. No small talk, just right to it.

"Do you have any people near Ukraine?" Jen asked.

Sarah said she had the best people there.

"I kept talking on both phones and my eyes were dilated and the nurse thought I was crazy," Sarah says. "I told her I had an emergency and had to leave and she said, 'You can't leave!' But I did anyway. There was nothing that was going to stop me from helping Jen."

Sarah and Jen had twelve years of history between them, and they'd built an unbreakable bond based on their shared persistence and resiliency. "We both like mountains and trying to move them," Sarah says. Sarah's husband, Sergeant Michael Verardo—they met in high school in Barrington, Rhode Island, as young teens—lost his left leg and much of his left arm in a devastating IED attack in Afghanistan in 2010. He was left with severe polytraumatic conditions that required many dozens of operations and a staggering amount of speech, visual, physical, and occupational therapy. "No one can fathom what men like my husband are going through," Sarah says. "The first time we spoke after his injury, he said, 'I don't want this for you.' I said, 'No, this is something that is both of ours.'"

The next several years for Sarah and Michael were more physically and emotionally wrenching than they could have imagined. Early on, when she was with her husband at a San Antonio, Texas, rehabilitation hospital, Sarah sat slumped in a chair in the waiting room and felt overwhelming despair. "Life had never seemed so dire," she says. A doctor saw her and came over. He gently shook her by the shoulders and said, "Sarah, the hardest part is yet to come. You will have to learn how to survive surviving."

Since then, Sarah has devoted her life to helping her family through its ordeal and helping thousands of others through theirs. She became a national advocate for not only injured veterans but also for their caregivers, and wrote a book, *Hero at Home*, about the compassion, teamwork, and understanding needed to care for wounded veterans.

When Jen Griffin called her on March 14, however, it was in Sarah's capacity as a cofounder of Save Our Allies, the global group proficient at helping get people out of war zones. Jen told Sarah what had happened in Kyiv and asked her to look into assembling a team. She told her to stand by for official word from Fox executives before setting her team in motion. Sarah left her doctor's office, went to her car in the parking garage, and sat inside and worked her phones.

The first person she called was a special operations veteran and former intelligence officer who went by the code name Seaspray.

She had first encountered Seaspray in Afghanistan, where he played a vital and mostly unsung role in evacuating thousands during the U.S. pullout in 2020. "That was a huge project for us and he worked with our ground team there," Sarah says. "He is one of the most talented people I have ever met. He is proficient in hostage extraction on five continents."

Seaspray was also quite mysterious. He was intensely private and trusted no one, and he'd been on hundreds of missions, most of them highly dangerous, some in a military capacity and some as a volunteer. He had at times been a paid contractor for SOA overseas.

"He is one of those guys who says, 'The government isn't doing this, so we'll just have to do it ourselves,'" Sarah says.

When she reached out to Seaspray on March 14, he was in an SOA command center in Poland. He'd been there for a while in preparation for the impending Russian invasion. "The writing was on the wall and I was doing assessments, feeling things out, figuring out how we could set things up and start helping people," he says. Seaspray surveyed warehouses, scoped out trucking companies, worked on logistics, and, in a more clandestine capacity, looked for vulnerable border-crossing points—disused railways, areas without fences. Gradually he solidified a vast network of contacts and established what he called "some really good capabilities."

Working with a contact with ties to the United Nations, and with the CEO of a powerful NGO, he witnessed, and helped coordinate, an amount of volunteer support for humanitarian efforts during the invasion "that is probably unprecedented in history," he says. Seaspray also identified a niche gap that no one in Ukraine was addressing.

"What nobody was doing is mobile medicine," he explains. "Having an ambulatory kind of evacuation capability, something like we did in Afghanistan. Nobody was really able to track people getting in or out of Ukraine in a timely manner."

On March 14 Seaspray was on the phone with Sarah—he was speaking with her while she was in the eye doctor's chair—when she said, "Hold on, I gotta take another call." When Sarah came back on, she said, "There's an emergency. A Fox News team was just hit. Can you guys find them?"

"I need coordinates and cell numbers," Seaspray responded with zero hesitation, almost as if he had been expecting just such a call. "What were they wearing? What was their last known location? Anyone they spoke with recently? Cell phones, passports?"

It was then around 1:30 p.m. on March 14, literally minutes after Jen Griffin first heard about the incident in Ukraine. Sarah didn't have any names or locations to pass on to Seaspray, and she was still waiting for Jen to give her the official word to get moving. Finally, around 2:20 p.m., Sarah opened a terse email from Jen.

"Please send your team ASAP," it read.

Jen also included Jock's cell number and a tentative last-known location, as well as my name, which Sarah quickly forwarded to Seaspray in Poland. Meanwhile, Seaspray was already formulating not one but two plans to extract assets from Ukraine. That was the way his mind worked: always have a Plan B. He put two teams together and had them buy two used ambulances and outfit each with as much emergency medical equipment, food, and water as they could find—enough to last at least two weeks, he insisted. He reached out to the contacts already in place in and around Ukraine and began the process of building a mobile operating room and having it available at some point in the extraction. He reached out to old military contacts and asked them to try to trace the cell phone numbers Sarah had given him, and perhaps even triangulate a location. He called contacts on the ground and had them canvass hospitals in Kyiv, looking for injured journalists. He gathered closed-circuit TV footage, hoping that a shot of our license plate could lead him to where we were.

Sarah and Jen started a group chat on an encrypted app, and that became the way they kept track of Seaspray. That afternoon, when Jock learned which hospital I'd been taken to, Jen put the information on the group chat. But when Jock tried to go into the hospital I was in, he was not allowed in—doctors only, he was told. Jock advised the team they would have trouble getting access to me in the hospital.

Sarah called the chief of staff for the minister of foreign affairs in Ukraine, someone with whom she had a long relationship, and began figuring out a way for Seaspray and his team to get in to see me.

Seaspray now had a file assembled for him by Sarah, with all the known information so far. Head shots, passport data, last-known outfits. Pierre was referred to as Blue Puffer Jacket because that was what he was last seen wearing. Sarah sent Seaspray screenshots and coordinates, hoping to steer him to the hospital where I was. No matter how many coordinates or how much data Seaspray had, that was going to be a monumental task. There were dozens of checkpoints between the SOA command center in Poland where Seaspray was based, and the city of Kyiv. Just getting to me, if it was even possible, would likely take hours and hours, maybe even a day. No one knew my condition, so they had to wonder if I could hold on that long. And there was always the chance that Russia would bomb the hospital at any moment. Time was everything.

Seaspray not only had to somehow sneak into Ukraine and Kyiv in the middle of a shoot-on-sight curfew, and then somehow find my location and physically get to me, he also had to provide me with expert medical attention as soon as humanly possible. I wasn't just trapped, I was in terrible shape. The doctor at the Military Medical Clinical

Center strongly recommended that I not be moved at all for at least three more days. Seaspray, it seemed, was going to need some pretty good luck to pull it all off.

What I would later learn was that guardian angels were already at work and looking out for me, in the form of two heroic Ukrainian girls named Anya and Anya.

ELEVEN

THE TWO ANYAS

The story of the Anyas began just a few days before the incident in Horenka.

An active-duty U.S. Army Special Forces lieutenant colonel—who we will call Dave—had an old high school friend, James Heller, who was also active-duty and stationed in Alabama. On February 25, 2022, Heller contacted Dave with an urgent request.

Heller and his family were in the process of adopting a sixteen-year-old orphan, Anya, who lived in Kherson, a port city in southern Ukraine that one day earlier had been invaded by Russian forces. Anya was living at a children's school for orphans when an order for immediate evacuation was issued as Russian troops swarmed the city's streets. In the chaos that followed, Anya was left without a guardian, passport, vehicle, or money—nothing but a few of her possessions. She was alone and trapped in a war zone under intense Russian shelling and gripped by mass panic, with nowhere to go and no one to turn to.

All she could do was send a text message to James Heller in Alabama. He told her to lie low, try to steer clear of Russian soldiers, and somehow get on a bus out of the city. He bought her a ticket and stayed in contact until she made it to the bus station. There, she encountered a massive throng of Ukrainians desperately trying to flee Kherson. Anya tried as hard as she could to get on the very last bus out of the city, but it filled up before she even got close.

That's it, Heller thought. *She didn't make the bus. She couldn't get out. That's it.*

But Heller refused to give up. By then he had already reached out to Dave, who in turn reached out to his colleague Seaspray, then on assignment in Poland. If Dave and Heller could somehow get Anya to Lviv, 560 miles north of Kherson, could Seaspray help get her across the border to Poland?

Seaspray said that if Dave could facilitate the border crossing and connect him to Anya in the busy city of Lviv, he would do it.

Seaspray drove into Ukraine, waiting four hours at the border. The wait to get out of Ukraine was estimated to be as long as ten days. In Kherson, Anya managed to find a ride to the adjacent city of Mykolaiv, which was only slightly safer than the besieged Kherson. There, she had to fight hard to get on a bus headed out, but at last she did, and she took the long, slow overnight crawl to Lviv.

As it happened, Dave's wife received a message from a twenty-year-old girl also named Anya. She was a member of their church in Krakow and had been visiting her family in Mykolaiv when Russian troops stormed Kherson. She, too, would need help getting away from the front lines and across the border to Poland. On her own, even if she could figure out how to get all the way to the border, the crossing would likely take longer than a week, and might not even happen at all.

Dave asked Seaspray if he could pick up *both* Anyas—A1 and A2, as they began referring to them—in Lviv. Despite how dangerous the situation was in Lviv—Special Ops soldiers at checkpoints were advising anyone heading in to Lviv to immediately turn around—Seaspray said he would try.

Remarkably, both Anyas managed to board buses and finally arrive in Lviv, where, miraculously, Seaspray found them both. "In an ocean of chaos, in the middle of the night, all three of them somehow linked up," says Dave, who was in Ukraine himself at the time, helping a family leave Kyiv. "Now the problem was the border crossings, which were so backed up the anticipated waiting times were over a week."

Dave communicated with his Polish Special Forces contacts at the Polish Special Operations Command (POLSOCOM) and fed information to Seaspray about which crossings were best. Unfortunately, every crossing was overrun and all but shut down by massive crowds. With fifteen miles still to go before they reached the border, Seaspray and the two Anyas found themselves stuck in standstill, bumper-to-bumper traffic. They had a better chance of running out of gas, it seemed, then they did of making it to Poland.

Seaspray made a decision. He went off-road and steered the rental sedan through miles of treacherously muddy hills and backwoods terrain. They made it about three miles before finally running out of road, still thirteen miles away from the border. Seaspray had another tough call to make—drive back and join a lengthy line of cars, or proceed on foot. It was still the middle of the night, and the temperature was well below freezing.

Seaspray phoned Dave and asked, "What do you think? That's a long walk and these girls aren't layered for cold. A1 has dress boots on."

Dave told him he'd heard from POLSOCOM that the lines of cars had only grown longer, sometimes by several more miles. "What's your water look like?" he asked.

"We've got enough as long as it doesn't freeze. I'm most worried about the cold. If we have to stop, I won't be able to prevent hypothermia."

"Your call," Dave said, "but I think this is a problem that only gets harder as time goes on."

Seaspray asked the Anyas what they wanted to do. They said they wanted to walk.

All three had now been up for over twenty-four hours with no sleep, and none had eaten much, if at all. Fatigue was setting in. The ice-coated mountains around them gave off a moist, chilling breeze that only made them feel more exposed. Deep inside the interlocking mountains, as they trundled up and down steep inclines, they lost all contact with Dave or anyone else. They would either make it to the border, or they wouldn't.

Finally, Dave got a message from POLSOCOM.

Seaspray, A1, and A2 had made it. They were at a crossing, and A1's feet were bleeding. They were all dazed with exhaustion, but they'd made it.

Even so, they spent ten more hours at the crossing, where they had their documents checked three times and advanced a total of 150 feet in line. Luckily, a Polish Special Ops team located the trio and drove them across the border in thirty minutes. Dave was there to take A1 and A2 to Krakow (Anya 1 eventually made it to the U.S. and was adopted by the Hellers, while Anya 2 made it safely back to her church in Krakow). After dropping them off, Seaspray went back to work. Just a few days later, he took a call from Sarah Verardos.

"Every process and relationship engaged to rescue the Anyas," Dave later told me, "would be revisited when the calls came on March 14th to respond to your situation. We basically cut our teeth getting them out."

• • •

Late on March 14, the day I was injured, Dr. Rich Jadick was in a small hotel near the Polish-Ukrainian border, waiting to hear what he'd gotten himself into this time. He was on a mission of sorts, he just didn't know exactly what that mission was. Finally, the team leader appeared with a very succinct briefing.

"We have to get into Kyiv and get this guy out," he said.

Rich Jadick gave the team leader a quick once-over. He knew him only as Seaspray, and he knew he was every inch the hardened combat operative, trained for dangerous missions and countless battlefield escapes. Seaspray had an authority, a presence—he looked the part.

"Meanwhile, I looked like a suburban dad," Rich says. "I was fifty-seven years old, with gray hair and a gray beard, in a lacrosse sweatshirt and a jacket. I hadn't changed my pants in four days and I had mustard stains all over them."

It was Sarah Verardo who had first recruited Rich weeks before March 14. She called Rich, an American naval surgeon and Bronze Star recipient, and reached him while he was teaching a surgical course in a hotel conference room in Tennessee.

"Hey, I got something for you," Sarah told him. "Do you want to go to Ukraine?"

"Oh no," Rich responded, "my wife is gonna kill me."

A Russian invasion seemed imminent, and through SOA Sarah was setting up a team near the border in Poland. She wanted Rich to fly in, assess the situation, coordinate with NGOs, and help them set up reception camps for people fleeing Ukraine. That kind of work was just about Rich's specialty. He'd met Sarah when they both worked with the Independence Fund, and they were both veterans of vast humanitarian efforts in far-off places. Sarah had a feeling Rich would say yes to Ukraine, and he did.

Growing up in middle-class Albany, New York, Rich was fascinated with military matters, even though he didn't have any relatives who were veterans. "I liked the team aspect of military units, relying on each other and doing things that were bigger than you," he says. He applied to the U.S. Military Academy at West Point, New York, but was physically disqualified due to a depth-perception problem—"a wandering eye," he says. During the Vietnam War an ROTC recruiter told him: he could work around the medical issue and enlisted him in the Marines; two weeks later Rich had an ROTC college scholarship. He graduated as a second lieutenant and served active duty with the

Eighty-Second Infantry Battalion in Norway, tracking the Russians during the Cold War.

After finishing medical school and a pediatric residency, Rich deployed to Iraq in 2003 as a senior medical officer and surgeon with a Marine expeditionary unit. He had a hundred soldiers with various levels of combat casualty training under his watch, nearly all of them twenty-two years old or younger. "Some of them couldn't even hook up an IV bag yet," he says. Their fiercest test was when they moved toward the front lines in Fallujah.

There Rich found himself running into the middle of street battles to retrieve wounded soldiers. "They say you have to keep the medic safely in the back, but the reality is that what decides if a soldier lives or dies is what happens at the point of injury," Rich says. "I can't stop them from getting shot, but what I can do is put myself between the point of injury and a body bag. That is where I belong—putting my fingers in bullet holes."

Rich's novel idea was to move mobile medical units as close to the front lines as possible. Medical doctors had always spoken of the Golden Hour—the first sixty minutes after an injury—as a soldier's best chance of surviving. But Rich believed it was more like a Golden Minute.

On his very first day on the front in Fallujah, Rich and his team were in the back of a windowless M113 armored personnel carrier when they heard an urgent radio dispatch: *A hundred meters to your south, Bravo Company is getting ambushed!* The M113 turned around and headed toward the fight, bullets pinging off its turret. At the scene of the ambush, Rich jumped out, kept his head down, and pulled a wounded Marine from the middle of the street. His name was Lonny Davis, and Rich knew him: Marine sergeant, Dallas Cowboys fan. Lonnie was bleeding profusely from a large groin wound. He was gurgling and looking up at Rich with fear in his eyes. Rich worked on Lonny's wound, but was soon pulled away to treat four other badly injured soldiers. By the time he got back to Lonnie, the young sergeant was dead.

"I was so scared," Jadick remembers. "I thought, *My idea is bad, we're all gonna die, the soldiers and the doctors.*" Every inch of Rich's uniform was covered in Lonny's blood, and Rich took sand and rubbed himself down so that the blood would turn black and the other medics wouldn't see how horrifying things were at the front.

Rich put Lonny in a body bag and went back out. He found another badly wounded soldier, Sergeant Volpe, who, like Lonny, had a severe groin injury. Rich learned from what happened with Lonny earlier that day and rushed over and put his hand in Volpe's wound and searched for the iliac arteries and managed to stop the bleeding. Volpe survived, endured twenty-seven surgeries, and, to Rich's great satisfaction, eventually went to college.

In that First Battle of Fallujah, Rich and his aggressive approach to combat casualties were credited with saving the lives of *thirty U.S. soldiers.*

There was something about the front lines of combat that called out to Rich, and energized him, and seemed to him to be the theater in which he did his very best work. That was why Sarah Verardo believed he would agree to put his teaching duties on hold and fly into Poland.

Which is just what he did.

Rich traveled there with Dakota Meyer, a former Marine, Afghanistan war veteran, and Medal of Honor recipient for his actions in the Battle of Ganjgal in 2009. Smart, fearless, and highly skilled, Meyer had helped Sarah and SOA in Afghanistan, and now he'd signed up for duty in Ukraine. Rich and Dakota worked on evaluating a four-thousand-person refugee camp in Warsaw before flying to an SOA safe house and command center in a village hotel nearer the border with Ukraine. It was late and Rich lay down and tried to grab a bit of sleep.

"I hadn't heard one single word about Benji Hall yet," he says.

Back in Washington, DC, Jennifer Griffin learned that Rich, her good friend and fellow Independence Fund board member, happened

to be in Poland on SOA business. She called Sarah Verardo and asked her if Rich could be part of the team that went into Kyiv. Sarah contacted Seaspray and let him know Jadick would be a huge asset.

At 6 a.m. that day, there was a knock at Rich's hotel room door. It was Dakota Meyer. "Listen, we're leaving at eleven, we have to pick up some vehicles and stuff by the Baltic Sea," Dakota said. Together they drove six hours to a tiny hamlet by the water and wound up in a man's backyard, where six old ambulances were parked. The plan was for Rich and Dakota to drive two of them back to the safe house. But before they could climb in, the man who owned them came over.

"Your check hasn't cleared yet," he said.

Rich and Dakota, who didn't have enough on them to pay for the vehicles, had no choice but to find a local place and order breakfast and wait. Finally, the check cleared, and they drove the beat-up old ambulances back to the safe house near the border.

Later that day, March 14, Seaspray briefed the rest of the team.

"We have to get into Kyiv and get this guy out," he said.

Rich Jadick might not have looked the part. But, in every way, he fit the bill.

"Okay, then," he said as soon as Seaspray finished the briefing. "Let's go."

• • •

At the InterContinental in Kyiv on March 14, Trey Yingst struggled to sleep and continued scanning posts and group chats for news about Pierre and Sasha. The next morning, Tuesday, March 15, he received a text from a source in the field: there was an understanding that Ukrainian soldiers were the ones who found us. In fact, Jock had connected with Song, the operative who rescued me, and learned that Song had picked up Pierre's camera. Song was on his way to return the

camera to the Fox News team in Kyiv, and wanted them to show him what Pierre had recorded.

Jock—who headed back to the InterContinental after getting kicked out of the hospital where I was a patient—arranged for everyone to meet in a large VIP suite on the hotel's first floor. In addition to Jock and Shane, Trey and Dudi, our second cameraman, waited in the suite for Song to arrive. Song entered carrying Pierre's damaged and bloodied camera in a plastic grocery bag. He put it on the conference table. Dudi took out the SD storage card and put it in his laptop, and they all watched what Pierre had shot.

There was about thirty minutes of footage, mostly showing us in the press van and the red car, and me doing stand-up spots in the abandoned village. At the very end, Pierre captured our car turning right on the highway and stopping at the sound of the first missile exploding in front of us. You could see the camera swivel as Pierre turned to film the explosion. You could see a tree begin to fall. And you could hear Pierre yell, "Reverse the car!"

An instant later, the second bomb hit and the footage cut off.

"What about Pierre and Sasha?" Trey asked Song.

"They were killed," Song said. "I saw Pierre's body at the site but could not take it. I saw the remains of a woman in the car."

Trey had hoped for the miracle but prepared for the worst. He had worked with Pierre often and he knew him to be the very best person to be with when things went wrong, and he believed Pierre could get out of just about any situation, so he held out hope. But he also prepared for the worst.

Song's news was the first confirmation for anyone at Fox that Pierre and Sasha were gone.

Jock and Shane delivered the information to Dragan Petrovic in London, and Dragan called Jay Wallace and Suzanne Scott in New York. Around then, Jock got a call from a source who told him Pierre's body and Sasha's remains were at a local morgue. Jock quickly left to identify Pierre.

At the morgue Jock had to wait a long time for local police to arrive before he was allowed to see Pierre. He got the phone number for Sasha's father in Kyiv and called him with the terrible news. He invited him to come to the InterContinental hotel, but the shoot-on-sight curfew in Kyiv was fast approaching, and Sasha's father did not want to risk getting stuck at the hotel. Instead Fox News arranged for someone to bring Sasha's duffel bag and belongings to him.

At the InterContinental, Trey and Dudi went through Sasha's bag and saw that her gear and clothes had been hastily stuffed inside it. They didn't want her father to receive her things in that condition, so they emptied her bag and carefully folded her clothes and neatly repacked her gear. "They wanted him to see that we cared about Sasha a lot," Jock says.

At the morgue, Jock was finally let through to identify his friend and colleague. Pierre's body was not in bad shape, and beyond some shrapnel and bruises his face was easily recognizable. "He'd obviously lost a lot of blood," Jock recalls. "There was blood all over his trousers."

Back at the hotel, Trey turned his attention to figuring out how to get Pierre's body across the border and back home to Ireland.

"Pierre and I had a pact," Trey says. "We agreed we would stay in Ukraine to the end and finish the story together and leave at the same time. So it was extremely important for me to be with him when they took his body out of the country. I wanted to honor our pact."

TWELVE

THE ONLY VIABLE OPTION

Near the Polish–Ukrainian border, early on March 15, Seaspray prepared to start the mission to get me out of Kyiv. He knew well how hazardous the journey from Poland to Kyiv would be. In an earlier operation he'd been on a Ukrainian highway when the Russians bombed it and took it over. He knew that even checkpoints manned by Ukrainians could be dangerous. "You would run into these burn-barrel type checkpoints that were unregulated and not in any comms with the Ukrainian army," Seaspray says. "It was the kind of thing where whoever the kid who was running the checkpoint was, you know, president of Ukraine for the day."

What's more, despite how surprisingly effective the resistance had been, Russian forces were still on the advance everywhere in Ukraine. On March 14, the day we were attacked, Russian rockets killed thirty-five people in western Ukraine, while a Russian missile launched from Donetsk in the east killed twenty more. The most intense assaults of all, against Mariupol in the south, showed no sign of letting up. And Kyiv, the capital, was slowly being encircled and cut off by Russian troops. The situation in Ukraine was bleak and dire, and in Kyiv conditions were more dangerous than ever before.

Seaspray knew all of this and prepared for it. At the SOA safe house, he had two QRF teams—Quick Reaction Force—ready to go: a backup Plan B team led by Dakota Meyer in one ambulance, and the other led by Seaspray. Dr. Rich Jadick would travel in the latter. The two vehicles were stocked and ready to go, and Seaspray laid out the plan.

"Here's the deal, guys," he said. "There's three missing plus two local drivers, and we don't know where any of them are. But we're going to go in anyway."

The key to making it safely to Kyiv, Seaspray believed, was projecting, and never straying from, a completely nonthreatening, de-escalatory presence. In a way, such thinking was counterintuitive. For starters, the two teams would travel in actual ambulances; that was why Seaspray arranged to buy them and not roomier, more comfortable vans. None of the team members would wear any kind of protective clothing, not even body armor, and none would carry visible weapons or high-tech gear. Instead they all wore bright orange jackets with conspicuous medical patches, so that they appeared to be an actual medical team. Their posture would be aggressively deferential, hopefully defusing any tense situation and allowing them ease and speed and safety of movement.

Seaspray believed they had to create a narrative of what was happening, and not let others craft one of their own. "It is about shaping people's perception of who you are and what you're doing," he says. "We're in bright colors. We're driving slowly. We've got our hands up. No weapons. We're trying to be as disarming as possible."

The teams set off and drove across a desolate part of the border, arriving at another safe house inside Ukraine. From there they split off in different directions. Rich Jadick was in the back of one ambulance with an interpreter, Seaspray and another operative, whom Rich knew only as Bo, a former paramedic and special operative who had been in Poland for a month helping with relief efforts. Bo drove the ambulance while Seaspray, who had a cell phone and a satellite phone, stayed in constant communication with contacts in the country, both figuring out how to avoid any Russian checkpoints and devising a plan to get me to the Polish border once they found me.

The ambulance was in terrible shape. It limped along at barely 15 mph and poured smoke out the back. Most of the time it was the only vehicle on the eerily desolate roads. "We were sitting ducks," says Bo. "And Seaspray was blaming me like I did something wrong. We were bickering like an old married couple."

Then the ambulance all but gave out. Bo managed to wobble it into a local garage. "It was kind of funny," says Rich, "because we got out and looked at it and these two big special ops guys looked at me and asked if I knew what was wrong. I said, 'Yeah, it's broken.'"

Somehow, they managed to get the ambulance running and kept going. They drove on back roads, through farmlands, across hollows, trying not to be spotted. When they came to checkpoints, they slowed down, smiled, and kept their hands up. At every checkpoint they had to get out and be searched. At some, they passed through easily thanks to Seaspray's contacts, who had called ahead and alerted the Ukrainian soldiers. At others, things got tense.

"You're on your knees and you're thinking you're going to get executed," Bo says.

The team was so intent on not being mistaken for Russians that they didn't even allow their interpreter—who had a thick, heavy Russian accent—to speak to the Ukrainian soldiers.

Along the way Rich was briefed on the mission: to get me, the only survivor of the attack, to the Polish border. The secondary part of the mission, which they hoped to accomplish concurrently but which could end up requiring a second trip, was to get the remains of Pierre across the border and deliver them to his widow, Mich, who would be waiting in Poland. On the way to Kyiv, Seaspray worked ceaselessly to arrange for my passage to the border. There were no specifics yet, only ideas. The biggest concern, by that time, was that the ride in the ambulance alone might kill me. "It was a really small old ambulance like the one in *Ghostbusters*, and the roads had a ton of potholes and shell craters," Rich says. "We would have to hope we didn't hit the really deep ones."

It took several hours, but Seaspray's team finally made it into Kyiv and used GPS guidance to pull through the gates to the National Military Medical Clinical Center on Hospitalna Street. A Ukrainian doctor was waiting for them outside. "I'm glad you're here," the doctor told Rich, who identified himself as an American surgeon. "I'm supposed to get my rifle and get on my post." Even the doctors in Ukraine were fighting on the streets. The doctor explained he was worried about moving me, but he was just as worried about leaving me there to possibly be victimized by Russian bombs again. No one wanted a Western journalist to die in their hospital.

Seaspray's team had been warned that Jock had been kicked out of the hospital, and they might have trouble getting in to see me. But Rich and Seaspray announced themselves as doctors and walked straight in. They climbed the stairs to my third-floor room, and Rich went in to see me while Seaspray waited outside. Rich walked up to me and asked my name and then asked if I was ready to leave. I warned him about the Russian spy nurses and the Russian assassin with a pistol in the bed. Rich made note of my medication-induced paranoia and assured me I was fine.

Then he quickly looked me over. There was a lot going on: a head injury, a drain tube in my skull, shrapnel the size of a matchbox right by my carotid artery in my throat, burns covering what remained of my left leg. Rich's main concern was my head and throat: he was worried the shrapnel would not allow him to intubate me. On the plus side, my vital signs were stable, and the doctors at the medical center had done a good job of wrapping my injuries. The bulky drain tube sticking out of my head, however, would likely get in the way once we hit the road. Rich asked the neurosurgeon if it was necessary, and the doctor explained that that was just the way they did things there. Rich took a photo of my CT scan on his cell phone and texted it to a neurosurgeon he knew in New York City.

"You can get rid of the drain," his friend told him.

But Rich decided to leave it in. It was going to be a very long ride, and the risk of dirt and dust entering the wound and causing an infection was high. I would have to be transported with my head contraption and my leg contraptions and an IV tube and arm and leg casts and wires sticking out everywhere. There was also no backboard available to keep me straight while moving me, further complicating things. But there was no time to fix these problems: the shoot-on-sight curfew in Kyiv was now in effect. Seaspray leaned into the room and said, "We have to go."

Just then two very large Ukrainian soldiers walked in.

My paranoia flared. Rich calmed me down as the soldiers explained they would accompany us out of the hospital and possibly on the trip to the border. Rich helped get me onto a gurney and wheel me and my IV tube to the elevator and out the front entrance. My ambulance awaited in the parking lot. Rich knew that Seaspray would not want Ukrainian military muscle accompanying us to the border, and he pulled Seaspray aside to talk it over. Finally, Rich spun around and told the soldiers they could go back. No discussion, just a declaration: *we don't need you.*

The soldiers grumbled a bit but stepped back and walked away. Just like that I was in the back of the old ambulance, and we were free to go.

"That's the best part of combat medicine," Rich says. "No paperwork."

What I didn't yet know was that getting the team into Kyiv and getting me out of the hospital had actually been the *easy* part of the mission. What lay ahead was going to be, at best, a miraculous confluence of fate and fortune and, at worst, a sheer impossibility.

Once the U.S. evacuated all its diplomatic and military personnel from Ukraine, the options available for my extraction became extremely limited. There were only three ways to transport me the nearly eight hundred miles from Kyiv to an as-yet-unknown border town in Poland: by car, by plane, or by train. Seaspray had exhaustively researched all three options. Commercial air travel was not available, so Seaspray reached out to a contact: a Polish pilot who was flying risky low-altitude flights across Ukraine on humanitarian missions. The pilot told Seaspray he would research possible flight paths as well as safe areas to land near the border.

Yet even if the contact had been able to devise a feasible route, nonstandard air transport was simply too risky anywhere near Kyiv, given the presence of Russian surface-to-air and air-to-air weapons. There was also a question about whether I could handle an airplane's low air pressure in my condition. Seaspray crossed air transport off our list of options.

Travel by vehicle, even an ambulance, was also highly risky. Rich had a real concern that the rough roads and constant bumps could dislodge the shrapnel in my throat and kill me. Driving eight hundred hard miles in the dilapidated ambulance at 15 mph would also likely take three excruciating days. There had to be a better and safer way to get me to the border.

Seaspray enlisted another close contact, an active-duty U.S. Army special forces lieutenant colonel under U.S. diplomatic mission in Poland. This was Dave. Dave made several calls to sources in his network who were part of the Ukrainian government and inquired about the possibility of getting me aboard a commercial train. "I was told the trains out of Kyiv were so packed, people were jumping off overpasses onto the trains to get out," Dave says. Loading me onto a train and finding room for me and my contraptions once I was on it seemed impossible.

The truth, says Dave, was that "the options available for an injured person's extraction out of Kyiv and to the border were severely limited to nonexistent."

Even so, Dave did not give up. He learned that, by sheer coincidence, a Polish government train was transporting the Polish prime minister into Kyiv for a highly clandestine, high-stakes meeting with Ukrainian president Zelenskyy. The train would also carry the Czech prime minister, Petr Fiala, as well as Janez Jansa, prime minister of Slovenia. They would be the first world leaders to venture into Ukraine and meet with President Zelenskyy. Their train would remain at the

Kyiv train station most likely overnight and possibly until noon the following day, before taking them back to Poland. Practically no one knew about the trip, and details about it were exceedingly scarce. Layers of security measures were in place.

Was it somehow possible to get me on that train—to put me aboard the Polish rail equivalent of Air Force One on the first-ever, highly sensitive Western diplomatic visit to Kyiv since the invasion, during the largest European conflict since World War II?

"Getting someone out of Ukraine on a high-risk diplomatic transportation platform required approval from the Polish prime minister of a submitted request from the U.S. ambassador to Poland," Dave explains. "That request would undoubtedly stand in contradiction to the official State Department advisory issued a month earlier regarding official U.S. support for evacuation efforts." That meant that, even if the prime minister's train remained in the Kyiv station until morning, Dave and Seaspray would have only a precious few hours—all of them in the dead of night—to secure written diplomatic permission for my evacuation (in violation of U.S. wartime policy), without which the mission to get me to Poland would be, as Dave put it, "dead in the water."

By then Dave was referring to this unlikely scenario as "the only viable option" to get me out of Ukraine. What it was, in fact, was a logistical, diplomatic, and security nightmare with only the smallest chance of success. It was a Hail Mary pass, an act of sheer desperation. Dave, a highly skilled, endlessly resourceful veteran of many such operations, had just the slenderest hopes it was even possible.

Yet, even if only in the most generous definition of the word, it *was* possible.

In the middle of the night on March 16, as Seaspray slowly wound his way to Kyiv, he received a text from Dave in Poland.

Hey man, Dave wrote, there's a potential option.

That's great, Seaspray responded, because our other options aren't looking too great right now.

THIRTEEN

THE PRIME MINISTER'S TRAIN

Sometime around 2 a.m. on March 16, Alicia's first sleepless night, the buzzing of her cell phone broke the silence. From the number, Alicia knew it was Fox News CEO Suzanne Scott in New York. They hadn't spoken since Suzanne's early calls the previous evening, alerting Alicia that something bad had happened. This time Suzanne did not even say hello or identify herself when Alicia picked up after one ring. She just got to it.

"Benji is fine," she said. "He lost a leg. He's in a hospital in Kyiv."

By then, Suzanne had decided to update Alicia as quickly and as thoroughly as she could about where and how I was, but also about the extent of the injuries I'd sustained. Her own father had lost a leg to diabetes, and Suzanne knew what a shock that could be to a family, as well as how much strength and positivity Alicia would need to help us all get through it. "It wasn't easy for my father or the family," Suzanne says. "I felt that Alicia needed to know the seriousness of Ben's injuries as soon as possible."

When Scott told her about my leg, Alicia's first thought was: *Thank goodness. He lost a leg. That is something we can deal with.* Her fear was that I hadn't survived, so this was news she could handle, a problem that could be fixed.

"Is anyone with him?" she asked.

Suzanne told her Jock was at the hospital but not allowed to see me in my room. Jock would try again later to get in. Suzanne also said they were waiting on any word about Pierre and Sasha. It was a short call, but Alicia felt greatly relieved. "Knowing Jock was there, trying to see Benji, trying to find Pierre, that was huge," she says. "It seemed like Fox News had it under control and were doing the right things."

Alicia could not sleep after that, so she waited out the night and was up getting ready before daybreak. It was a school day and Alicia had to feed the children and get them to school. She hadn't told the girls anything about what happened, and she decided she would wait to tell them when she was on firmer footing herself. Children are intuitive; they can pick up cues and sense when something's wrong with their parents, and Alicia did not want them to see how devastated and afraid she was. She wanted to keep the girls in the dark about their father for as long as she could.

But that would not be easy. Word was getting out. Alicia's very good friend Katie had texted her earlier; her husband had seen something on the wires about a wounded journalist in Ukraine. By morning, the Facebook post with my press pass had been picked up by the media, and texts and calls from concerned friends came in on Alicia's cell. She didn't want to answer them because she didn't know what she could tell anyone or what help she could ask for. "I didn't even know myself how to help," she says.

Her first concern was Hero, Iris, and Honor, then two, four, and six years old. Alicia did not want them to hear about their father from someone else, and wouldn't that be what happened if they went off to school? Surely some child or some parent would say something. Alicia texted the school headmistress and told her I had been injured in Ukraine and asked if she should keep the children home.

Send them in, the headmistress said. We'll take care of them.

This was an assurance Alicia needed to hear. It was going to be a very long day, and to know the children would be safe at school, and protected from rumors and remarks, was something like a lifeline. Next, Alicia sent a group text on a WhatsApp chat that included all the parents in our daughters' classes. She asked for their help in making sure the girls didn't find out about what happened in Ukraine.

Alicia got dressed, went downstairs, had breakfast with the children, and prepared to drive them to school. It was important, she felt, not to stray from the routine. She arranged it so they would be a few minutes late, to avoid the crush of cars at the school drop-off. Just before it was time to go, she heard a knock on the basement door that was level with the street outside our home. She opened the door and saw her great friend Natasha Parker, Tash to everyone, standing there with her young son, who went to the same school as the girls. Alicia fell into Tash's arms and, for the first time since the call from Suzanne Scott the previous day, she let the tears go.

"I just started crying because suddenly it all felt very real," she says. "I'd thought I could take the girls to school, but when I saw Tash, I realized that I couldn't have. I would have absolutely crumbled."

So it was Tash who drove our little ladies to school that morning, and they were besides themselves with excitement because they loved Tash and this was something out of the ordinary for them, and what child doesn't like something new and out of the ordinary? Tash's presence, too, was a lifeline, a blessing.

Alicia's posture changed after that. She would no longer passively wait for information. She would be more proactive. She would make things happen. She texted Suzanne Scott and asked if she could arrange for some sort of private medical assistance to be with me in Kyiv. She did not want me to be alone. She also asked for more specific information about my condition. How critical was it? Could I be moved or not? Alicia was more demanding of details. "The main thought I had was that Benji could not stay where he was," she says. "I didn't think he would survive Kyiv."

My grandfather Alastair and his children—from left, Ian, Connie, Alastair, and my father, Roderick—in the Santo Tomas Camp in Manila in 1945. The photograph was taken by an American GI after they were saved.

My father, a U.S. Army private with the 7th Infantry, at the approximate border between North and South Korea at the end of the Korean War. He called his time in the military "the best experience."

After the war, my father tried his hand at bullfighting in the Andalusian region of Spain. "He had an adventurous spirit," says his sister, Connie. "If he failed, he just picked himself up and marched on."

That's me on a ride with my mother, Jenny, in Hampshire, England. She taught me so much, including how to barter with bazaar merchants—a skill that came in handy as a journalist.

Sitting in on a backwoods voodoo ceremony in Petit-Goâve in Haiti in 2010. There's a pin-pierced voodoo doll in that little blue casket beside me.

Documenting a rebel firing against Gadaffi's forces in Misrata, Libya, in 2011. Moments later an RPG hit the wall and injured the rebel. *Photograph by Rick Findler*

When we were stuck in a port in Misrata in 2011, Rick Findler and I took an ill-advised dip as shells landed in the near distance. The Jellyana (behind me) eventually got us out. *Photograph by Rick Findler*

Reporting from a rebel cave in Taftanaz in northwestern Syria in 2012. Rick and I slept there surrounded by AK rifles, RPGs, grenades, and other ammo. *Photograph by Rick Findler*

Dodging sniper fire in Aleppo, Syria, in 2013. Our Syrian fixer, Rizgar, was a sprinting champion who liked to race us from shelter to shelter as snipers shot from above.
Photograph by Rick Findler

With Syrian rebels staging a protest in the town of Taftanaz in 2012, not long before Syrian Army soldiers opened fire on the protesters.
Photograph by Rick Findler

Rick and I with an African Union soldier at the parliament building in Mogadishu, Somalia, in 2014, moments before one of the bloodiest battles I've ever witnessed.

Alicia and I in Norfolk, England, in 2014.
We grew up just a few streets apart.

Our wedding day at the Brompton Oratory in Knightsbridge in 2015. My niece,
Daisy, is the flower girl on my left; on Alicia's right is her goddaughter, Beatrix.

Filing a report for Fox News from Kyiv in 2016, on the anniversary of Ukraine's Independence Day. By then, Russian forces had already made inroads in eastern Ukraine, and many of the soldiers pictured wound up in combat in the Donbas region. *Photographs by Mal James*

Reporting from a hilltop above the town of Baghouz, Syria, as Syrian forces wiped out the last ISIS troops in the caliphate in 2019.
Courtesy of Fox News

As Baghouz was being destroyed, I covered the exodus of ISIS fighters and families into the desert north of the town, on their way to prison camps.
Courtesy of Fox News

Pierre and I talking to children in the al-Hol prison camp in northeastern Syria in 2019. Some who spoke English just shouted, "We're all going to kill you."
Photograph by Tim Santhouse

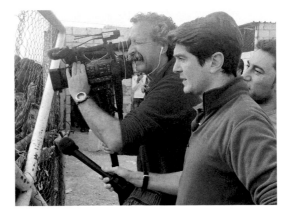

Pierre and I on horses in a rare recreational moment in the mountains of Afghanistan in 2021, one of our final assignments together. When I think of Pierre, I picture him this way.

Reporting on a protest in Sderot, Israel, the town closest to the Gazan border, in 2018. The Israeli protesters rallied against a ceasefire proclaimed in Gaza.

Anchoring a show on Veteran's Day in the Fox News bureau in London in 2020.
Photograph by Tim Santhouse

Early morning in Derik in northeastern Syria in 2019, with Pierre and our producer Tim Santhouse. Soon after we headed to the front lines to cover Turkey's invasion of Syria.
Photograph by Tim Santhouse

A pile-up on Daddy in our home in west London: from left, our baby, Hero; Iris in the middle; and our eldest, Honor.

Our daughters adored their grandfather Rod (out for a stroll with us in Kensington Gardens).

Alicia and I with (maybe) a couple of prospective journalists, Honor and Iris, in the Fox News Bureau in London.

Alicia and I with the girls in 2021. This was the picture Dave showed to the Polish commander to persuade him to let us on the prime minister's train.

On a balcony of the InterContinental Hotel in Kyiv, Ukraine, where I anchored our nightly show in early 2022. By then, Kyiv was nearly encircled by Russian troops.
Photograph by Dudi Gamliel

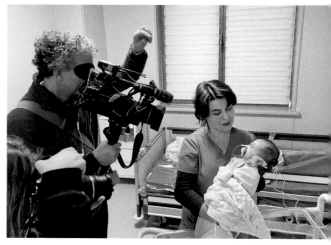

Pierre filming our visit to the Children's Hospital in Kyiv on March 13, 2022. There we met the last unevacuated child, whom hospital staffers nicknamed Prince Charlie.

Our tireless fixer, Oleksandra "Sasha" Kuvshynova, was a brave and idealistic Ukrainian journalist.

Sasha and I about to get into our media escorts' car and travel to the village of Horenka, where the attack occurred, on March 14, 2022.
Courtesy of Fox News

Pierre filmed me on March 14 as I reported on the heavy damage to Horenka, which had been abandoned and all but destroyed. Shells landed a few miles behind me.
Courtesy of Fox News

The moment right after the first bomb landed twenty feet in front of us as we were leaving Horenka on March 14. Pierre yelled out, "Reverse the car!"
Courtesy of Fox News

Dashcam footage from the car of the man who found and saved me on March 14. That's the shell of our bombed-out car, and that's me in my helmet near the light pole on the right.

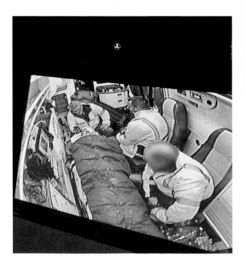

A team of specialists spirited me out of a hospital in Kyiv and to the train station on March 15. Dr. Rich Jadick is behind me in the ambulance.
Courtesy of Save Our Allies

Seaspray (long hair) and others carried me off the prime minister's train after we crossed the border into Poland on March 16.
Courtesy of Save Our Allies

A U.S. soldier helped Seaspray, Bo (blue T-shirt), and Dave (black jacket) carry me onto a UH-60 Black Hawk helicopter on a tiny landing strip in Przemyśl, Poland, on March 16.
Courtesy of Save Our Allies

I was strapped tightly into the Black Hawk, given noise-canceling headphones, and covered with a sheet to keep dust out of my wounds.
Courtesy of Save Our Allies

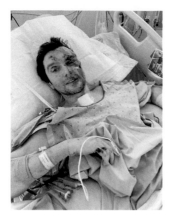

I finally made it to the U.S. Army's Landstuhl Regional Medical Center in Landstuhl, Germany, where I spent the next ten days.

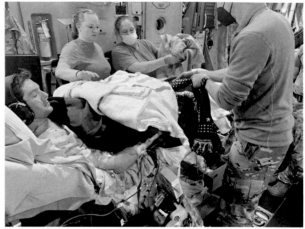

Getting buckled into the U.S. Air Force's massive C-17 cargo aircraft for the challenging twenty-four-hour trip from Landstuhl to San Antonio, Texas.

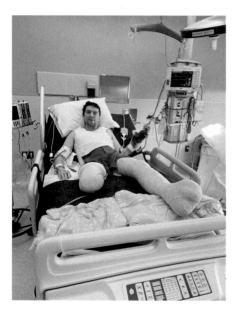

In my room in the ICU at Brooke Army Medical Center (BAMC) on Joint Base San Antonio–Fort Sam Houston on April 4. A pair of leeches are at work on my injured left hand.

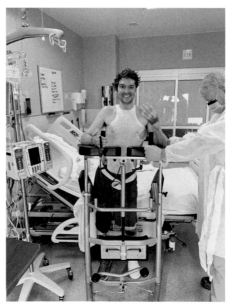

Standing up on my crude temporary prosthetics at BAMC on May 7. That's my PT Kelly Brown urging me on.

Getting a welcome visit at BAMC from my Fox News colleague Jen Griffin (left) and Sarah Verardo of Save Our Allies—both of whom helped save my life.

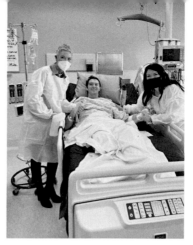

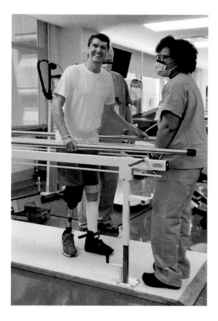

A happy day at BAMC—me doing a little salsa dance with Major Kendra Howard, chief of occupational therapy, on May 18.

At Fisher House with my new friend James; his wife, Cynthia; their daughters, Kimber and Oakleigh; and their healthy newborn, Rossi.

I'm up and about at the Center for the Intrepid (CFI), on my actual prosthetics, alongside the man who led my team of specialists, Dr. Joe Alderete.

Celebrating my fortieth birthday with a chocolate cake and my incredible physios at BAMC.

Suzanne Scott, Fox News CEO, and Jay Wallace, president, showed up at BAMC with a giant birthday card signed by all my Fox colleagues.

I grew especially close to the great team of ICU nurses at BAMC who tended to me and lifted my spirits every day around the clock.

My mate Rick Findler paid me a welcome birthday visit at BAMC. We hope to work together again one day soon.

Back in Washington, DC, Jen Griffin, Fox News' national security correspondent, had been told about the existence of an option to evacuate me from Ukraine. She was given few other details, and when she pushed for them, she didn't get them. The mission was simply too sensitive. Jen organized a group call with Alicia and pulled in top Fox executives, including Lachlan Murdoch, the cochairman of News Corp and the son of its founder, Rupert Murdoch. It was Lachlan who spoke directly to Alicia, introducing himself and asking for her permission to transport me out of Kyiv, despite my fragile condition.

"All I knew was that they'd concocted some top-secret plan for an evacuation, and they wanted my blessing," Alicia says. "I knew there were only two options: stay or move." Alicia also knew what I would have wanted her to say. "Benji is a mover," she says. "He would never have wanted to stay perched in any situation. He would want to go. I told them, 'I think the right thing to do is move him, even though there are risks.'"

Jen quickly called Seaspray in Ukraine and connected him to Suzanne Scott and Jay Wallace in New York. They would have to be the ones who officially signed off on moving me. In essence, they would be authorizing Seaspray to assume control of the entire operation to get me to the border, even though they had their own security teams in place, and even though they knew hardly anything about Seaspray, and even though Seaspray could not divulge any details about the plan to transport me. "I didn't know anything about Seaspray, either," says Jen. "But I had to trust him and I did. And I told everyone in New York they could trust him, too."

The Fox executives signed off on the move.

While on the call, Jay Wallace asked Seaspray how things were going in general. As they spoke, Seaspray could see explosions lighting up parts of Kyiv in the near distance. The Russian shelling hadn't let up in days. And there we were, outside a military hospital up on a hill,

The moment of our joyful reunion: Alicia rushed onto the plane that brought me home to London on August 21, 2022.
Photograph by Rick Findler

I finally made it home, much to the delight of our young daughters and my chocolate lab, Bosco.
Photograph by Rick Findler

Honor, our eldest—whose voice I heard after the attack in Horenka—holding on to me when I walked into our London home for the first time in six months.
Photograph by Rick Findler

A scene I dreamed about: happy at home with the girls. Hero is holding Blue Jumpsuit, the little hedgehog toy I carried with me through my entire ordeal in Ukraine.

With Hero, Honor, and Iris a few days after my return. The simplest things now bring me the greatest joy.

With Alicia, Honor, Iris, and Hero a few days after my return. We're all on a journey together, and as long as they're with me, I know I'll be okay.

• • •

That Seaspray and his team had been able to get me out of the Military Medical Clinical Center in Kyiv was, on its own, quite a feat of daring. As much as the Ukrainian doctor did not want to see me perish in his hospital, he was still reluctant to let me leave. I was in no condition to be transported anywhere, much less through a war-torn country. The doctor needed to be convinced that handing me over to Seaspray and the team made some kind of medical sense.

"We had to make him feel comfortable that we were all actual medical professionals and that we were qualified to safely transport you," says Seaspray, who is *not* a medical professional. "The doctor knew the condition the roads were in, and he knew what condition you were in, and he was understandably hesitant to let you go."

Seaspray responded with authority.

"My recommendation is that we have to get him out," he advised the doctor. "He needs care in less than forty-eight hours that you don't have the ability to give him. He's inside a massive military target. If we want to move Ben, this is the time to do it."

What Seaspray couldn't share was the most persuasive point he had to make—the possibility of getting me on the Polish prime minister's private train. The operation was highly sensitive and would be undermined, even ruined, if word about it was leaked. Seaspray needed to be highly discreet. He leaned forward and spoke to the doctor in a whisper.

"We have a way out," he said. "It would take less than fifteen hours, and it would be the smoothest ride possible, with no bumps. Would you take that option if you had it?" The doctor said he would.

"Okay, well, that's what we have," Seaspray said, ending the talk.

Still, there were two problems. One: we *didn't* yet have that option. And two: Fox News had to authorize moving me anywhere.

an exposed valuable target, with a seventy-two-hour shoot-on-sight curfew in effect.

Seaspray was blunt with Jay: "The situation's not too great."

• • •

Seaspray and Rich wheeled me out of the Medical Clinical Center and loaded me into the ambulance. Seaspray and Bo were up front, with Rich tending to me in the back. The doctor left us with a long list of everything that needed to be done for me in the next forty-eight hours, and Rich handled what he could with the rudimentary supplies available in the ambulance. Jock had arrived at the hospital and was now in the ambulance with us. From there on out, Jock would be part of our team.

We sat in the ambulance outside the hospital for a long while—too long, as far as Seaspray was concerned. There was still nowhere for us to go. Seaspray continued coordinating with his fellow operative Dave in Poland, getting updates on the eleventh-hour operation to secure permission to get me on the prime minister's train, and pushing everyone to move faster.

In his home office in Krakow, Poland, Dave was doing two things. He was working urgently to secure the written permission needed to get me on the train, and he was coordinating with his special ops contacts in Poland and having them reach out to their Ukrainian counterparts and help secure our passage through the tricky checkpoints between the west side of Kyiv, where we were, and the train station clear across the city.

Dave had, at most, the next several hours to make it all happen. Once the prime minister's train left Kyiv, there would be no other feasible options to get me to the border.

Then things got exponentially worse.

Dave got word that, in an unexpected turn of events, the Polish delegation's meeting with President Zelenskyy had adjourned earlier than anticipated, *by about six hours.* The prime minister's train would now be leaving Kyiv far earlier than the morning, and most likely within the hour.

That meant Dave now had less than one hour to resolve a bureaucratic and diplomatic challenge that would ordinarily require days if not weeks to untangle. *Less than one hour.* If he failed, I'd be stuck in Kyiv.

Dave quickly called the Polish Special Operations Command deputy chief of staff and asked him if the approval for special access to the train could be waived. He was told the Polish State Protection Service could not legally authorize access to the train without the U.S. ambassador's request and the Polish prime minister's approval of that request.

Dave then called the U.S. defense attaché and asked if there was any update from the U.S. ambassador to Poland regarding the request for special access. Dave was told yet again that U.S. strategic policy on evacuations out of Ukraine had to guide the U.S. ambassador's position. In other words, don't get your hopes up.

"My heart sank," Dave says. "I'm not going to lie, and at that point I felt a bit defeated. We were so close, and I felt sick that I might have to watch things decline with nothing to do except monitor the situation."

Dave sat back in his chair in his home office, staring at the ceiling, racking his brain to devise a solution. He looked down and saw his three-year-old daughter, who had wandered into his office and was playing with chess set pieces, arranging the kings, queens, and pawns into little family units, while at the same time munching dreamily on Goldfish crackers. His daughter's carefree innocence moved him, and he had a single thought:

Ben Hall's kids need a father.

Then Dave looked at the wall across from his desk. There hung a photograph of Marine sergeant Benjamin Bitner.

Bitner had been team sergeant on Dave's first special forces team years ago. "He was one of my best friends," Dave says, "and the best soldier I have ever had the privilege of serving with."

Dave thought back to a moment when he and Bitner were together in Afghanistan. Dave was standing twenty feet from Bitner when Bitner's interpreter stepped on an IED. The explosion mortally wounded the interpreter, and fatally injured Bitner as well. Dave rushed over and prayed over Bitner's body in his final minutes.

"It was this visceral prayer of desperation, powerless rage, and frantic resistance to the finality of the moment," Dave says. Reluctantly, he helped load Bitner onto a helicopter, and watched the helicopter disappear over the horizon. By the time it landed at Kandahar Airfield, Bitner was gone.

Dave sat in his home office and remembered the terrible phone call he had to make to Bitner's wife, informing her that her husband would not be coming home. He had never felt as helpless to fix things, to make things better, as during that phone call. "And now, ten years later, I was trying to get another man named Ben back to his family," Dave says. "I decided then and there that I would refuse to let this Ben die."

Dave placed a second call to the deputy chief of staff for the Polish Special Operations Command (POLSOCOM). He told him the U.S. embassy was asking for POLSOCOM's support. The deputy chief of staff asked if Dave had received a signed memo from the U.S. ambassador.

"I am working on getting that," Dave said.

Then Dave told him that if I weren't on that secret train, I might not make it back to my family.

"I understand," the deputy said.

Dave found a picture of me and Alicia and the girls in his dossier about me, and he took a photo of it with his cell and sent it to the deputy chief of staff at POLSOCOM. The deputy hand-delivered it to the POLSOCOM commander in Krakow, along with the information that the prime minister's secret train would be leaving Kyiv imminently, and that it was my only medical and tactical option. "We need immediate authorized access to the train," the deputy said.

The POLSOCOM commander had a question: *Has anything changed in getting the required signed memo from the U.S. ambassador, or even a phone call from the ambassador making the request?* All the deputy could say in response was what Dave told him—that this was my last, best chance to survive.

The commander picked up the photo of my family and me and he looked it over. Then he put it back down on his desk.

"Get him on that train," the commander instructed his deputy. "Whatever we need to do, I'll make the calls to get it approved."

Dave forwarded our passport information to the office of the mayor of Kyiv, the former boxer Vitali Klitschko, and to the chief of police, notifying them that an ambulance transporting a wounded journalist would be crossing Kyiv during curfew. Then he sent a text message to his contacts in the U.S. Dave is a man of faith, and he had already asked his wife and many others to pray for the success of the mission. And because of Dave, hundreds of people *were* praying for us. Now he had a simple message for all his contacts:

We are at a critical juncture. Pray for God's hands to move and protect.

• • •

Seaspray got a call on his cell. It was Dave, who gave him the cell number for the Polish ground commander. "You can start coordinating your movements with him," Dave said.

Seaspray knew Dave could sometimes be less than entirely

specific about things, and he wondered if that meant Dave had finally secured formal permission to get me on the prime minister's train.

"You should be good," Dave answered.

"Hey, Dave, man, you know I hate it when you say, 'We should be good,'" Seaspray said. "I'm either good or I'm not good."

Dave said, "No, yeah, yeah, you should be good."

"Dude, are we good? Are we *good*?"

"If I were you, I'd probably get moving," Dave said, "but all I can say is, you should be good."

"All right, man, thanks," Seaspray said. That was the most he was going to get out of his friend, and it was good enough for him.

Seaspray called the number for the Polish ground commander, who was in theory paving our way through the checkpoints in Kyiv. The commander answered and seemed surprised. He said cell phone towers were down all over Kyiv and they were losing connectivity with contacts there. He was amazed to be talking to Seaspray on a cell at all.

The connectivity issues, the commander explained, made it impossible for him to communicate with his counterparts in the Ukraine special forces. That meant, as Seaspray put it, "there was no deconfliction with the Ukrainians at checkpoints." The Polish side knew that Seaspray would be on the move through Kyiv during the shoot-on-sight curfew. But the Ukrainian side, the side that mattered most, would *not* know.

"Does that mean I'm good to go?" Seaspray asked.

"Well, you're good to get on the train," the ground commander said. "That's all I can tell you. But it's up to you to get yourself to the train."

"Okay," Seaspray said, "how much time do we have?"

"I can't tell you that over an open line. I can't give you a window. I just know if you guys don't leave right now, you're not going to make it."

Kyiv was under continual aerial attack. No one without express authorization was being allowed in or out of the city for the next seventy-two hours. Ukrainian soldiers at checkpoints would be on high alert and in active engagement mode, poised to confront Russia's lethal Spetsnaz counterinsurgency teams. "At that point," Seaspray says, "the risk of driving across Kyiv was extremely high."

But Seaspray knew it was even riskier *not* to go.

He chose not to tell anyone else on the team how tight their time frame was, or how risky the next hour was going to be. All he said was "Hey, we're approved, let's get on that train." He reminded everyone to continue with their aggressively deferential approach. "Smile and wave, smile and wave," he told them. Seaspray switched on all the lights in and on the ambulance and slowly pulled out of the hospital parking lot. He drove at precisely 4 mph, no faster, so as not to appear threatening, and he told everyone it was to protect my neck and head.

"We're just gonna take it nice and slow," he said.

There were no other cars on the road. No buses, trucks, nothing. No streetlights, either; the electricity was off. Kyiv was an eerie ghost town. The only signs of life at all were the sporadic and massive militarized checkpoints we would need to navigate. As Seaspray approached the first one, he slowed the ambulance down to a near crawl.

Still, as soon as the soldiers at the checkpoint saw us, they ran out of their stations with guns drawn and pointed at the ambulance. From inside the ambulance, Seaspray continued smiling and waving. He slowly drove up as far as he could before a soldier stepped forward and held up his hand in a stop gesture, and for a moment there was a strange standoff, with neither the soldiers approaching the ambulance nor Seaspray or anyone getting out. Finally, a Ukrainian soldier came to the window.

The soldier was aggressive. He yelled at everyone to get out of the ambulance. Seaspray stepped out with his hands up and said, "Medic humanitarian, medic humanitarian," and "English American." He spoke slowly and softly to, once again, project not even the slightest trace of a threat. The soldiers surrounded the ambulance and looked inside and pointed at doors they wanted opened. One or two soldiers peered into the back and saw me laid out. They looked me over, trying to determine if I was truly injured or only faking injury. Apparently they were not satisfied that I had indeed been hurt.

A soldier entered the ambulance and reached down and began pulling back my bandages, exposing my gruesome wounds. That seemed to do it. Outside, Seaspray held up his cell with a mapped GPS route on the screen, and pointed at it as if to say, *Here is my map, we're going to the train station, that's all, no funny business.* "It was a lot of pointy talkie stuff," Seaspray says, "selling the story, smiling, waving, being nonthreatening."

It worked. The soldiers let us pass.

Before the next checkpoint, Seaspray got a call on his cell. Not many people had his number; he preferred to be as close to unreachable as possible, except to those who absolutely needed to reach him on a particular mission. It was not some quirk of his personality; it was, to him, a matter of life and death, part of his meticulously wrought efforts to mitigate the risk in the many impossibly dangerous scenarios he put himself in. Seaspray did not recognize the caller on his cell and answered tentatively.

"Who the hell are you?" the caller loudly demanded. "How do I know who you are or what you're doing? How the hell do you think you're going to get an American across the border without my permission?"

Seaspray hung up. His cell sounded again. Seaspray picked up and it was the same caller, even angrier now. Seaspray hung up on him again.

We've got a problem, Seaspray thought. *Something is wrong.*

• • •

Jen Griffin was back at the Pentagon around noon on March 16, after her own long and sleepless night. She had not stopped working, calling, connecting, planning, and badgering since the moment she first heard from Sylvie Lanteaume in Corridor 9 that journalists were hurt in Ukraine.

Jen had made the crucial call to Sarah Verardo that ignited the mission to rescue me, and she'd spent hours reconstructing our comings and goings in Kyiv over the last twenty-four hours, so she could forward that data to Seaspray. She connected with Jock and learned who had been with the same Ukrainian press escorts a day earlier—*New York Times* reporter Andrew Kramer. She called him and asked for his help. She put on her reporter hat and asked endless questions: *What checkpoint did they pass through? When were they due back? How long did they plan to be out?*

Jen eventually learned from Jock that I had been found and was in a hospital. She also learned that the remains of Pierre and Sarah had been left at the site of the bombings. Jen knew as well as anyone, and surely better than most, how dangerous that particular area outside Kyiv was, and she was hesitant to authorize anyone to go there in any capacity. In fact, she sent a message to Seaspray specifically telling him *not* to go to the scene.

Jen, Seaspray wrote back, it's okay. This is what we do.

Jen's mission now had a new dimension. In addition to recovering the remains of Pierre and Sasha, she had to find a way to get me out of Ukraine. She was aware that Dave in Krakow was working on a secret plan for the evacuation, and she knew the plan would likely end up involving some kind of trickery. She stayed in touch with Dave and kept pushing for details she could pass on to Seaspray, as well as to her contacts in the U.S. military, with whom she was separately working to arrange a pickup point for me on the Polish border. Most of all, Jen knew there was only a tiny window of opportunity to make the plan work. There was zero room for error.

All of this was happening as she was preparing to go live on-air with a report on weapons shipments to Ukraine for the evening broadcast.

Then Jen received a text from Seaspray. He was clearly angry.

Who the fuck gave this guy my number? NEVER GIVE ANYONE MY NUMBER!

Jen dug into what happened. She realized who had called Seaspray—a U.S. military attaché assigned to Ukraine who had not been consulted about the secret evacuation. When the attaché learned about it, he got his hands on Seaspray's cell number, which Jen had discreetly passed along to Pentagon spokesperson John Kirby and his chief of staff, Elizabeth Trudeau, so they could coordinate my pickup at the Polish border. "I made the decision to share Seaspray's number with them because I felt I had to," Jen says. "I did not expect him to get a call from someone acting like a tough guy. There always has to be a fucker in the middle of anything."

Now the attaché was trying to stop the evacuation. By then Jen was hooked up and microphoned in the chair in the Fox News media booth at the Pentagon, minutes away from her live report. She swiveled in her chair and called the military attaché and politely explained that they were moving a British American citizen out of Ukraine and did not need his help. Then she called Trudeau and told her the attaché was trying to stop the evacuation.

John Kirby wasn't there to help—he and Secretary of Defense Lloyd Austin were aboard a U.S. Air Force E-4B over the Atlantic on the way to NATO headquarters in Brussels for discussions about the Russian invasion. So Trudeau reached out to a high-ranking government official, who phoned the attaché and ordered him to stand down.

The attaché was not heard from again during the mission.

Jen had a minute or two before going live. The first piece on the evening's broadcast had been an emotional tribute to Pierre. Jen had not planned to be part of the tribute; she was set to follow it and go directly to her straight news story about weapons. "You don't need to talk about Pierre and Ben," a producer told her. "We have it covered."

But Jen made an executive decision and rewrote the top of her report on the spot.

"A word about our colleagues Pierre, Sasha, and Ben Hall tonight," she began. "The loss and pain we feel is enormous, but if ever there were a time when the world needed journalists and reporters risking their lives to tell these stories, to tell the truth, it is now. Without a free press the autocrats win. We will redouble our efforts to honor these colleagues and all reporters in harm's way tonight."

• • •

Thanks to Seaspray's smile-and-wave strategy, we made it through the first checkpoint in Kyiv. But it was only the first of a series of extremely tense stops. A few times we got through relatively easily. Most of the time the team had to get out and be questioned and searched. At every stop the procedure was different, creating a helpless sense of dread and uncertainty. At some stops the soldiers rifled curiously through the supplies in the ambulance. Seaspray happily traded tourniquets and bandages for permission to get through.

Finally, after about an hour on the road, we arrived at the sealed-off outer cordon of Central Station Kyiv, where the Polish prime minister's secret train, Seaspray hoped, was still on a track.

Seaspray stepped out and approached the Ukrainian secret service agents manning the cordon. They were not happy to see him and had no idea why he was there. Seaspray called the Polish ground commander, the contact Dave gave him, and luckily the call went through. The commander spoke with an Ukrainian agent, but the conversation did not go well.

Several more minutes passed. Eventually some agreement was reached. A bomb squad with bomb-sniffing dogs was summoned and swept the ambulance; soldiers did mirror sweeps beneath it and looked through every supply box in the back. That took several more minutes. Then the soldiers told Seaspray to wait. He got back in the ambulance and sat there and waited as more precious time ticked off the clock.

At last, it all seemed to come down to one Ukrainian soldier.

The soldier waved Seaspray forward. "To me," says Seaspray, "it looked like the whole thing was kind of a show to let the others know who was in charge." The soldier frowned and looked up at Seaspray, who towered over him. The soldier's English was poor.

"You American?" the soldier asked.

"Yeah, American," Seaspray said cheerily. "Medical, medical."

The soldier nodded his head.

"Yep, okay," he said.

And that was it. Seaspray jumped back in the ambulance and followed the soldier in his car through more checkpoints and to a passageway beneath the train station. We drove up to within several feet of the prime minister's dark-blue-paneled train. Seaspray and Rich Jadick prepared to move me from the ambulance into a compartment on the train.

Immediately it was clear that they would not be able to get me aboard on a rigid gurney. There was no way to navigate it through the narrow door and up the steep steps and turn it sharply into a compartment.

Rich had secured a bright orange emergency blanket from the hospital in Kyiv, roughly the size of a bedsheet, with handles on the ends and sides. That would have to do. Rich and Seaspray gently grabbed hold of me, counted to two, and swung me swiftly from the gurney onto the blanket. I was in and out of consciousness, and on the last legs of the morphine I'd been given at the hospital—the last that would be available to me until I reached Poland—and I cannot remember if the move onto the blanket was painful, though the others were certain it had to be.

But I do remember that just a few minutes later, I began to feel the worst waves of pain I've ever felt in my life.

Seaspray put the ambulance in a parking space and removed the battery. Hopefully, he could retrieve it later. Then Seaspray, Rich, Bo, and Jock all took one corner of the blanket and hoisted me to the train. The door was so narrow there was only room for one person at the head of the blanket and another at its foot. Seaspray and Bo each grabbed an end and carefully pulled me up the stairs, trying their best to keep me centered and not allow the blanket to buckle too severely in the middle. Without solid backing, however, the blanket was going to buckle. Rich stayed near and watched to make sure my head did not accidentally hit anything.

"That was my job," he says. "To yell, *Watch the head!*"

The first attempt to get me aboard failed. They had taken me in feetfirst, and, like a newborn, I could only pass through headfirst. I was lowered out and carried back up, nearly sliding off, bending at the middle, in and out of consciousness. Somehow we made it on board. I was lugged down the three-foot-wide corridor to a small, dark compartment with two sets of bunk beds on either wall and very little room in between. They put me in the lower right bunk, and Rich stayed with me to rebandage my wounds. Jock refused to leave my side and took the bottom bunk on the left.

Seaspray snapped a photo of me in my bunk and sent it to Dave. "It was a blessing to see you alive on the train," Dave told me later.

On the train, Rich tended to my injuries and asked me to rate my pain on a scale of 1 to 10. I told him it was 5.

"I could see on his face there was no way it was a five," Rich says.

"He had to be in a lot more pain than that. But all I had to give him was Tylenol. No morphine, no opioids. It was going to be a long, long trip."

Yet I only had one request, which I kept repeating over and over. Not for food or medicine—all I wanted was my cell phone.

All I wanted to do was call Alicia.

FOURTEEN

THE EXTRACTION PLATFORM

The prime minister's train trundled west across northern Ukraine, toward the Polish border. The heaviness of the train, the solidity of its iron wheels, and Ukraine's extra-wide-gauge tracks were a comfort in a world of crumbled buildings and buckled roads. Ukrainian trains never stopped running during the invasion, endlessly shuttling out refugees and bringing in humanitarian supplies, and providing the country's only reliable link to the outside world. Yet trains, too, could be bombed, or attacked, or hijacked, and travelers were advised to sleep with their heads away from the windows, in case of explosions outside.

I had been placed in a lower bunk with my head under the window. As the train left Kyiv I was, as I had been since waking up in the military hospital, in and out of consciousness, catching only glimpses, little snapshots, of my surroundings. Mostly I had only a sense of what was happening—that we were moving quickly, that there was urgency, that danger was all around us, and, most crucially, that I was in safe hands. I remember watching Seaspray with his roguish long brown hair and beard, this classically dashing American figure, and even in my unstable state I could tell he had a good plan and knew how to execute it. I understood I would have no input into the plan or anything else, that I was just a passenger, and so my only option was to trust Seaspray—to literally put my life in his hands. And I did.

Somewhere along the way it occurred to me that the way I felt being rescued by Americans was an echo of how my father must have felt when U.S. soldiers saved him from the Japanese in Manila. How moved he was that those soldiers had risked their own lives to save someone they'd never met. The relief, the gratitude, the awe of American prowess and might—everything my father had talked about, it was all there for me. War, it seems, not only makes history, but repeats it.

By the time the prime minister's train left Kyiv, the morphine I'd been given at the military hospital had all but worn off. For really the first time since the bomb blasts, I became conscious of the pain. The pain could be measured in levels of intensity, and the levels kept rising, even after I thought they couldn't rise any more. It felt as if my body were putting out an alert that something was seriously wrong, and that alert was a deep, persistent throbbing throughout my body. I looked down at my legs and saw the metal rods sticking out of them, holding what was left together. Everything below the knee was missing, and at the stump there was an intense radiating pain, not like the pain you get from a cut, but something much wider and deeper, something that ripples inward and outward.

All these differently intense sensations of pain got progressively worse and more searing as the morphine wore off.

I had never felt such pain before. In my career I'd seen a lot of people in what seemed like intolerable pain; people with lost limbs and gaping wounds and holes blown through them, writhing at the very edge of what humans can endure. My heart had broken for them, and I always had the same question:

How would I react if I was the guy on the gurney?

And then I was. The pain that was now pulsing in waves through my body was unlike anything I could have imagined. But how would I react? How would I handle the pain?

Without any real painkillers available, all I could do was turn the pain into a mind game. I had to tell myself—*convince* myself—that the pain didn't matter. I had to teach my body to ignore the pain and teach my mind to block it out. I had to, in essence, put the pain away.

The only way to do that was to absolutely believe there was something more important than the pain that needed my attention, and that thing was my *survival*. I had to tap into the pure animal necessity we have to stay alive and get home, to drag ourselves along like a wounded dog. I had never had to do that before, but now I did, and I reached *past* the level of pain and found another level I never knew was there. Perhaps that sounds simplistic or self-aggrandizing, but that is truly what I did—I marshaled every bit of my focus and put it on the only thing that mattered: to survive, to escape, to get back to Alicia and the girls.

That was not an easy thing to do. Try focusing on just one thing for a long time. Try focusing on that for *hours*. But that was the only option I had aboard that train. There were no physical or medical solutions, only mental games. I had no choice but to reach for that next level, the level beyond the pain, and hope that I could find it, hope that it was there.

It was the only way I would make it through my descent into hell.

● ● ●

I lost track of time on the train. It was dark outside and dark inside, and the hours passed but the darkness persisted, and I tried to sleep but I also wanted to remain conscious, remain alert, to honor the mission we were on. Dr. Jadick had re-dressed my wounds, then climbed into a bunk and passed out; he'd been up for days. Jock stayed awake in a bunk across from me, always watching, on alert. Seaspray came back to visit five or six times, checking on how things were going. He never

asked "How's the pain?" or "Are you okay?" It was always "How are things going?" I appreciated that. I didn't want the focus to be on me and how I felt; I wanted it to be on the mission. And my job during the mission was to be as low-maintenance as someone in my condition could possibly be. No complaints, no requests. So I'd always tell Seaspray, "Everything's going great."

Seaspray insisted that I eat something, and though I wasn't hungry I gobbled down the military ready-to-eat meals he gave me, one after another. Again, I was complying, going along with the plan, doing what I had to do. All I thought was: *Food is good. Food is protein. Eat the food. Eat everything they want you to eat. Stay fueled, keep fighting.*

Seaspray had not stopped thinking, planning, or working since we'd climbed aboard. He felt a bit of relief that we had made it on the train and the train was moving, but that did not mean he could relax. Someone like Seaspray can't afford to feel relaxed in the middle of a mission, ever. "That part of your brain never shuts off if you're from this world," he says.

On the train, he was thinking about options. What if the train got bombed? What if it stopped and couldn't go on? How would we get to the border then? Seaspray had that covered—the second ambulance, holding the backup team led by Dakota Meyer, had made it to Kyiv and was now shadowing the train. That ambulance was fully loaded with gear and supplies. If it came to it, that would be our Plan B. Seaspray kept in constant communication with Dakota and updated him on the train's location, so the ambulance could keep its distance but remain within reach should we have to get off the train.

As the hours dragged, I noticed something was going on with my brain. I simply could not turn my mind off for even a moment. I had entered into some kind of hyperadrenalized state and my synapses were firing relentlessly. Every few seconds, another thought. Odd thoughts, random thoughts, crazy thoughts. I would think about the

sky, then about clouds, then about storms, continually breaking down my thoughts into smaller, more arcane components, an incessant spiral of meaningless busy-think.

I would ponder things. *I hope these rails were laid well*, which would lead to *I wonder if the steel came from a mine in Poland*, which led to *Imagine what it's like to be the guy laying tracks all day*, and on and on. I feared my brain had gone haywire, or was otherwise broken, and I wondered if it would ever shut off. It was like in a movie when a doctor tells someone, *Stay with me. Do not sleep.* That was me—I felt like I absolutely should not sleep, like I had to remain alert and engaged at all times, and my brain slipped into a bottomless stream of consciousness that all but precluded rest.

The fact was, I had suffered a traumatic brain injury. Shrapnel hit my left temple and carved out a piece of my skull. The extent of the brain damage was unknown, though a frontal contusion and concussion seemed likely. The chaos in my brain did not spontaneously arise: it was part of whatever process my mind was using to heal itself.

Somewhere in the long stretch of time we spent on the train, I thought about Pierre and Sasha.

I hadn't asked about them, and I hadn't heard about them, but I knew that if Pierre had been rescued, he would have been with us on the train, and there was no evidence that he was. Perhaps I already knew the truth, but I had to find out the facts, just to be sure. I turned to Jock.

"Where are Pierre and Sasha?" I asked.

Jock didn't answer. I asked again and he said, "Pierre is in Kyiv."

That was all he would say. I let it go. An hour later I tried again.

"Is he dead?" I asked. "Is Pierre dead?"

Jock took a long pause.

"Yeah," he finally said, "he didn't make it. Neither did Sasha."

I closed my eyes and tried to remember the exact scene of the bombing. Where I was, where Pierre and Sasha were. I remembered Pierre

lying on the ground a few feet in front of me. Clearly, he'd gotten out of the car first and was ahead of me when the third bomb it. I pictured him lying on the sloping stretch of road. I could not see all of his body, but his face was turned toward me. His arms were slightly above his head, as if he'd instinctively raised them to protect himself from the blast. When he spoke to me, he did not move his body at all—he just talked.

Pierre, it turned out, had been struck in the thigh by a small piece of shrapnel that severed his femoral artery. The artery starts near the groin and runs down to the knee, and it's the primary vessel supplying blood to the lower body. If it is severed, and there is no treatment, the blood loss can cause a person to slip into unconsciousness and die.

A severed femoral artery is what caused the death of the great war photographer Tim Hetherington in Misrata, Syria, in 2011, at the same time I was there. After Tim's death, freelance journalists were offered classes—called RISC, or Reporters Instructed on Saving Colleagues— on what to do if they encountered someone bleeding out. Simply stuffing a T-shirt into the wound and pressing and holding it there could keep the person alive long enough to get them to a hospital. A T-shirt could have saved Tim.

Could a T-shirt have saved Pierre?

That I simply couldn't say.

• • •

Hours into the train ride, everything was quiet. There had been no surprises, no unforeseen holdups. I had not yet learned I was on board a train with three world leaders conducting historic wartime diplomacy, but at some point the Polish prime minister, Mateusz Morawiecki, sent an envoy to my compartment to ask how I was doing.

There came a time when, even with my efforts to mentally overcome my pain, I felt like I just couldn't bear it any longer. I blurted out, "Does anyone have a painkiller?" as if they were lying around and they just forgot to offer me one. Jock looked around and found two lowly Advil pills. I took them, but I remember thinking, *Where are the fucking real pain meds?* though of course I didn't say that out loud.

I had another request for Jock. I asked him for my cell phone.

Up until then there hadn't been time, or I hadn't been conscious enough, to think about calling Alicia to let her know I was okay. But in the train, that was all I wanted to do. I had asked for my own cell a few times, but I never got it. Now I needed a phone. I needed to call Alicia.

Jock handed me my cell. It was early in the morning in London. Alicia was in the kitchen making breakfast for the children and she heard the specific ringtone she'd assigned me—a delicate crystal sound. She'd spent the last two days waiting for calls, not necessarily from me, but from anyone with news about me. And, she hoped, possibly from me. Now the familiar ringtone.

"Benji? *Oh my God Benji!*" she said.

"It's me, Alicia. It's me," I answered, as if I were calling from the market. "I am fine, don't worry, I'm okay, I'm okay."

I think I said the word *okay* ten times.

On her end, Alicia took note of my voice. "I remember thinking, *It sounds like Benji, it really sounds like Benji,*" she says. "*He sounds like himself.* And to hear that he was still Benji, still the person I knew as Benji, what an enormous relief that was. I exhaled for the first time."

"I love you," Alicia said.

"I love you, too. I'm okay, I'm okay. I love you."

It was a short call, but it was unlike any call I'd ever made before. Quite obviously something had changed; I had been badly injured, nearly killed, and our lives would be different from here on out. But it went deeper than that, far deeper. When I got off the call with Alicia, I thought about our children, our three beautiful daughters, Hero, Iris, and Honor, and I felt something that I'd never felt before, something I didn't even recognize.

It was a deep feeling in the pit of my stomach, a physical thing, something that seized me and took me over. Even through the pain, I felt it. And as I felt it, I realized what it was, and what triggered it.

That feeling was the result of having shrunk my world down to one single thing—my family.

The thought that I had survived the explosion and was making it out of Ukraine, that I was going to see my wife and children again, that I would have the chance to *hug* my children—just that thought filled me with an intense love and wonder and happiness. *Now* I felt my breath taken away. I was surprised by how powerful the emotions were: it was as if, just like I found a higher level beyond my pain, I had now discovered a new and brilliant level of emotion that hadn't been available to me before.

When I thought of my wife and children, it felt like the absolute pinnacle of my life and of my experiences and of my very reason for being. *I am going to see my family*, I thought. *I am heading to them now. I am going to hold my children again. And there is nothing in the world that matters besides that. Nothing. Nothing at all. Just—them.*

• • •

After Jen Griffin connected Seaspray to Fox executives in New York, and got them to sign off on moving me, she turned her attention to Poland—specifically, who was going to pick me up at the border?

As soon as she got off the phone with Seaspray in Kyiv, Jen sent an email to Pentagon spokesperson John Kirby, who was aboard a U.S. Air Force E-4B with Defense Secretary Lloyd Austin, on the way to NATO headquarters in Brussels. Now that I was on the move, and anywhere from ten to twenty hours from the border, Jen needed Secretary Austin to authorize the U.S. military to set up a pickup point for me in Poland.

Jen knew the lay of the land in the Middle East and Eastern Europe. She'd been covering the War on Terror for a long time. She knew that the U.S. Army–operated Landstuhl Regional Medical Center in Germany had treated the thousands of U.S. soldiers injured in the wars in Iraq and Afghanistan. The medical center was staffed with elite doctors, surgeons, and staffers proficient in treating blast injuries and trauma. It was about 835 miles from the Polish border, or roughly a two-hour flight. It was the obvious place to take me, except for one thing: Landstuhl was only for members of the U.S. armed forces, military retirees, and family members.

Jen Griffin would need to secure an exemption to have me admitted to Landstuhl as a non-military patient, and that meant getting approval from the U.S. defense secretary, Lloyd Austin.

Jen's email to Kirby advised him that I was on my way to the border. She wanted to further update Kirby and Secretary Austin and was hoping to arrange a phone call. While she was walking outside with her earbuds in, trying to sneak in some exercise, her cell phone sounded.

"Can you accept a call from the office of the defense secretary?" an operator asked.

Kirby came on the line. Jen succinctly filled him in on the details of the train trip and tried to convey the urgency of the situation. *It's go time*, she said. *We need to cut the bureaucracy. Minutes will matter.*

Kirby had an obvious question—where along the three-hundred-mile border Poland shares with Ukraine was Seaspray going to hand me over?

Jen had already asked Seaspray for that location, and he told her he couldn't give it to her. Not yet, anyway. "I told her, 'Here's the deal. They gave us this extraction platform and the only thing they asked in return was we don't say anything about the location until they feel like they're in a safe spot,'" Seaspray says. "The whole trip was supersecret and you've got world leaders on the train and they don't want to be attacked. So I had everybody constantly hitting me up, Jen, Kirby, asking, 'Where do we put the helicopter?' I just couldn't tell them yet."

If anyone knew how frustrating that could be, it was Seaspray. He'd been on the other end of that conversation too many times to count. On pins and needles, having to wait, not knowing what you need to know.

But he also knew that helicopters move fast, and U.S. military assets on the Polish side of the border could scramble to get into position on short notice. The U.S. Army's Eighty-Second Airborne Division, which a year earlier had played a huge role in airlifting troops out of Afghanistan during the pullout, had moved over to the Polish town of Rzeszow, just sixty miles from the Ukrainian border. The Eighty-Second was in place and up and running, providing thousands of U.S. troops to help NATO with humanitarian missions and refugees streaming in from Ukraine.

What's more, the division was under the command of Major General Chris Donahue, the last U.S. soldier to board the final plane out of Afghanistan—and someone Jen Griffin knew well. Seaspray was confident the Eighty-Second could have a helicopter at the border pickup spot with no more than thirty minutes' notice. "They wanted to know the location twelve, eleven, ten hours out to have everything ready, and they weren't very happy with me when I wouldn't tell them," Seaspray says. "Periodically they tried to get me to change my mind, but I held my ground."

For several hours while we were on the prime minister's train, as few as two people on our team knew the exact drop-off location. Seaspray was one of them. Dave in Krakow was another. Dave had been recruited for the mission by Sarah Verardo, who had close contacts inside the Department of Defense. In essence, Sarah got the military to deputize Dave, who was still on active duty, to serve as the liaison between the Department of Defense and Save Our Allies, Sarah's organization. Dave had been contacted by John Kirby, who told him, "If you need anything at all, the secretary wants you to know you have our full support."

Yet Dave couldn't divulge the exact location, either. For the longest time Sarah and Jen Griffin and everyone else knew only that Seaspray had a secret capability, an access point, that he called "the extraction platform." They would have to wait to find out any more than that.

Meanwhile, Jen still had to secure Secretary Austin's permission to not only use the U.S. military to pick me up, but also to get the military hospital in Landstuhl to accept me. Jen understood how the military works, and she knew that securing permission like that could involve many, many layers of military bureaucracy, and, in normal situations, likely many days. But Jen only had a few hours to pull it off. She would need an executive decision by Secretary Austin, the only one who could cut through all the red tape. She would also need Austin to make that decision while flying over the Atlantic on his way to a crucial NATO meeting about the worsening war in Ukraine.

So when Kirby called her from the E-4B, she pushed him to take the matter directly to Austin. "John said something to me along the lines of, 'I will take this to the secretary, and I can't see him *not* signing off on it, but, you know, you never know,'" says Jen.

Only later did Jen learn that when Kirby walked the request up to Austin on the E-4B over the Atlantic, the secretary looked it over and said, "Yes, get me whatever you need me to sign. Just do it, no delay."

• • •

Things moved quickly after that. Secretary Austin alerted four-star general Tod Wolters, then NATO's supreme allied commander in Europe, that I was on the move and headed for Landstuhl. Eventually Austin's authorization would have to pass through the Judge Advocate General's Corps (JAG) to affirm its legality, but that would come later. There was no time for it now. Major General Chris Donahue, commander of the U.S. Army's Eighty-Second Airborne Division in Rzeszow, Poland, was also alerted, and a medical team was scrambled while a Sikorsky UH-60 Black Hawk helicopter was readied to transport me.

All that was needed now was the precise location of "the platform."

On the prime minister's train, Seaspray and Rich Jadick stayed in close comms with the U.S. medical team in Poland, feeding them my vital signs and updates about my condition. A Ukrainian secret service colonel occasionally came back to visit Seaspray and bring us food and ask about me, but Seaspray never pushed him for permission to divulge the pickup point. He knew the permission would come when it came— when it was safe to give it.

We'd been on the train for close to nine hours. I had no sense of time or duration, so I had no idea if we were nearing our destination. I don't remember anyone giving me a proper briefing of what was happening and what was going to happen while I was on the train, but at some point, I became aware that the U.S. military would play a part in getting me to safety. How or when, I didn't know.

It turned out we were very close to the border. A Polish special ops commander on the train went to Seaspray's compartment and told him, "You're good to go. Good to give the Americans the location."

Seaspray immediately jumped on the encrypted operational chat that included all the mission's participants and relayed the location of the pickup—an airstrip in the southeastern Polish border city of Przemysl—as well as the train's current location and an ETA. Polish special ops dispatched an ambulance to meet me at the border train station in Poland, while in Rzeszow, the Eighty-Second Division staffed the UH-60 Black Hawk with Army paramedics and got them in the air.

Everything was in motion.

Before I knew it, Seaspray appeared in my compartment and I was taken out of my bunk and carried down the train corridor on the bloody orange transport blanket. I was carefully lowered down the stairs, where five paramedics and several special ops agents met me on the secured train platform. They lifted me onto a gurney, wrapped me in a gold thermal blanket, strapped me on securely, and checked my

bandages. Then they wheeled me out of the station and to the waiting ambulance.

Our team piled in—Seaspray, Bo, Rich, and Jock—and in a few minutes we pulled onto the grassy airstrip in Przemysl.

As soon as Seaspray and the others moved me from the back of the vehicle to a gurney on the tarmac, I saw it—the gunmetal gray UH-60 Black Hawk, its four blades churning the air. I saw U.S. Army soldiers in their green camos and helmets moving with uncanny precision, wasting not a single moment. Once again I felt what my father must have felt in Manila—a profound gratitude and sheer exhilaration— and it struck me even then how our separate experiences mirrored each other in a way. "The sky was full of strange single-engined airplanes," my father later wrote about his rescue in Manila. "It took us only a minute to realize they were American. We watched as they flew across and around, in dogfights with Japanese airplanes. We were so excited we ran out to collect the shrapnel as soon as we saw a piece fall."

And now, nearly eighty years later, there I was, on the tarmac, just as excited as my father had been, and just as grateful to see the U.S. military had arrived.

That was the moment when I knew I was safe.

Seaspray and Bo stepped back and let the Eighty-Second Division soldiers take over my care. The soldiers lifted me into the helicopter and secured me to a slot on the right side of the aircraft. Seaspray filmed the scene with his high-tech, camera-loaded Ray-Ban sunglasses and transmitted the footage to Sarah Verardo in North Carolina.

"I was on the cell with Seaspray and I could hear the Black Hawk in the background," Sarah says. "He sent me the video from his glasses and said, 'Wheels up. Benji's on his way to Germany.'"

FIFTEEN

LANDSTUHL

I've always wondered what it would feel like to hang out of an airborne Black Hawk with an Army gunner, just like you see in movies. As a journalist I thought I'd one day get the chance. But pulling away from the airstrip in Przemysl, I knew it wouldn't be that day. I was strapped into place with noise-canceling headphones on and a sheet covering me to keep debris away, perfectly immobilized, though even then the visceral stimuli of being in a Black Hawk—the chop-chop of the blades, the rumble of the engines, the blast of cold air—jump-started my consciousness.

I still didn't really know what was happening: the extent of my injuries, what kind of rehabilitation I'd need, even where I was going. For the past forty-eight hours, all I had cared about was escaping, getting out, fleeing. But once I realized I was out of Ukraine and safe, I entered a new phase of this adventure I was on. Right there in the Black Hawk, my physiology switched from flight to fight. I was now in fight mode.

We descended after ten minutes in the air and landed at a U.S. air base in Poland. Dr. Jadick and Jock stayed close while I was taken to a small hospital on the base. The hospital seemed quite strange to me because it was so *normal*. Soothing colors, clean floors, staffers in tidy scrubs, relative calm. I guess I was no longer accustomed to "normal" after a month in Ukraine. Three or four doctors came to my side and began a quick examination. One of them told me they had three medical students there, and did I mind if they looked in?

I glanced at the students, who seemed young enough to be in high school. I told the doctor it was fine, and the students shuffled into positions around my gurney and stared at me intently. That felt odd. I was a broken, shredded human being, as vulnerable as could be, and here were these three kids ogling me like I was some kind of rare specimen.

In a weird way, however, those students helped me. Up until that moment, it hadn't quite hit me that the person going through this incredible journey out of Ukraine was, in fact, me. As a journalist I'd never been the story, and I never, ever wanted to be. But now I *was* the story. I was the focus. Everything was about me. In fact, as the students watched, the doctors examined every inch of me—arms, legs, groin, eyes—poking and prodding, lifting and turning, dissecting me into a collection of parts and ailments. I was, and would continue to be, the object of everyone's scrutiny.

That was something I was going to have to get used to.

What made it easier was that I was, as I said, in fight mode. I was still on a mission, but the mission had changed: the goal now was getting better and getting back home to my family. Whatever was required, whatever I was asked to do, I would do it. There was no room for vanity or pride (not that I have a lot of those qualities anyway, or at least I don't think I do). Any unpleasant step on the way to the goal was insignificant.

All that mattered was Alicia and the girls.

• • •

A few hours after I called Alicia from the prime minister's train, she got another call from Suzanne Scott in New York. This time Suzanne told her I was safely across the border and on my way to Landstuhl Medical Center. She asked Alicia if she wanted to fly to Germany to see me.

For Alicia, it was all very sudden. "I felt enormous relief and I called everyone to say, 'Benji's through, he's through,' but to me, just because he was across the border didn't mean he was out of danger," she says. "He was out of *one* kind of danger, that's all. He was still very seriously injured."

Alicia had not yet told our daughters what happened, and she did not intend to do so for a while. With so much uncertainty about everything, it didn't seem like the right time. The idea of suddenly packing up and disappearing on a trip to Germany didn't seem right to her, either. Alicia had never left the girls for any longer than a day, and she didn't want to vanish on them now. But she also wanted to see me. "I decided if I could somehow go in and out all in one day," she says, "I would do it."

Fox News arranged a private plane for Alicia. By air, it would only take her an hour to get to Landstuhl. Now she had to figure out who would take care of the girls in her absence. Her sister had hurried back from her vacation and was already with the children. Alicia's good friends Katie and Tash were already in place to drive the children back and forth to school all week. Alicia's mother wanted to fly in from Australia, but there was a problem getting her a new passport. My agent, Olivia Metzger, went into what she calls "Alicia mode" and reached out to Fox News, and they stepped in and cleared the way for Alicia's mother to fly in, too. After that, Olivia focused on helping Fox do what they could for my family. Fox sent food and gifts and boxes and boxes of toys for the girls. They were among those who knew straightaway that Alicia and the girls would need as much help and support as possible. This would be a battle for our whole family.

Along with Fox News, so many of Alicia's remarkable friends and family rallied around her and made it so she didn't have to worry quite as much about the children's care and safety while she sorted through all the issues involving me. "People were coming out of the woodwork to ask how they could help," says Olivia. "Everyone jumped in."

Not very long after hearing I was safely out of Ukraine, Alicia prepared to fly to Landstuhl and help me begin this new phase of our lives.

• • •

I did not stay at the air base in Poland for long. The doctors there only made sure I was stable and, mercifully, gave me painkillers. A fairly good dose of painkillers, I'd say, judging from how quickly I slipped into semiconsciousness. I can't remember much at all about the short flight from Poland to Landstuhl.

The medical center in Landstuhl is a massive complex near Ramstein Air Base, headquarters of the U.S. Air Force in Europe, in far western Germany. It is jointly staffed by members of six service branches but under Army command. More than 100,000 wounded soldiers have been treated there since 2001, including soldiers with some of the very worst injuries sustained in Afghanistan and Iraq. I was a civilian and I'd been granted Secretary Designee Status—permission from Defense Secretary Lloyd Austin—allowing the staff at Landstuhl to care for me. I was still groggy when I was wheeled in, but I was aware of doctors quickly surrounding me, with one of them taking charge. I remember being impressed with their speed and efficiency. They had a quick discussion and I was rushed away somewhere.

On March 18, four days after I was injured, a doctor at Landstuhl briefed me on my injuries. Until then I had only been vaguely aware of different problems, though I did realize my right leg was gone just below the knee. But my eye injury, for instance, was a bit of a mystery to me, as were many others, until the very kind doctor at Landstuhl filled me in.

"Let's go from top to bottom," he said. "You have a depressed skull fracture, which means you basically have a hole in the skull that's been pushed in a little bit, not too much, and based on how you're perfectly cognitively intact, my understanding is there are no plans at all to perform any neurosurgery on you."

So far, so good, I thought. A dent in the head, I could handle. The neurosurgeons were stepping aside and waving in the next set of specialists.

"Then there is your eye," the doctor went on. "You have retinal detachment on that side. Apparently, they need the hematoma behind it to somewhat liquefy for them before they can do any laser surgery. They are planning on surgery in two days."

I had lost my iris, my lens, and my cornea, and I couldn't see out of the eye at all, but even all that sounded manageable to me, too. The doctor moved on to my left hand, much of which had been blown off, sheering off much of the skin and exposing the tendons on the back of my thumb. There was a fragment at the base of my index finger that seemed problematic. My left thumb metacarpal was almost completely shattered and some of it was missing, a common situation, the doctor explained, when really small bones encounter high-velocity projectiles. For now the doctor had molded bone cement around it for support; eventually I would need surgery there, too.

Still—so far, so good.

Then we got to my lower body: "On your right leg you have amputation just below the knee and [on the left] you are missing a fair amount of calf muscle and you need lower extremity amputations." A reasonably functional kneecap remained, but it wasn't clear if I would get to keep it. "If necessary," the doctor said, "we will go through heroic measures to save it."

There were also significant burn issues, which I expected, since I woke up on fire after the third explosion. There were serious burns from the top of my left leg to the bottom, most of which would require deep skin grafts. The back of my left hand was also badly burned, and that, too, would need grafting. The burns, I was told, were in some ways the most immediately pressing injuries, because they could cause deadly infections.

"Then there's the left foot issue," the doctor said with a bit of extra gravity. "Have you seen pictures of the X-ray?"

I told him I hadn't, nor had I seen the condition of the foot.

"Your foot has some issues with it," the doctor diplomatically began. "I don't want to have too heavy a conversation with you about it, but I also try to be a straight shooter. I will give you as optimistic a picture as I can without lying to you. And I would be lying if I told you your foot would ever work as a foot again."

Now things were serious. For starters, I was missing a fair amount of calf muscle in my left leg. The doctor said I would need "lower extremity amputations." To be missing one foot was bad enough. But to be missing both? The X-rays revealed that a good portion of the left foot had been destroyed, and much of it was missing altogether. I later saw a photo that showed a hole the size of a baseball right through the foot. To save the upper part of it would require very complex limb reconstruction or perhaps a novel surgery technique that, as the doctor put it, "has never been described." Rebuilding and preserving the left food was going to be a very long shot, which meant I might be looking at another amputation. "The tendons that power the toes have all been erased," the doctor said. "The area that provides blood supply to the foot has also been erased. Your big toe is intact, but it is not long for this world if the blood supply to it is gone."

Complicating everything, the doctor explained, was that I'd already had my lower right leg amputated.

"The conversation changes a bit when you're missing the leg on the other side," he said. Optimally, if another amputation was needed, the doctor hoped to be able to save at least the lower half of the left foot.

We spoke for the next twenty minutes about the foot. There were

so many options, so many possible outcomes, but it was too early to know anything for sure. The discussion helped me clarify my goals. If I wanted to, as he put it, "have a left foot to look at it," it would likely take two years of intense, complex surgery and rehab, which, in the end, might not even be successful. If, however, my goal was simply to be able to walk again—"to play with your kids," as the doctor put it—that could be achieved much more quickly with an amputation and prosthetics.

My goal, I realized, was to walk again, as quickly as I could.

•　•　•

At Landstuhl I had the impression I was being taken care of by the best of the best. I had multiple teams circling me around the clock, each hyperfocused on their area of expertise, each determined not to waste a moment in making me better. Col. Jodelle Schroeder, Landstuhl's chief nursing officer, coordinated all the moving parts that went into my stay—including speaking with Alicia several times to keep her informed and assure her I was in good hands. "We were already on high alert and we sprang into action when Ben arrived," Jody says. "It was especially important for me to be able to help Alicia navigate the process and make decisions about Ben's care." Jody's calm yet purposeful demeanor was enormously comforting, and I was happy when I was surrounded by these incredible professionals. The problems happened when I was alone at night.

I was receiving a good amount of pain medication, and I was grateful for it. I had endured twelve hours without it and discovered new levels of agony, so to now be hooked up to a steady supply of Dilaudid and morphine was wonderful. The medication, however, led to hallucinations.

My mind was already spinning deliriously, leaping from topic

to topic and never shutting off. Now the medication intensified the chaos. At night, with no procedures or discussions to focus on, I lay perfectly awake in my hospital bed, thinking crazy thoughts and having twisted visions. I did not die in these visions, but I was always trapped somewhere existentially frightening—at the bottom of a dark, impenetrable dome, for instance, or in a dense forest where I was tied to the ground.

These thoughts and visions never let up; they just rolled on and on, one after the other, a steady stream of darkness and dread. The feeling of utter helplessness was crushing. All I could do was press on the two buttons that released my two pain meds, one in my left hand, one in my right. *If I press the buttons*, I thought, *I can get out of this dome.* So I pressed them and pressed them and pressed them—*bad thought button, bad thought button.* But the visions kept coming, trapping me in a hideous alternate reality. It got to the point where I would apologize in advance to the nurses on night watch for anything crazy I might say. Later I saw the notes I had scribbled about that time: "Totally out of it. Lying there as if tied to the ground. Mind can't stop. Everything coming at me fast. Can't make decisions."

Those first several nights in Landstuhl were *lifetimes.*

Inevitably, I would make it to the light of day, and anything that happened then, I could handle. That included any number of indignities, such as being asked for a stool sample in the presence of a team of nursing students while completely unable to move.

Submit to everything, I told myself. *Don't fight it. Make it work.*

A few days into my stay at Landstuhl, I was told that the U.S. secretary of state, Tony Blinken, wanted to speak with me. He and I had met a few times while I covered the State Department, and I was touched by this gesture of support. A call was arranged for three o'clock that afternoon.

At two o'clock, a doctor and some medical students entered my

room. "We need a new catheter from your arm to your heart," the doctor announced. He turned to the students and asked, "Who's going to do it?"

"Not me," one nursing student quickly declared, which might not have been the gung-ho attitude they were looking for in nurses.

"I'll do it," another nursing student said. The group then stretched out these wide plastic sheets and covered my entire body with them, like you'd cover a car with a tarp. Apparently the procedure could get bloody.

The student cautiously approached me and inserted a drip line in my right arm, slowly pushing it farther and farther upward. She was concentrating intently and obviously wanted to get it just right. But it was slow going. Blood was dripping out of the injection site, and before long the plastic sheet was red. The IV tube in the student's hand was bloodied, too. She kept working the tube, focusing even more intently—for forty long minutes. Meanwhile, blood kept trickling out. The student suddenly looked a bit unsteady, and the color drained from her face.

The next moment, she flat-out fainted.

She crumbled and collapsed to the ground. With my left hand I made a grab for the IV tube as she was falling so it wouldn't pop out, but it did and blood spurted out of me in a miniature geyser. For a moment I felt like I was back in a combat situation, like it was all happening again. The other students bent over their colleague to see if she was okay, while I lay bloody in the bed, clutching the IV tube.

"Guys!" I finally said. "Up here!"

The nurse was fine, thank goodness. But just a few minutes later, the telephone rang. It was time for my call with the U.S. secretary of state. Naked beneath bloody plastic sheets, frantic nursing students swirling around me, I was grateful Blinken wouldn't be able to see the gruesome scene. After a short delay—he was in a meeting with President Joe Biden discussing, among other things, Ukraine—Blinken was on the line. I casually said "Hey, Secretary Blinken," like I was talking to an old mate.

"I am so glad to hear your voice," Blinken said. "We have been thinking about you, praying on you, and we're really just so glad that you are out of harm's way. We were all powerfully moved by what happened, and I am so deeply sorry for the loss of your colleagues."

It was a great comfort to hear his voice. It felt like a tiny little step on the way back to normalcy. In fact, my journalistic instincts took over and I treated the rest of the call like an interview.

"What do you think Putin's endgame is?"

"Will he be happy with the land bridge he's got to Crimea and the cities up north?"

"Why hasn't he hit Kyiv yet?"

Blinken was generous with his time and insight. I knew that after we hung up, he'd be on his way to Brussels and then Poland, trying to answer these very questions. His message for me was that my injuries, and Pierre's and Sasha's deaths, were not in vain.

"Bringing the reality of the war to people around the world has done more than anything to get countries to stand up and do what they can to support the Ukrainians," he said. "The foundation of everything is a small handful of people like you who have the extraordinary courage to bring this story to the world, and that is where it all starts."

When we finished the call, I was frustrated by not having been able to communicate more effectively. I felt I could rectify that by writing an article about my call with Blinken for Fox News. I had the call transcribed and started there, but I found that I couldn't read even three words in a row. I wasn't so much reading the transcript as staring at a bunch of words.

I spent hours trying to type up something on my iPhone. But there was just no way I'd be able to write and edit a coherent article—not under the kind of medication I was on. Finally, I gave up.

• • •

The care I was getting at Landstuhl was brilliant, but it was also preliminary. I would need to move to a larger facility that could provide long-term, multi-trauma care. The two medical centers that could best handle the array of my injuries were the Walter Reed National Military Medical Center, in Washington, DC, and Brooke Army Medical Center, at Fort Sam Houston in San Antonio. Alicia and I talked it over and were leaning toward Walter Reed. The downside, of course, was that I would be across an ocean from my family and my girls, who I was so very anxious to see and talk to and hug. I could almost feel them in my arms.

But I had to accept that I wasn't quite ready to see them, nor them me. Not long after I arrived at Landstuhl, I FaceTimed Alicia and caught her putting our littlest one, Hero, to bed. Hero always took the longest of all the girls to get to sleep, and I'd be the one to finally carry her there and tuck her in. I asked Alicia if I could speak to her, and Alicia said, "Absolutely not, unless you turn off FaceTime. She's not ready for that."

Alicia was right, of course—I was a sight. There were shrapnel scars all over my face, the front of my head was bandaged, and my left eye was shut. I disconnected FaceTime and, at last, spoke with one of my daughters. "Hi, Daddy!" she said cheerily, as if nothing at all in the world had happened since we last spoke, some two weeks earlier. Her innocence and her sweet little voice had always moved me, but now they nearly had me in tears. Alicia listened in and was relieved that I almost sounded like my old myself, and that Hero and I were able to have an ordinary chat.

The next day, Alicia took a car service to Farnborough Airport, a private, corporate airfield outside London, and got on the plane that Fox News arranged for her. She landed in Germany and was taken to Landstuhl by a grumpy local taxi driver. Apparently he was angry he'd been made to wait half an hour, and he complained about it to Alicia in German, which she does not understand. He dropped her at the gate, where Jock and my case manager, Marti, were there to greet her. Another tiny hatchback car ferried them past the security checks and to the medical center. Alicia hadn't brought much, but she had packed a Ziploc bag with little mementos for me—photos of the kids, a miniature book of Wordsworth poems my mother had given me, and Honor's music box.

"I didn't want to bring things," Alicia says. "I wanted to bring memories."

Alicia was led down a long, wide corridor, though nothing of her surroundings registered. She was in a daze, just following orders, much like I had done in Kyiv. Jock led her to my room, and outside the door she ran into my brother Barnaby, who had driven in from Switzerland and been with me until that moment, reading me all the lovely messages of support I'd received from around the world.

Just beyond Barnaby, Alicia could see me.

When I saw her, I felt a rush of excitement and I smiled. I smiled a child's broad, goofy smile. A smile that people who know and love and cherish each other share. The smile alone assuaged one of Alicia's deepest fears—that a traumatic brain injury might have wiped out the man she knew. "Then I walked in and he smiled and I knew he was still Benji," she says. "I thought, *Oh, that's him, there he is.* And I was so relieved."

Alicia came over and tried to hug me but found there wasn't much there to hug. Tubes stuck out everywhere, and she'd been advised not to put pressure on any of my wounds. So she sort of cradled my head, the only spot she could find. Meanwhile, I reached out to her and just seized her, gripping her around the waist and pulling her toward me.

"We're all fine, Benji, we're fine," Alicia kept repeating. "We're here now. We will get you better."

She handed me the Ziploc bag with all my little keepsakes, and I immediately took out the photos of my daughters and looked at them and felt my love for them in the pit of my stomach. I took the photos and slipped them under my blanket and under my shirt and put them right on my chest. The photos stayed there, near my heart, for weeks.

During Alicia's visit I was alert but not quite all there, and we didn't talk about my injuries at all. The only question Alicia asked me in the room was about my hair, much of which had been shaved off around my head wound. "Has the hair been blown off, too?" she wondered. There I was, blown up and missing a leg, and Alicia was worried about my hair.

The visit was short; I was needed for some procedure or another. Alicia spent the rest of the day conferring with doctors. Colonel Jean-Claude d'Alleyrand, an American doctor living in Germany and my primary doctor at Landstuhl, briefed Alicia on my various injuries. There were no notes to give her; everything that happens at Landstuhl is too confidential to write down, and anyway the doctors are far too busy to spend time scribbling notes. Colonel d'Alleyrand explained he had left my remaining toes purposefully unbandaged, so I could see them. He told Alicia the toes would have to come off because of the grave risk of infection, but he wanted me, the patient, to notice how abnormal the foot looked, how black the toes already were, and make the decision for myself. Alicia gave him her blessing to do whatever he thought was necessary to get me back home.

By then, Alicia and I had already spoken about my problematic left foot. I simply called her one day and said, "So, they say they're going to take off my foot. I think that's okay, isn't it?" This was typical of me—downplaying things, taking a huge, seemingly unmanageable problem and whittling it down to a small annoyance. In this case, I did it because I did not want Alicia to worry about me feeling devastated by the loss of a limb.

"Yeah, I think it's okay," she answered. And that was that.

The day passed in a flash for us both, and Alicia came back to my room in the evening to say goodbye. She had already planned her next trip to Germany to see me a few days later, before I flew off to the States. On the plane ride back to London, Alicia felt the enormity of what had happened hit her all at once. She realized that under the immense pressure of such a catastrophic event, anyone could crumble. Anyone could buckle. But Alicia didn't buckle. She is not the buckling kind. I wasn't dead, I was alive, the only survivor out of five people in that car, and for that Alicia felt deeply grateful. Everything that came after that, she resolved, was something she could handle. She understood on that plane that she would be able to get us both through this.

SIXTEEN

C-17

The body of our beloved colleague Pierre Zakrzewski remained in a morgue in Kyiv for several days after the attack. Now that I was safely in Landstuhl, the team that retrieved me went back to bring Pierre home.

Jock made sure I was settled in the hospital before flying from Germany to Krakow, Poland, about two hundred miles west of Lviv. Pierre's wife, Michelle Ross-Stanton, a thirty-year veteran of the media industry as a journalist and production manager, had also flown in to meet Pierre's body when he crossed over from Ukraine.

First there was a great deal of paperwork involved in taking Pierre's body from the morgue, as well as medical exams and certifications that the body was not carrying any diseases or unexploded ordnance. By then, Seaspray had already returned to Ukraine in anticipation of helping bring Pierre home. He knew the bureaucracy was going to take a while, but when he learned that Pierre's widow, Mich, was already waiting for her husband at the border, Seaspray went into double time. "This woman had been through enough already," he thought. "We needed to pull out all the stops."

Seaspray reached out to Dave in Krakow, and together they worked their contacts in the Polish government to secure permission to move

Pierre before the paperwork was done. Seaspray had earned the trust of his high-level contacts in Ukraine and Poland, and when he kept his promise not to divulge the location of my drop-off point at the Polish border, his credibility among his contacts was solidified. Government officials agreed to facilitate the paperwork and even provide what is known as a peace escort—police accompaniment of Pierre's body across Ukraine.

The first stop was another morgue in Lviv. There the team was joined by Fox reporter Trey Yingst and Fox cameraman Dudi Gamliel, who had arrived earlier from Kyiv. A Fox producer and a good friend named Andrew Fone had persuaded a local Irish step-dancing school to sell them an Irish flag they'd been using, and in Lviv, Dudi and Trey draped it over Pierre's casket. They paused for a moment and Trey let his hand rest at the foot of Pierre's casket. "We paid our respect to him," Trey says.

The team made it across the border and finally reunited Pierre with Mich, and together they all drove three hours to a funeral home in Krakow. There Mich asked to see Pierre's body. "The Irish like to have an open coffin at their wakes," Mich says. "I needed to see how he looked."

The coffin lid was raised and Mich looked down at her husband. She saw shrapnel on the left side of his face, and his body was ice cold, but otherwise he didn't look too bad to her. The next day, Mich accompanied Pierre's casket as it was flown from Krakow to Dublin.

Pierre finally did make it home.

Two weeks later, my great friend Pierre Zakrzewski, a seeker of truth, a teacher of men, was laid to rest in Dublin. His loss was grieved but his life was celebrated, and stories about his generosity of spirit were told to laughter and tears. The time he waltzed into the offices of the feared Iran Revolutionary Guard and announced, "I'm Irish, my name's Pierre, give me a visa stamp" and wound up sitting for tea and kabobs with the fighters. Or the time he asked the Dalai Lama if he'd like a nice pint of Guinness and the Lama playfully pretended to kick him in the butt. "He treated everyone the same—Mother Teresa, the Pope, freelancers he met in the field," his wife, Mich, said. "This wasn't a job to him, it was his life. He breathed the news and loved being out on the road."

Pierre's beautiful, valiant spirit will live on in me, and so many others, forever.

So, too, will the memories of Mykola Kravchenko and Serhiy Mashovets, the proud Ukrainian servicemen who were our press guides on March 14, and who perished in the bombing of our car. Kravchenko had a PhD in historical sciences and founded a small publishing house in 2014, during Russia's war on the Donbas, to spread the truth about his country's battle for sovereignty. He left behind two daughters; Mashovets left behind one. Both were true heroes to their cause.

The same can be said of Oleksandra Kuvshynova, who we all knew as Sasha, and who also perished in the car. I may not ever meet anyone as passionate and patriotic and full of fervor as Sasha was. When she was still a schoolgirl, she slipped unnoticed out of her house and without her parents' permission to help translate texts at a media center during Ukraine's bloody Revolution of Dignity in 2014 (a few hours after she left, the center burned to the ground and twenty-two lives were lost). She signed up with Fox News so she could play her part in exposing Putin's atrocities. Sasha had other interests, of course: photography, poetry, electronic dance. But what moved her most was the plight of the country she loved.

Sasha died far, far too soon at the age of twenty-four.

• • •

In Landstuhl I still hadn't found a way to escape my nighttime hallucinatory chaos. My mind simply never stopped working, and if I closed my eyes, it only ran faster, producing new dark, troubling thoughts every second. I honestly believed I was losing my mind. At some point I determined that my only hope of shutting down the hallucinations was to get off the cocktail of painkillers I was on. At night I would beg the nurses, "Please, take me off the medicine, I can't do it anymore," and they would say, "Yes, okay, we will." But when the pain became intolerable I had no choice but to get back on the painkillers.

Part of the challenge of those first few days in Landstuhl—and perhaps the most important challenge—was accepting my situation. It came down to doing whatever was needed and knowing that something worth fighting for was waiting at the end. I was a model patient, going along with everything I was asked to do and with no complaints.

Toward the end of my stay in Landstuhl, I got a visitor in my hospital room. His name was Irwin, and he was an American soldier who'd been stationed in Afghanistan and had suffered nearly the same injuries I had. He'd lost part of one leg and his other foot, and he came into my room in a wheelchair, wearing cowboy boots and a big cowboy hat.

"Yo, what's going on, man?" he asked in a southern twang.

His message to me was that he'd gone through what I was about to go through, and he'd come out on the other side, and so would I. He spoke candidly about his injuries and his setbacks and about what I could expect.

"Your prosthetic leg will be fine," he said. "The prosthetic feels like a leg and it's great. But what's left of the foot, that's going to be harder. It's all bone and skin. That's gonna be your big challenge."

I appreciated his frankness, but even more than that, I appreciated what he was doing. It was like he was saying, *Welcome to the club. It's a lifetime club, and we're all really tight about it. You're gonna be okay.* We both understood it was not a club you ever wanted to join, but once you were in it, it wasn't so bad, and most importantly, you weren't alone. There were other people there for you, people you could learn from, people you could lean on. In other words, it's not quite the nightmare you're afraid it might be. Irwin's kindness and honesty, and his casual

but no-doubt hard-fought acceptance of his situation, changed the way I was thinking.

• • •

Most of the decisions regarding my care at Landstuhl, and my future care wherever I ended up, were being handled by Alicia. It wasn't easy for her. She was hit with a ton of technical medical jargon and often felt she was being asked to make decisions about matters she didn't fully understand. She consulted with my brother Barnaby, but he really wasn't any more medically savvy than she was, and he deferred the decision-making to her. Once my condition had been stabilized, the biggest decision we had to make was which hospital I would go to next.

The chief of trauma at Landstuhl wanted to send me to, as I've mentioned earlier, either Walter Reed National Military Medical Center in Washington, DC, or Brooke Army Medical Center, aka BAMC (pronounced "bamcy"), in San Antonio. The consensus seemed to be that Walter Reed was the best place for me. But Eric Ahnfeldt, my burn doctor at Landstuhl, told Alicia he thought I should go to BAMC. They, too, excelled in every facet of care I would need, and had possibly the best burn center anywhere. Only later did Alicia and I learn that there was a sort of friendly rivalry between the two institutions, and both valued the experience that working with a complicated patient like me would offer their teams of young surgeons. I was like a top draft pick being recruited by the best colleges.

Alicia and I finally decided on Walter Reed. The next day, an external voltage incident caused damage in the intensive care unit there and, at least for that day, Walter Reed could no longer accept new patients. That settled it—we were headed to Texas.

My accepting physician at BAMC would be Lieutenant Colonel Alicia Williams, a remarkable doctor and burn surgeon with the U.S. Army Institute of Surgical Research at Joint Base San Antonio–Fort

Sam Houston. She was a veteran of two tours of duty in Afghanistan and had also treated many dozens of burned and wounded U.S. soldiers during her residency at Walter Reed. After speaking with doctors at Landstuhl, Dr. Williams put together a team of consultants who would be involved in my care.

Alicia spoke with one of these specialists, the chief of surgical oncology at BAMC, Dr. Joe Alderete. He gave her a very preliminary estimate that I would need to stay at BAMC for the next two years. That was much longer than Alicia had expected, and much, *much* longer than I'd thought. Alicia had been told by several people, including Dr. Alderete, that patients recover best when they're surrounded by their families, and now we had to decide if Alicia and the girls would come to live with me in Texas for what might be two years.

The fact is neither Alicia nor I thought that was the best option for us. From my perspective, I did not want anything to even slightly interfere with the all-absorbing concentration I was prepared to focus on my recovery. I did not plan to spend two years in Texas. I planned to be out of there in six months. And as much as I would have loved to be with Alicia and the girls, I knew that my attention would be divided if they were there: I'd either be worried about how much Alicia was having to endure, or about how the girls were reacting to seeing me in the state I was in. I truly believed that if I was left alone to recover and rehabilitate without any distractions, I could be back with my family in just a few months, and in the kind of condition I wanted them to see me in—upright, walking around, no ghastly scars or bandages.

The truth is, I have never wanted to be a burden on anyone. I can't stand the thought of that. Even when I was semiconscious on the Polish prime minister's train, I felt the need to call Jay Wallace, president of Fox News, just to let him know he needn't worry about me anymore. Suzanne Scott jumped on the call with him. Jay had only recently heard that I was on the train, and he never dreamed I'd be in

any condition to phone him, and, really, I wasn't, but when we spoke I was determined to downplay what had happened and stop being a burden for him.

"My assistant came in and told me, 'I've got Ben on the line,' and I thought, *You've got to be kidding*," Jay says. "He's half a world away and he just rings me up at my desk. But that's when I knew he was going to live, and he was going to make it home."

I had the same instinct about my family moving to Texas to be with me. It just seemed far too disruptive a move to force them to make. Alicia, of course, was ready to do it. She would have done anything she needed to help me with my recovery. But on her own she'd come to the same conclusion—that uprooting our family might not be the best move for us.

A lot of people simply assumed that she and the girls would be going to Texas with me. "So when are you moving?" they'd ask. Many others suggested she really had no choice but to be with me at BAMC. "There is no way Benji can do this alone," she was told. "You cannot leave him there by himself." Kim Dozier, a journalist who was seriously injured in Iraq in 2006 while working for CBS News, told Alicia that her family never left her side and slept next to her at Walter Reed for weeks until she was better. "Benji will need help with everything," they said. "You have to be there for him, or someone does."

Sarah Verardo, who ran Save our Allies and was behind my evacuation, told Alicia the opposite. She explained how she had moved with her young children to a military hospital where her husband was being treated and spent several months with him there. "It was a disaster," Sarah said. "It wasn't helpful. Living on a military base was very hard on the children and on me. Do not go. Ben's a big boy. Holding his hand is not going to make him better."

Finally, Alicia sat down and thought about what was best for *me*.

She knew me better than almost anyone, and she understood my nature. She believed, rightly, that whatever I had to go through to get better and return to my family, I could do it, and I could do it alone. She also knew that I hated the idea of having everyone's attention focused on me around the clock for months. I wasn't, as the friend had said, someone who needed my hand held.

"Benji *did* need me to be there for him during it all," Alicia says. "But he didn't need me to be *there*, by his side. I knew before I even asked him that he'd say he didn't want me to stay so he could do it on his own."

But Alicia also knew that I would need some help. As Kim Dossier had strongly urged, I would need to have a patient advocate with me at the hospital. And so, on her second trip to Landstuhl, Alicia sat down with Jock outside my hospital room. She didn't know Jock all that well, but she trusted him, completely, and she needed to ask him a very big favor. "I didn't know how to phrase it, it was such an enormous ask," she says. Finally, she blurted it out.

"Do you think you could go with Benji to the U.S.?"

Alicia knew Jock had his own family and children he hadn't seen for a long time. She knew he had lost a friend in Pierre and hadn't had a moment to grieve for him. How could she now ask him to uproot his own life for the next several months?

"Yep," Jock immediately responded. "That's fine."

Alicia held back tears. Knowing Jock would be with me stripped away a good part of her anxiety.

We made the decision together. I would go to San Antonio with Jock, and he would stay in housing near the hospital for as long as he could. Sarah and the kids would remain in London so the girls wouldn't be uprooted and stuck in new surroundings. Perhaps not everyone would understand why Alicia and the girls weren't with me, but that wasn't really our concern. We knew what was best for us, and this was it.

• • •

Right after Pierre's funeral in Dublin, Jock hopped back on a plane and returned to Landstuhl to be with me. He would accompany me on the long flight from Germany to Washington, DC, and then on to Texas. Two days before my scheduled departure from Landstuhl, a special air rescue medical team came by and prepared for my transport across the Atlantic. They spent two days figuring out how to keep me stable on the flight. Transatlantic flights, I learned, can be hell on medical patients. One team member worked only on what meds I would need; another would handle dressing my wounds; a third was in charge of my many monitors.

I would be traveling the more than five thousand miles from Germany to Texas aboard a McDonnell Douglas/Boeing C-17 Globemaster, the cavernous military transport aircraft you see in movies carting soldiers and tanks from base to base. The C-17 is 174 feet long with a 169-foot wingspan, and its maximum takeoff weight is nearly 330 tons. It is a colossus. The best thing you can do when you get on one, I was told, is try to sleep until the flight is over.

At the time, I hadn't slept a peaceful hour in more than ten days.

On the day of the flight I was loaded onto a hard gurney that felt like a steel sheet. Medics from the XVIII Airborne Corps, office of the corps sergeant, then moved a metal U-shaped device over my chest and onto the gurney, leaving only an inch or two in between. On top of the device, they attached all the tubes and devices I would need to be hooked up to for the entire flight. It was a little terrifying, to be honest, because I felt like I couldn't move. Yet even though this rather scary preparation took several hours, I was still very excited to go.

Finally I was wheeled up and fit into a stretcher slot in the bare belly of the plane. They strapped me in tightly and I was all set.

We sat on the tarmac for the next four hours.

I realized then that the long flight was going to be a test of will.

We finally took off and climbed into the clouds until the aircraft flooded with freezing air. The weather was choppy and there was quite a bit of turbulence, and I felt every bump and bang and jolt. The roar of the engines was absolutely deafening, even with my ear protectors on. Then a drop of condensation from the plane's ceiling landed on my face. Then another. My arms were somewhat trapped beneath the metal cage and all I could do was endure what felt like drip torture. It was a confluence of pain and unpleasantness that began to drive me mad. I lay beneath my metal harness and struggled to find some state of being that I could tolerate.

Several hours in, I begged one of the medics, "Please do something to me, I can't handle this." They said they couldn't put me to sleep because they needed me to be alert, but they said they could give me ketamine, a short-acting anesthetic that can cause hallucinations.

Then the hallucinations began.

They were like the ones I had back in Landstuhl, only more intense. I had strange, unnerving thoughts about my legs, and I was convinced one of them was a miniature oak tree, while the other was being out-fitted with a slender little pink ballet slipper. A bit later the oak tree had grown by several feet and the ballerina foot was dancing in a per-formance. I even asked someone to take a picture of my legs because I wanted to see what was going on down there.

I also became totally paranoid. There was some guy exercising in the back of the C-17 and I was certain he was engaged in a swordfight, trying to save the plane from enemies. Back and forth he went, thrash-ing away against an invisible foe, their swords clashing loudly. I was out of my mind with terror and feared for all our safety. Immobilized by my sheath and addled by sleeplessness, I knew this was the low point of my entire journey since the bombing—worse than anything that had come before it by far. I lay there and, between hallucinations, tried to stay strong, as I had so many times before, but this time I just couldn't do it. I gritted my teeth and thought, *I am in fucking hell.*

Then a figure appeared before me. He was special forces and he was flying home. In my mind he looked like one of those heroes I'd seen in war movies when I was young, returning to his hometown after saving the world. At that point I was the very opposite, at my very lowest, at my bitter breaking point. From across the plane he noticed me and came over. He stood beside me and put his hand on my shoulder. I assumed he was there to tell me off because I'd done something wrong, that I was in the wrong place, that I was broken and no longer of any use. Instead, he simply said two words:

"Gummy bears?"

It may not sound like much but sharing the little candies he had in a bowl with me was a simple gesture of kindness that changed my whole world. The gesture instantly stopped my paranoia, stopped me thinking we were all doomed, and provided the tiny spark of goodness that brought me back to life. He stayed with me for a while and asked how I was doing and where I was headed. He told me he was on his way to North Dakota, near the Canadian border. I told him I'd be at the other end of the country, in Texas near the Mexican border.

"I guess guys like you and me, we just end up on the borders, man," he said. "We live our lives on the edge."

Then he patted me gently on the head and walked off.

There was bad weather in Washington, DC, too, so we circled the airport for four hours, then sat on the runway for another four hours, and finally flew the final five hours to San Antonio. All told, I was strapped to my private prison for twenty-four sleepless hours.

But by then, I was okay with it all. For most of the trip I'd felt like I was dead while still alive. But my moment with the special forces guy gave me all the strength I needed, and I would think of that moment many times in the future when I needed to be strong. He showed me that not everyone was out to get me or harm me or blow me up—that there were plenty of people who wanted nothing more than to help me. I wasn't in hell after all. I was simply alive.

High up over the Atlantic, I was saved by gummy bears.

SEVENTEEN

MOGADISHU

The monstrous C-17 touched down on a dedicated military airstrip at San Antonio International Airport, just a short drive from Joint Base San Antonio–Fort Sam Houston, the Army base that is home to Brooke Army Medical Center. It was 2 a.m., and I was relieved beyond measure to be on the ground.

We taxied for a while before the big ramp opened and three medical professionals strode on purposefully and settled at the foot of my gurney. At first they talked about me, not to me, wasting not a second in checking my vitals and resuscitation data from the long flight. Finally, the doctor in charge, a fifty-year-old man with a fit build and short brown hair and the posture and demeanor of a soldier, stepped forward and addressed me.

"Hi, I'm Dr. Joe Alderete. We spoke with everyone in Landstuhl and we heard what a brave person you are, and how you fought through everything, and I want to tell you not to worry, because we are going to continue all that here. We've got you. You are with us now. Let's get to it."

I could not have asked for a more rousing greeting: *Let's get to it.*

Colonel Dr. Joseph Alderete was the chief of surgical oncology at BAMC. He was, I would soon learn, a very impressive guy. His father had been a B-29 pilot in World War II, and from the age of six Joe "never wanted to do anything other than be in the Army and lead soldiers," he has said. He attended West Point and went to medical school at Penn State, and in the early parts of the Afghanistan War he was deployed with the 555th Forward Surgical Team (the "triple nickel"), in support of the 173rd Airborne in Jalalabad, the scene of heavy fighting. He set up an innovative mobile surgical unit that treated not only U.S. soldiers but locals, tribal chieftains, and even the Taliban. "We wanted to allow them to see the massive medical heart of the American soldier," he says.

At BAMC he performed a groundbreaking above-the-elbow arm replant on a woman whose arm had been severed by a guardrail. He also once performed a complex reconstructive surgery that lasted *thirty-three hours*, outlasting several shifts of residents. I liked that he was aggressive and relentlessly positive. I felt like I couldn't have been in better hands.

On the C-17, Joe was encouraged by what he saw. He was surprised I was as alert and articulate as I was, despite the in-flight medications, and he and his fellow surgeon and longtime colleague Colonel Dr. Jennifer Gurney exchanged shorthand glances that meant, *You know, he's not that bad.* Had he told me that, I would have asked, *Compared to what?*

By then Joe had already assembled a team of attending surgeons, handpicking burn and reconstruction specialists and having them review my records a week earlier so they could start envisioning a treatment plan. He would end up with a group of eight to ten surgeons, each of whom would play a vital part in my recovery.

Because I'd been injured in a bomb blast, I had what is known as polytrauma. The phrase was coined during the wars in Iraq and Afghanistan, when roadside bombs and other IEDs caused devastating and widespread injuries to soldiers. A typical polytrauma case might feature burns, missing limbs, visions issues, brain injuries, shattered bones—trauma from top to bottom. Because so many U.S. soldiers injured in those wars were treated at BAMC, it became one of the leading polytrauma treatment centers in the world. Dr. Williams and Joe Alderete had top specialists in every relevant discipline available to them for the team.

When I touched ground in San Antonio, Joe's team was more than ready to go. I was wheeled off the C-17 and taken by ambulance to the main campus of BAMC, a 425-bed center that is the Department of Defense's largest medical facility, with a staff of more than eight thousand military and civilian personnel. I didn't need to go to the OR for any operation right away, so I passed quickly through the trauma unit on my way to the burn unit, where I would be under the supervision of Dr. Alicia Williams. Based on the data they had received from Landstuhl, they had decided my burns required the most immediate attention.

I was taken into a vast, highly air-conditioned room and lifted onto a big metal table with drains at every corner. There were machines and monitors and endless wires surrounding the table, with countless more computers behind a glass wall. Dr. Williams was there, as were several other doctors and staffers who swarmed me and got right to it. What happened next is called a Trauma and Burn Tertiary Survey.

Joe Alderete calls it "unwrapping the Christmas presents."

My gown was stripped off and my bandages were unraveled, until I was naked and exposed on the table, stumps and wounds and all. Joe and his team examined every inch of me, even reopening some of my sealed wounds in search of hidden infections.

In that instant I properly understood that I wasn't so much a person anymore, as I was a *patient*. I had no function in that room other than to lie there, inert, so I could be poked and prodded and examined.

Bloody hell, I thought.

But by my very next thought, I had switched gears. *This is going to be everything that it is going to be*, I said to myself. *Embrace it. Maybe even try to enjoy it. These people can help you, so just let it happen. Help it along.* The nurse in charge, a sweet, long-haired guy who was also named Ben and looked like Jesus, was the only one in the room who addressed me during the procedure, putting his hand on my forehead and saying, "It's all going to be fine, you're okay." I later learned that Ben was a devout Christian who led his church group, worked the night shift so he could be with his family, and had a side business selling Lego parts. His kind and gentle demeanor helped me more than he could know.

. . .

The next morning, I went under the knife for the first time in the U.S. (I'd already had several surgeries in Kyiv and Landstuhl). Just before noon I was taken to an OR, intubated, sedated and anesthetized, and washed with a germ-killing Hibiclens solution. The surgeon was Dr. Williams, my burn doctor, and the operation was mainly to irrigate and debride (remove damaged tissue) my burn wounds. I'd suffered burns to some 17 percent of my body, of which less than 10 percent were third degree burns. Joe Alderete scrubbed in for that operation and was happy to see that the doctors at Hospital No. 7 in Kyiv had done an admirable job of amputating my right leg. "Ben could have easily come to us with an amputation that was above the knee," he says. "That it was below the knee was a huge break."

I was still groggy from the sedation when I awoke after the operation, and the first thing I saw was a photo of my daughter Iris up on the wall. My hallucinatory paranoia kicked in and I assumed I was in the back room of a dry cleaner serving as a front for Russian operatives who had, it seemed, kidnapped my daughter. I thrashed in my bed and kept trying to get up and yelled, *What are you doing with Iris, let her go!* An attendant held me down long enough for me to figure out what had happened: Jock—who was given a room in housing across from the medical center, and who stayed with me just about every waking hour—had simply put some of the photos Alicia gave me of our children up on the glass wall of my room.

My hallucinations continued at BAMC. Once again, I had to try to find a balance between pain eradication and clarity. The more medication I was given, the more I tended to hallucinate. Yet without the medication I would have been a goner. In the long, long months I spent at BAMC, I was administered medication of some sort (lots of eye drops, plasma, and IV drips but also plenty of painkillers) more than 5,600 times. Medication was an indispensable part of my rehab and recovery, and I would have to learn to live with it. So, the hallucinations continued.

In those early days at BAMC, I realized that most of my muscles had atrophied and basically given out on me. I hadn't moved very much in two weeks and trying to lift what remained of my left leg even one inch was all but impossible. I'd always been extra active, and literally not being able to move a muscle left me feeling more than a bit of despair.

"Don't worry about it," Joe assured me. "It's completely normal. Keep trying, it will get better."

And it did. At BAMC I measured success in physical increments. Lifting my left leg another inch? That was progress. That was meaningful. I could build on that. I had five problem areas that were all being treated at once—my burns, my left eye, my left hand, my right leg, and my left foot—but mainly I was focused on my legs. In order to get out of the hospital, and back to my family, I knew I had to be ambulatory. I had to be able to walk. And to walk, I would need prosthetics, one on each leg. Getting to the point where I could begin wearing the prosthetics and learning how to walk in them was, really, just about all I cared about.

The men and women who would help me get there were as expert as they come. Before I arrived at BAMC, John Ferguson was eating in a coffee shop when he got a call from Joe Alderete, asking him to familiarize himself with my case. John Ferguson is the chief prosthetist and division director of the Center for the Intrepid (CFI), a cutting-edge rehabilitation center housed at BAMC. CFI's mission is to help casualties who have suffered amputations, burns, or functional limb loss. One article about John's prowess in the field of prosthetics referred to him as a "legend." John brought in an equally skilled CFI prosthetist, Del Lipe, and these extraordinary men became the heart of the team that would try to get me walking again.

My prosthetics, however, would have to wait. "The burns were more of a concern, so all we could do early on was monitor the tissue coverage and see how much could be preserved," John says. "While we waited, Del and I sat down and worked on an aggressive treatment plan. His case was complicated, but our thinking was *Everything is surmountable.*"

While I was still based in the burn center, other specialists came in to work on their areas of concern. My hand surgeon, Major Casey Sabbag, who was also the vice chair of BAMC, began rebuilding my left hand. The thumb metacarpal had been shattered and I was missing much of it. The muscles and cartilage had been torn out and my whole thumb was just barely hanging on. After extensive surgery it was covered with a flap of skin brought down from my elbow.

On April 1, just a couple of days after my first surgery, the blood was flowing to my hand quite well but it wasn't draining properly. Major Sabbag showed up with a glass jar and asked a nurse to cut the cast and bandages on my left hand. Then she retrieved something from the jar and deftly placed a small, black shiny thing on my hand wound.

It was a leech. Two leeches, in fact.

The doctor held down the leeches with small pinchers until they'd properly latched on to my hand and begun drinking my blood. They would start out as tiny little things but within ten minutes they would swell to two inches long and an inch around, bursting with my blood. Their purpose, I understood, was to suck away excess blood and allow freshly oxygenated blood to flood the area and accelerate the healing process. When the leeches were done feeding and fully engorged they would simply drop off and tumble to the bed, and two more would be retrieved from a jar and latched on to my wound. I became a round-the-clock, all-you-can-eat leech buffet. On and off, two by two, twenty-four hours a day, seven days in a row. At first I was a bit uneasy about it—it seemed sort of medieval. But after a while I didn't mind the leeches at all, and quite enjoyed watching them feast and blow up.

"Hey, look at this one!" I'd call out to one of the nurses. "He's really drinking fast, this one!"

I was happy to see just about all my doctors, but the ones I came to somewhat dread—through absolutely no fault of their own—were my eye doctors. Technically, my left eye suffered a retinal detachment—tissue pulling away from blood-supplying vessels at the back of the eye—and aphakia, the loss of the lens behind my iris and pupil, and aniridia, the loss of the iris, and also the loss of my cornea, felled by a piece of shrapnel. I'd also had a corneal transplant at Landstuhl, but the new cornea was already defecting, while the fluid pressure in my left eye kept rising. The specialists were concerned I might lose the eye altogether, and they came to see me every day to check on it. Eventually I had a small tube inserted in my eye to drain the liquid building up inside, which was just as unpleasant as it sounds. I had an ongoing joke with the eye doctors that I would always try to be somewhere else, having some other injury treated, when they came by on their rounds. But they were relentless, and inevitably they'd find me.

One day the doctor walked into my room and expressed his concern that my eye was not healing quickly enough. He told me he was going to have to insert a special contact lens and then sew my eye shut.

That's right—sew my eye shut.

"When is this going to happen?" I asked.

"Right now," he said, pulling out a sewing needle, handing it to one of his doctoral students, and telling her to go ahead and insert it through my eyelid. Then the doctor fitted a round metal ring in my eye socket. Wedging it in and keeping it in was extremely painful; it felt like a piece of shrapnel being shoved in there. Finally the doctoral student sewed up my eye, which to me barely seemed to shut around the metal lens.

I was raised to be strong and resilient, as my father had been in Manila, and I made a point of never complaining no matter the situation. You would never hear me describing an injury or explaining how much something hurt. But at BAMC, I learned a valuable lesson. My recovery depended on me being honest and straightforward about how I felt. I was asked to, and I happily did, tell everyone how I was feeling, good or bad (mostly, it was good). Just as I'd been physically exposed on day one, I was also, for the first time in my life, required to be emotionally vulnerable.

What I learned is that sharing how I felt with someone made me feel better. *Crying* made me feel better. Sometimes I cried out of happiness, because I knew I'd been given the chance to see my wife and children again. Sometimes I cried from the pain or out of despair, as I did after my eye was sewn shut. The crying felt good. It righted the ship. I was still determined to be strong and resilient, but that didn't mean I couldn't express my feelings or even cry now and then. That might not sound like much of a revelation to some, but to me, it was.

I had learned an important lesson about being human.

• • •

In the same way I had to adapt to my new reality in Texas, back in London Alicia had to plan for life without me for the foreseeable future.

Her friends and family continued to rally around her, helping take the girls to school or minding them while Alicia tended to one or another facet of my care. Weeks into my stay at BAMC, we still hadn't told our daughters about what happened to me. All they knew was that I was sick, nothing serious, and that I had to stay in a U.S. hospital for a while. Our goal was to minimize their fear and anxiety as much as possible until I was better and my return was more predictable. As my facial injuries healed, I was able to jump on FaceTime with the girls, and we dealt with my absence the same way we did when I was off on assignment—with lots of laughs and giggles over the phone. It was all I had, and it kept me going.

Meanwhile, Alicia dealt with the challenges and emotions of having a polytraumatized husband. "Early on I almost couldn't believe it was happening," she says. "I would go around asking, 'Is this our lives now?'" One of the biggest adjustments was responding to the onslaught of sympathy she was receiving. Another was figuring out how to talk about me. When her plane landed at Heathrow after flying back from Landstuhl, the man checking passports on board asked her, "Business or pleasure?"

Alicia laughed and heard herself say, "Do you really want to know? Well, my husband is a journalist and he's just been blown up and I went to see him, so that's the reason for my trip."

The man looked shocked and quickly shuffled past without looking at her passport. Alicia was shocked, too—she couldn't believe she'd said something so horrible and inappropriate. But there were no rules for how she was supposed to act, no handbook she could consult. Was she not supposed to mention what happened to me at all? If she did, was that unfairly burdening someone with her grief? Whenever she did tell someone what happened it would usually provoke an "Oh my God, I'm so sorry" reaction, which made Alicia want to explain that she didn't mention what happened just to get sympathy, and they would say, "Oh, I know you didn't," and then everyone would be uncomfortable.

Finally Alicia gave up on acting how a traumatized wife should act, whatever that meant. She just focused on keeping the girls' lives normal and consistent, and on helping me however she could from London.

Alicia and I discussed her and the children visiting me at BAMC at some point. I wasn't especially keen on it happening anytime soon. As desperate as I was to see and hold my wife and my children, I still didn't want the girls to see me in such physical disarray. Alicia agreed, and we put the question of visiting aside. I would speak with Alicia several times a day, and with the girls as well, but I simply didn't want many physical visits from anyone—I didn't want to spend hours accepting sympathies when I could have spent them toiling away at my recovery.

What made it tolerable for me was the sense of mission: I had to get out of the hospital and back to London as soon as humanly possible. Early on I had a discussion with Joe Alderete about the time frame of my stay. Just as he'd told Alicia, he told me a two-year stay was his best estimate.

"That included three or four months of reconstruction, surgical endeavors, the learning process, unplanned hiccups and infections, and maybe a return to BAMC for some advanced rehab," Joe explains. "Benji listened and said, 'I want to get back to my family as quickly as you can make it happen. Let's make it work.'"

What I was thinking, however, was, *No way, that's not happening. I am going home way before then. I'm thinking months, not years.* It did not matter to me if that was realistic or not; I needed to believe it was possible and I needed to have it as a goal I could work relentlessly toward. I understood I was going to have to be at BAMC for a long time; I wasn't delusional about the extent of my injuries. And early on I didn't dare pick a target date for getting out, because I knew it wouldn't be based on anything concrete. My feeling was that if I kept pushing hard—and got up on my prosthetics—I would soon see a clear path to getting out, the light at the end of the tunnel, and that would be all I needed to keep me going.

To that end, I leaned especially hard into my physical therapy. Dr. Sarah Flores was my wonderful lead physical therapist (PT) at BAMC, though I spent most of my time with a PT named Kelly Brown, who worked with me from Wednesdays to Saturdays, anywhere from three to six hours a day. We started our therapy together within a few days of my arrival at BAMC. He was just about the nicest man I'd ever met, a wholesome country boy who loved to fish and told incredible stories about his life. It was Kelly's job to get my muscles back into shape, so that I would not, as he put it, "be as weak as a kitten." Born in Tuttle, Oklahoma, Kelly had attention deficit hyperactivity disorder as a child and found relief in helping his dad, a logistical engineer, rebuild an old Chevy truck in the garage. Kelly needed to put his hands on things, get under the hood, drag in broken farm equipment, push and pull levers into place. Except for the farm equipment, he is still doing that now.

"They always say doctors save lives and nurses keep them alive, and physical therapy gives them a life," he says. "Our whole thing is *function*."

Kelly was limited in how he could help me in the early going. His work required that he put pressure on certain parts of my body, and there weren't many parts of it that could sustain any pressure at all. We focused on lower extremity strengthening, as well as on the fingers on my left hand and even my right arm, technically my only "good" limb. We couldn't let those muscles atrophy, either. "With Ben, we probably had five hours of things that needed to be exercised every day: shoulder rotation, glutes, knees, arms," Kelly says. "There were at least a dozen separate moves we had to put him through every day."

Kelly paid extra attention to the muscles in my legs to prepare me for when I'd be fitted for prosthetics—the day I could hardly wait for. He wheeled me down to the large rehab gym at BAMC, and I'd lie on a mat while he leaned over me and manipulated various parts of my body, having me push against his resistance and always strive for more flexibility. He would hook a strap around my ankle and have me lift small weights, and he took me through leg extensions to work the muscles above both knees. It was often extremely painful, and Kelly would always ask me about the pain, and I'd always tell him I was fine, though he could surely tell from my grimace that I wasn't.

But I loved it all. I didn't shy away from any of it. I never once begged out of a gym session, or any other procedure or treatment at BAMC. I tried to approach every exercise, every surgery, every IV tube insertion with energy and enthusiasm. Kelly told me he was going to steal my blood and bottle it and give it to other patients.

There were so many other physio workers and nurses and doctors who helped me in the same thorough and dedicated way, and I could write a book about all of them. Russ, a chess champ who'd taken shrapnel in Somalia when the Black Hawk Down episode happened. Tosh, the best ICU Jenga player out there. Patti, Christy, Sara, Adam, all enormously encouraging. And Berlew, who pushed me to go a bit further every day. One thing I know for sure is that the work they do is hallowed work—they give people back their lives, their freedom, their families. That's what they were doing for me, and I saw them as my heroes.

My days at BAMC took on a familiar rhythm. Regular visits from doctors and specialists, preparations for surgeries, therapy, procedures, painkillers. I was given multiple skin grafts—taking healthy skin from other parts of my body and transplanting them to the burned areas— and my wounds were constantly dressed and re-dressed. There was never a day when nothing happened; it was usually several things all day long, sometimes even at night. I began to crave anything that broke up this routine, even for a moment or two. I know now there is something called ICU delirium, which refers to what can happen if you lie in your bed on pain meds and stare at the same ceiling long enough.

What can happen is you go bonkers.

There were moments for me at BAMC when things got dark. As positive as I tried to be, the hallucinations and setbacks and pain flareups sometimes left me shattered. On some nights different moments from travels to war zones would suddenly pop into my head— explosions, hurried escapes, near misses, men with guns. Sometimes the moments were benign, like the time a rebel held a loaded pistol to my head in Syria as a joke, or what he thought was a joke. I recalled my uneasy laugh when it was over.

Sometimes at night I would see things that weren't benign at all.

• • •

I was back in the hall. The long hall on the first floor of the parliament building in Mogadishu. It was 2014, and just a few minutes earlier I'd been drinking beers with Rick Findler, not a care in the world. Then suddenly we were in the hall. And what we found there was hell.

We'd heard that the local government was paying journalists to fly to Somaliland, the autonomous region in the north of Somalia in eastern Africa. It was a promotional thing to encourage investment or something like that. Rick and I had always wanted to go to Somalia, and we figured we'd let them fly us over for the promo, then sneak down to Mogadishu when we were done.

We wanted to go to Somalia because the extremist Islamic terrorist group al-Shabaab was fighting a violent civil war against the Somali government in Mogadishu, laying waste to parts of the city. But when Rick and I got there, everything was quiet. We spent the first four days at a hotel, monitoring the news and occasionally going out with our fixer in a Land Cruiser, rap music blaring from the speaker—the driver's choice, not ours. We spent the next four days at the United Nations mission, mostly hanging around and chatting with diplomats. On the ninth day, we were booked to fly home.

The night before we left, Rick and I were having a few beers with some UN staffers when an urgent news bulletin came over the radio. Some twenty al-Shabaab troops had seized control of the parliament building in a huge attack. We threw on our body armor and ran madly to the convoy en route to the parliament. When we got there, the building was surrounded by African Union troops, as well as a throng of curious civilians. Al-Shabaab was holding hostages inside, and snipers were firing out the windows in our direction. One man next to us moved to his left to get a better look and took a bullet in the thigh; he crashed to the ground. We wanted a scene, and we had found it.

Suddenly Ugandan special forces troops working with the African Union stormed the parliament. There were explosions, hundreds of gunshots, people running everywhere—pandemonium. Rick and I looked at each other and both said something like, "We have to go in." We followed the sounds of the fighting and snuck into the first-floor hall.

The fighting was still going on. Bodies were everywhere, shot, butchered, mutilated, torn apart. Limbs cut off, torsos tossed in piles. Soldiers dragging corpses down the hall. White walls now bright red with blood. Rick took photos and I just looked. And I thought, *This is death. This is death up close. This is what hell looks like.*

Outside the parliament, it was just as bad. The Ugandan forces had annihilated al-Shabaab and were now throwing their bodies over fences and into stacks. Blood ran in little rivers, and I could hear the crack of skulls as they hit the ground. The Ugandan soldiers no longer looked human—they had satisfied some ancient bloodlust and were brutal, mindless zombies now. Were they the good guys or the bad guys? Did it even matter?

Rick and I had witnessed savagery before, but nothing like this. Never anything like this. Nor were we prepared for it. Other times the tension had been ratcheting for days, but in this case, we'd been having beers only minutes earlier, and now we'd been dropped into a horror movie, so bloody and so gruesome it didn't even seem real.

That is what really got to me—that it didn't seem real. That the bodies were thrown away like refuse and fell to the ground like sandbags. That all life had been so callously extinguished, and all humanity, too. That such a scene could even exist in a sane world. We flew home the next day and for the first time since I became a journalist, I dreamed about what I'd seen. In the daytime I was quiet, moody, shut down.

I had always had a system in place to divide myself into two people who existed in two different worlds. But now the system was showing cracks.

Eventually I managed to continue cutting back and forth between my normal life and the extremes of war. The dividing line was thinner, but still I managed to walk it. And then I went to Ukraine, and the line was forever erased. Because now the bad stuff came home with me.

• • •

By my third week at BAMC the strain of all the surgeries and procedures, and the terrible sameness of the fluorescent lights and sterile corridors and bland white walls, left me feeling like I was trapped. I was wrapped up in a protective cocoon with no hope of wiggling out.

Then Kelly Brown set me free.

One morning he walked into my room and just asked, "Hey, Ben, do you want to go outside?"

It was really that simple. I was lifted into a special bed and Kelly wheeled me down a hallway and to a little outdoor balcony on the third floor. There wasn't much of a view: just some other buildings and maybe a courtyard below. But that didn't matter, because there *was* something I hadn't experienced in three weeks. Fresh air. Sunshine. The *outdoors*.

I sat there and took a deep breath and felt a wave of emotion wash through me. To me, that breath of air was like the breath of life. I'd felt safe in my hospital snow globe, with my friendly little leeches and my lovely helpful nurses and Jock playing cards or chess with me. But I'd also felt trapped. I'd forgotten there was an outside world, a *real* world.

Then, there it was, within my grasp: the blue sky, the cottony clouds, the warm air of a hot Texas spring. The feel of the sun on my battered face. This was, in a way, my first step back into the world, even though I was still hooked up to my drips. I could see that it was all there, waiting for me, and that as long as I kept moving forward, getting better, I would be all right.

It was right around then, in my fourth week at BAMC, that John Ferguson and Del Lipe stopped by my room with a small, curved, thermal-molded piece of plastic about the size of a softball.

"It's a test socket," they explained. "It's temporary. It's how we'll figure out the prosthetic for your right leg."

There it was—the clear path. The light in the tunnel. The endgame.

It was the first tiny step toward learning to walk again.

EIGHTEEN

ROBOT LEG

A month into my time at BAMC I started a video diary. I recorded myself on my iPhone providing updates on my condition, my moods, everything. In my first video entry, I summarized the project:

"This is the diary of the recovery of a man growing back his limbs and coming back to society."

That made it sound like I was being reborn, which I believed I was.

"Growing back" my legs would not be easy. There were major problems with each. The amputation of my right leg below the knee left me with only about five inches of my tibia, the lower leg bone that connects the knee joint to the ankle joint. That was about two inches less than is optimal for the attachment of a prosthetic, and quite possibly not enough to even allow for a prosthetic at all. Dr. Joe Alderete said it would be the least amount of existing tibia he'd ever had to work with.

The problem with my left leg was the foot, which had a hole blown through it, essentially leaving me with only a working heel. My left ankle had also been badly damaged and would need major adjustments before it could be functional. To walk again on my left foot, I would need some sort of partial prosthetic that would stabilize my gait. Imagine walking with only a heel and no forward foot. That was the challenge I faced.

From the start, Joe had a directive for the team—get me up and walking as soon as possible. "People do better when they are ambulatory," he says. "It's the standpoint of considering the whole human being. Weight bearing was the priority." With the right leg, he considered three different options to deal with the short tibia.

One was tibia elongation, which was risky, more theoretical than practical, and extremely time-consuming. Bones can be lengthened through distraction osteogenesis: slowly pulling bone segments apart and allowing new bone to grow and fill the gap. But I had no bone below the tibia to connect to, which would make it very hard to grow new bone. That meant that to lengthen my tibia I would need an endoprosthetic—a synthetic 3-D printed titanium tibia that docked to my native tibia.

The second option was taking the tibia from my left leg, cutting it in half along with its dominant artery, attaching it to my right tibia, and sewing up the arteries so the tibia could get a supply of blood and grow. Joe called it the "double-barrel" technique, and it was even riskier than the first option. It would also have drastically slowed down the progress with my left leg until the left tibia could be returned.

The third option was the simplest: trying to attach a prosthetic to the very short tibia I still had.

John Ferguson, the prosthetist, believed option three was worth a try. He and Del Lipe had worked with short tibias before, and they told Joe that if they didn't pull it off, the other options would still be available. Joe—who had to be cautious but was also setting a fast pace for everyone on the team—gave John and Del eight days to make it work with my existing tibia while he prepared for one of the surgical options.

The race was on. John took a mold of my right stump and fashioned the plastic test socket for the leg. It was basically a plastic cup with an adjustable liner that my stump slid right into. It was only temporary, but it allowed John and Del to quickly swap it out and fiddle with it and see what worked and what didn't. For me it was much more than that. It was a license to finally, finally get out of my wheelchair.

I had a coconspirator in this effort to speed things along: my remarkable assistant physical therapist Kelly Brown. As aggressive as Joe and the prosthetists were, Kelly was even more confident I could bear weight on my right leg without surgery. He created a crude padded boot that I could slip my left foot into, so I'd be able to put at least a bit of pressure on it. Then, as soon as I was fitted with the test socket on my right leg, Kelly wheeled me to the gym and moved a chest-high, padded walker in front of me. He adjusted a cushioned rehab mat table so that it was fourteen inches off the ground—exactly the height of my right leg with the socket on it. He pulled the table right up to the tall walker.

Then Kelly helped me stand at the walker with my arms braced on chest-level padded mats, my left leg (with its makeshift boot) on the ground, and my right leg resting on the fourteen-inch-high mat table.

"Kelly," I blurted out, "look at me. I'm *standing*!"

Indeed, I was, holding tightly to the walker but in an upright position, with both my legs, as they were, beneath me.

Then, instinctively, I began to move. I lifted my right stump up and off the table, then put it back down and in turn lifted my left foot. Then I did it again. And again. To my astonishment, I was marching in place.

"Kelly, I'm *walking*!" I said.

There were several other people in the gym, and they spontaneously erupted in applause. My jubilant, relieved, bewildered grin was ear to ear. I hadn't been upright under my own power since before it all happened. But now I was, and not just standing—marching! Walking. *Moving*.

"Okay, Ben, don't overdo it," Kelly said.

The next day, the prosthetists John Ferguson and Del Lipe stopped by to see me in the gym. When they took a look at me standing in my walker, marching in place, their eyes widened. "We'd figured the socket was just for him to get used to," John says, "and there he is taking imaginary steps on it in the gym. We were so surprised to see that, and it flipped a switch. We knew we needed to be even more aggressive because Ben got ahead of us. We had to keep up with Ben now."

I was greatly, greatly encouraged that I'd been able to get on my feet so soon after arriving at BAMC, and I felt as if nothing could stop me now. But then I had a talk with Dr. Joe. During the talk, he noticed something was wrong. "He was suddenly a little more loopy and a little less alert," Joe says. "It's something you look out for in trauma patients. The rug is suddenly pulled out from under them." Personally, I felt a little more than loopy: I was shaking maniacally, freezing cold one moment and boiling the next, and completely unable to speak.

The technical term was *septicemia*, which is the persistence of pathogenic bacteria in the bloodstream. In other words, small hidden infections that are easily missed. "It makes you think you might be leaving a wound unanswered," says Joe. "It means you have to take a step back." What I had was a rare fungal infection that is often contracted after blast injuries, when dirt is blown into the wounds. I was quickly loaded up with medications that, after two weeks, fixed the problem and spared me a surgical solution. Still, it was a frightening moment and a real wake-up call for me. I was not some superhuman patient capable of astounding physiological leaps. I was human and as susceptible to rogue bacteria as everyone else.

It was a definite setback, and it slowed down everyone on the team and tempered expectations, which, in the end, was probably a good thing.

• • •

My days were long in the hospital, but back home Alicia's days were even longer. She was effectively a single mother, taking care of not only her own obligations but everything I would have handled as well, while also striving to keep the girls' lives as normal and consistent as possible—and all while setting aside hours every evening to make calls to me and my doctors in San Antonio. The responsibilities she had to shoulder were huge.

Early on she had the help of her sisters and friends and especially her parents. Her mother, Scarlett, flew straight in from Australia, and she made a big difference. "I had more children than hands," Alicia says. "My mother was that extra pair of hands for emergencies."

As Alicia puts it, she basically traded me for her mom.

Alicia stayed on top of every facet of my care, which wasn't easy because it was changing every day. There were so many stops and starts, potential options and medication issues—as well as fluctuations in my condition—that no one knew what the next week or even next day would look like. Alicia spoke mostly with Joe Alderete and my burn specialist, Dr. Alicia Williams. It was Dr. Williams, as kind and giving a soul as there is, who managed most things for Alicia, particularly when it came to my medication and trying to reduce it. "I wanted Alicia to feel like she didn't have to be there sitting with her husband every single day and I tried to centralize things so she didn't have to talk to ten different people," says Dr. Williams. Instead, Alicia would text her with all her questions and Dr. Williams would call and update her on a particular surgery or procedure. Every decision we had to make had a trade-off, and with Dr. Williams' help my wife versed herself in it all and made sure everyone always did what was best for me. She knew me better than anyone and she worried that because I was always so eager to try anything to speed things along, my team might move a bit more quickly than it should.

Alicia and the children were accustomed to me not being there—before the injury I'd been away in Washington, DC, for months—and so our daughters were not initially concerned by my absence. Yet while we agreed to hold off on telling the girls exactly what happened to me, we both knew we would have to tell them eventually, particularly about my lost limbs.

I knew it would fall on Alicia to do it.

She was determined not to worry the girls unnecessarily, and to do that she had to be calm and assured in her discussions with them about me. One afternoon a few weeks after the incident, Alicia had Honor, Iris, and Hero in the car with her after picking them up from school. She seized the moment and said, "So Daddy had an accident in Ukraine but he is absolutely fine and everything is under control. He's going to be in hospital for a while, but you needn't worry about him."

The girls had a few questions, and Alicia further explained that something hit my car and I'd been hurt but was okay. She gave them whatever details she could without mentioning my injuries. It wasn't time for that talk yet. Honor, our eldest, appeared the most worried by it all.

"Look at me," Alicia told her. "Do I look worried?"

"No."

"Well, if I'm not worried you don't need to worry, either."

What helped us both feel better about the children was that, as soon as my face healed and my shrapnel scars weren't quite as visible, I was able to FaceTime with them every day, just as we had when I was in DC. Those calls were loose and funny and typically chaotic (young girls can get distracted by pretty much anything). One of them noticed a small shrapnel scar on my nose and, inexplicably, the girls all became obsessed with it.

Daddy, how is your nose? Does it hurt? they constantly asked. I was happy that the small scar was all they had to worry about.

As the weeks and months passed, and it became clearer that I was going to have a prosthetic, Alicia looked for ways to break the news about my legs to our daughters. She bought a children's book that was written by Sarah Verardo, the cofounder of Save Our Allies and the wife of a military veteran who had lost a limb. The book was intended to help spouses talk to their children about amputations and prosthetics. The cover featured an illustration of a man with a prosthetic lower leg, and at first Alicia simply left the book lying around in the living room. She watched as the girls idly picked it up and looked through it.

"Is that a robot leg?" one of them finally asked.

"Yes, it is," Alicia said. "It's a robot leg and you can run faster on it and it's really cool." The girls absorbed that and, as girls do, moved on.

Alicia also pointed out people on the street who were in wheelchairs or on crutches, not linking them to me but just making the girls aware that such injuries are not uncommon. When I got closer to having my own prosthetic, Alicia found a moment to tell the children about my limbs.

They were sitting together having dinner, and Alicia said, as if it were just an aside, "You know, Daddy doesn't have his leg anymore. It wasn't working well after the accident so we decided to get him a robot leg."

The girls considered this. Alicia could already tell it would not be earth-shattering news for them. She had brushed over it, and the children would now likely just move on to something else. But Iris, our middle child and perhaps the most inquisitive of the bunch, had an odd question.

"What happened to his old leg?" she asked.

"Well, it just wasn't working that well anymore, so we replaced it with a robot leg," Alicia said.

"Yes, but where did the old leg go? What happened to it?"

Iris tends to ask pointed questions and doesn't like it if the answers aren't direct as well. Alicia did the best she could without telling her all the grisly details, and finally satisfied Iris with, "It's just not there anymore."

That was as far as the discussions went. I continued FaceTiming with the girls every day, and playing little games with the toy hedgehogs, Yellow Jumpsuit and Blue Pants, which they absolutely loved. We all progressed this way through the long weeks, just as we had before.

"Benji was still Benji," Alicia says. "Their daddy was still there. That's all that really mattered to them."

• • •

I recovered from the septicemia and resumed building up the strength I would need for my prosthetics. I'd been zipping along on what Joe Alderete called "the reconstructive ladder," and though I'd had a setback that cost me valuable time, I was determined to pick up where I'd left off. Everyone was pleased with how quickly I adapted to the new socket, and Del Lipe fashioned a pylon that connected to the socket and met a temporary foot on the ground—a crude placeholder for my eventual prosthetic leg. Kelly Brown, my physio, continued working me hard in the gym while also making sure I didn't get too far ahead of myself. Joe, too, realized the pace had been accelerated, and he was ready to accelerate with it. He came to see me one day to discuss what lay ahead.

"This is a Benji moment," he told me. "This is your time. We are at the point physiologically where I feel good about your progress and where you are. Now we're going to beat you up."

"Okay," I said with a big smile. "When do we start?"

In truth, all the leg work I was doing hurt like hell. Putting weight on anything was extremely painful, and so was Kelly exerting pressure on different parts of my body. Sometimes I'd have to power up on extra painkillers to make it through a session. Still, I didn't want him to know how bad the pain really was. I was afraid that if he saw how much it hurt, he would ease up on me. I know I said that expressing my pain was key to my recovery, but I felt reasonably sure the pain was not a factor of something being wrong, other than that hard materials were abrading against the damaged tissue around my stumps. I got pretty good at disguising my grimaces and hiding the pain.

There were other annoyances. My damaged and burned left hand was a continual, slow-healing nuisance. The burns were still very raw, and stripping away the skin on the hand hurt more than I could sometimes bear. I would have given *anything* to make that particular pain stop.

On one occasion, a certain type of dressing I'd become allergic to was mistakenly put on skin graft donor sites on my butt and thigh. The only option was to slowly pull them off, which, in effect, was the same as peeling away the new skin and the nerves. It was torture. This was the one time I could not keep my screams in. I found out later that patients heard me screaming many corridors away.

I had other problems with skin graft donor sites. Most of my back had been stripped of skin for grafts, and stubbornly the raw spots had refused to heal. For several weeks my back was essentially skinless. I couldn't sleep, couldn't properly lie down or sit up. My doctors tried every known method to heal my back, but nothing worked. Finally, I decided that we should stop putting anything on my back at all, and I would sleep facedown and get through the pain and see what happened. It took a long, *long* time, but eventually my back got better.

One of the most frustrating things for me was that I couldn't really bathe myself. I had to lie naked in bed while someone wiped me down and shampooed my hair. Eventually I'd have showers in a shower room, but they were hard, too. I'd lie in a big metal tray and someone would start up a big hose and hold the nozzle and spray me down and scrub me clean. These were not my favorite moments at BAMC. What helped is that the attendants who bathed me were all wonderful people who always played music during the shower. "What do you want to hear?" they'd ask. "Country music all the way," I'd say. "I'm in Texas, let's hear it all." I heard a lot of George Strait, Johnny Cash, and Tim McGraw, and it all made me feel like I was getting used to, even embracing, the Texas way of doing things.

Every little bit of progress I made was like seizing another small sliver of the freedom I once had. There came the day when I finally wheeled to use the toilet and took care of business all alone. Let me tell you, that was an *amazing* day. I felt like I'd grabbed a huge piece of freedom back.

Everyone at BAMC worked all day every day just to help people like me recover quicker and better. The folks there went out of their way to, as Joe put it, treat "the whole human being." My emotional state, my moods and feelings and energy levels, were just as important as any other data about me. The nurses acted like family and boosted my spirits when I was low, playing games with me, asking about my wife and children, making my recovery their own. As a result, I always felt like I was trying to get better not just for me but for them, too.

Early on, I spoke with a staff psychiatrist who asked a lot of questions about how I was doing. Very honestly, I was able to tell him that everything was going really well. I *did* feel positive about my progress, and I wasn't lying when I said I never moped or wallowed. In fact, I told the psychiatrist, I felt a little guilty about how well I believed I was doing.

The doctor jumped on that one word—*guilty*.

I knew what he was getting at: Was I feeling any survivor's guilt about being the only one of the five who made it out of that car?

I had thought about that a lot. I knew I would think a lot more about it as time passed, too. I knew it was something I would have to confront, along with all the other complicated emotions left in the wake of the incident. But the truth was, I could not do that then. I had to invest *all* my energy into one, singular goal: getting better, getting on my feet, getting home. I am not saying the mental and emotional side of my recovery was any less important. I just simply didn't see any way I could handle both recoveries at once, and it became more important to me to get back to my family. Just as my physical care and rehabilitation would continue long after I'd left BAMC and reunited with my family, so, too, would I have to try to heal all the other things about me that were broken.

One day I received a stark reminder of how difficult that healing process could be. The cousin of a friend of mine came to see me in the ICU to give me some advice. He'd lost both his legs in Afghanistan, and he was one of the funniest, most confident guys I'd met in a while. We talked about several things, and then he casually mentioned that he'd tried to take his life more than once. If I hadn't realized it already, I certainly realized then that beneath the external bravery of so many amputees, some very real demons can be lying in wait.

Therapy, however, can come in many forms, and some of my most healing moments had nothing to do with analysis or prosthetics or even medicine. Early on in my stay at BAMC, I learned that former president George W. Bush wished to speak with me. Bush was a Texan and his ranch was only a three-hour drive north of San Antonio, and the idea he wanted to call me and wish me well heartened me more than I can say.

"How are you, Mr. President?" I asked when he came on the line.

"Ben, I'm doing a hell of a lot better than you are," he said, the first of several times he made me laugh. We talked about the remarkable capabilities of U.S. military hospitals like BAMC, and about how I was doing and how strong I was going to come back. I assured him I had big plans for my future.

"Well, get yourself one of those prosthetics, get yourself a mountain bike, come on over to the ranch and I'll kick your ass," President Bush said. "You'll be back. I'm really proud of you. Fight on. I'll see you when you get out."

I was also greatly buoyed by the kindness of all the people who traveled to Texas to see me, including Suzanne Scott and Jay Wallace from Fox News. When they came into my room at BAMC they both gave me a big hug and presented me with a giant card signed by all my colleagues at Fox. Suzanne and Jay said they were happy to see me smiling and feeling positive, and I told them how grateful I was to them for literally saving my life. My Fox colleagues Dragan Petrovic and Bryan Boughton also came to see me, as did Jen Griffin and Sarah Verardo.

Even Seaspray made the trip—all the people who did so much to bring me safely back home.

Meanwhile, Sean Hannity, on whose nightly show I'd appeared, wrote me a moving letter: "My prayer for you is that God gives you the strength to face each day with the same resolve and courage you showed as a war correspondent," Sean wrote. "Thank God your three children will have their courageous dad back home where he belongs."

Bret Baier, the anchor of *Special Report* on Fox, was another colleague who warmly reached out. His son was born with congenital heart defects and has had four open heart surgeries and ten angioplasties. Bret reminded me in one of his emails that whenever they were in the hospital, they would all look at each other and say "we are one day closer to getting home," and they would celebrate that. It was something I reminded myself of every day—one day closer, one day closer, and with all the support in the world.

I also received a letter from Fox News host Johnny Joey Jones, a military veteran who lost both his legs in Afghanistan. In his letter he very kindly complimented my work before getting straight to what he called "the real talk." What followed was honest and practical advice that also managed to be inspirational. "This is a one-day-at-a-time game," he wrote. "Set small goals and celebrate the hell out of them." He told me to "get acquainted with pain, he's a stubborn friend," and to "voice my concerns and frustrations" rather than keep them bottled up. Most of all, he advised, I had to understand that I was not alone.

"Starting with the people who love you and are by your side already, and then the people who care for you, like myself, and want to help in any way we can and even those millions of Americans who have been thankful for your work, and now worried for your health—you are absolutely not alone," Johnny wrote. "Of all the things you may worry about, please don't let that be one of them."

Johnny was right. I wasn't alone. I was never alone. My brothers Peter and Michael came to San Antonio to see me at BAMC, as did my cousins Brent, Bennet, and Joe—even though I couldn't really sit with anyone for longer than an hour or so before I had to be off for therapy or treatment. Later on, my aunt Connie and her son Bob came by for a visit. Connie had been there with my father in Manila in the 1940s. She told me that of all my father's children, I was the one who most reminded her of her brother Roderick. "The adventurous spirit, and how you both just keep going forward, marching ahead" was how she put it. Connie also told me how my father used to call her whenever I went away to a war zone and ask her to join him in a prayer for me. In San Antonio, when we finally saw each other, we both began to cry.

"Oh, Benji" is all she said.

Connie had been by my father's side in Manila, and now, God bless her, she was by mine.

Perhaps the best therapy of all that I received at BAMC came from a helper named Huckleberry. He was short, had shaggy black hair, wore an orange vest, and did a lot of panting. He was a Labradoodle. He was part of a group of canines brought in by volunteers—in Huckleberry's case, a kind soul named Kris—to serve as therapy dogs for the patients. I was sitting in the physio gym, a big bandage around my eye after yet another procedure, when Huckleberry first came over.

He had a tennis ball in his mouth and dropped it in my hand. I threw the ball across the room. Huckleberry galloped after it and brought it right back to me, gently laying it in my hand again.

I lost it. I utterly broke down. I had cried before, little snivels here and there, but this time I wept for five minutes straight. I simply couldn't stop. Poor Huckleberry looked at me like he'd done something wrong. I reached down and hugged him close and continued crying. That Huckleberry had brought the ball back to me, just like my big chocolate Lab, Bosco, did at home, this mundane little game that we play with our dogs, struck me as the most wonderful thing I'd ever experienced.

It felt so perfectly, beautifully *normal*, and normal was all I wanted in the world—the way things used to be.

• • •

Kelly Brown spent more time with me at BAMC than probably any other professional (except for Jock, who never left my side). His focus as he put me through my rigorous resistance exercises and walking sessions was intense. He constantly examined and reexamined my right stump while we worked, looking for bleeding or pressure sores or anything out of the ordinary. Like me, he didn't want any setbacks. Also like me, he lived for the breakthroughs.

Before I even had my permanent prosthetics in place, Kelly had strengthened me to the point where I was more than ready for them. He had me walk along between parallel bars in my temporary boot and pylon, building up my upper leg muscles and my core, and every day I walked a little more and got a little stronger. I remember thinking I was fortunate to have the rare adult experience of learning how to walk. It happens when we're young and we can't even recall it, but I was doing it all over again. I found that I enjoyed the process of teaching myself how to take steps—it was another way I got to embrace the experience of being reborn.

One day, a patient in the gym was playing Latin music, and out of nowhere I asked Kelly how long he thought it would be before I could dance. He called over Major Kendra Howard, chief of occupational therapy at BAMC, and told her he needed her help with a matter of grave importance.

"Ben needs a salsa partner," he said.

Major Howard, God bless her, got right in between the bars with me and did a couple of cha-cha moves, and I copied her with one hand on the bars and the other in the air and my legs shuffling side to side. I didn't even have my prosthetics yet and there I was, *dancing*. We danced for just a few seconds, yet those were some of the greatest few seconds of my life.

NINETEEN

STRENGTH AT THE CORE

Things were going so well for me at BAMC that my two months cooped up in the burn unit's ICU finally came to an end. I was up and around on my temporary legs for short periods every day, and I regularly struck up nice chats with anyone I could find in the halls or the elevators or the gym, and I constantly corralled the nurses into games of Jenga and trivia contests. Dr. Williams, the burn specialist, even smuggled me out to San Antonio for lunch one day, as if I were any old tourist.

I think someone noticed all my gallivanting and said, "Maybe it's time for him to move on."

In mid-June, I moved out of the ICU and spent a week in a room elsewhere in the main hospital. Then I was transferred again, this time to a housing facility connected to the Center for the Intrepid (CFI), the prosthetics division at BAMC. The place was called Fisher House and it was one of ninety-eight Fisher Houses in the U.S., each designed for the families of military patients. My wingman, Jock, had been staying there since our arrival, and now I'd be moving in with him.

Jock—a name he picked up during his service—was my savior. He'd been with me from the very beginning, *before* the beginning. Since the bombing, he'd never left me, other than to return Pierre's body from

Ukraine. He was with me on the prime minister's train, with me in Landstuhl, by my side on the C-17 for those twenty-four excruciating hours. For just about every second of my stays at BAMC and Fisher House, Jock was my shadow.

Jock had served at the pinnacle of the British military. He had a slight but solid build and a deep Scottish brogue. He didn't say much and he always had an air of mystery. He looked the part of the silent tough guy watching out for you. But once Alicia asked him to accompany me to Texas, Jock essentially switched jobs. He became the best caregiver, and the best friend, I could have ever asked for.

Jock did *everything* for me that I couldn't. He rebandaged my wounds. He administered my eye drops. He gave me my meds. He taped up the photos of my children on the wall of my room so I would see them first thing when I woke up, and as Alicia sent me more drawings and letters they made for me, Jock taped them up, too. He played chess with me, and card games, and whatever there was to pass the time. He helped me reply to anyone who wrote a letter to me—hundreds of people. When we moved to Fisher House, he even rented a car and drove me on short day trips, to the Alamo and the National Museum of the Pacific War, and sometimes even for ice cream. Once in a while he would tell me about his far-flung adventures in the military, or about the mountains he climbed or the high-altitude jumps he'd taken out of planes.

The next minute he would clear some gunk out of my eye.

He wasn't only my right-hand man; he was Alicia's as well. When she sent me rules about staying off social media, it was Jock who enforced them. If she wanted something done for me, it was Jock who did it. He approached his job as caregiver with every ounce of seriousness and professionalism that he applied to everything else he's done. The tasks involved were different. The devotion was the same.

Our relationship changed over the months we spent together in Texas. We started out as colleagues, proficient in our different disciplines. We became quick friends, but then at BAMC our friendship

deepened. Finally, Jock transitioned into something like a father figure for me. My own father had passed away only a few months earlier,
and while I was strangely grateful that my father wasn't there to see
me go through this ordeal, I missed him terribly. Then Jock stepped
in. He helped me when I struggled, willed me on when I needed it,
encouraged me and reminded me of my goals. Jock reacted to me with
care and concern and even discipline when it was needed. Every day, I
was just so immensely *impressed* by how Jock conducted himself—he
helped other patients when he could, opened doors and carried pack-
ages, and even mopped floors if they needed mopping. He was, in every
sense of the word, a true savior.

Even so, I don't think Jock was thrilled when he learned I'd be
moving into his room.

To be fair, it was a tight fit. Suddenly we weren't together twelve or
fourteen hours at a time—we were together twenty-four hours a day.
Our beds were side by side, and I took over half the room, basically
invading the only sanctuary he had. The short two-hundred-yard trip
from Fisher House to the ICU had allowed Jock the sense that he was
on a mission—that he had somewhere important he had to be. But now
I was just there, with him all the time. I imagine it took the wind out
of his sails a little bit. Of course, he was a trouper about it, like he always was.

For me, Fisher House was a huge milestone. It was where I'd begin to learn how to live life again. Cooking, cleaning, other routine
chores. The first time I slipped into my normal, nonhospital bed, I was
totally overwhelmed. Something I took for granted my whole life was
suddenly a monumental blessing. Just my arrival at Fisher House em-
boldened me enough to envision a target departure date. I moved into
Fisher House on June 14, and my fortieth birthday fell on July 23. That
was it, I decided. I would be back in London in time to celebrate my
birthday with my family.

• • •

The move to Fisher House sped up the process of fitting me with my pros-thetics. Fisher House was next door to the unique and highly regarded Center for the Intrepid (CFI). It is an incredible complex that was built specifically to provide care for servicemen and women injured in Iraq and Afghanistan. It has taught hundreds of disabled servicemembers to use state-of-the-art prosthetics, learn how to perform everyday tasks and eventually reintegrate into society, and its success in this field has left CFI with no equal in the world.

CFI was also where John Ferguson and Del Lipe did all their fabri-cation work. Now they wouldn't have to spend time at the burn unit to work with me; they could just walk a few feet and find me in the CFI gym and try something out and go back to their workshop and tinker with it some more. John and Del worked out a strategy where John would handle my right leg while Del focused on my left foot.

Del, it turned out, had the harder task. The left foot was always going to be the bigger problem. It had been uniquely damaged and was in such fragile condition that one doctor asked me if I wouldn't rather just cut it off. But that was not an option—I wanted to keep whatever pieces of myself I could, even though I understood that could change in the future.

One big issue was that there was practically no place on my left foot and leg that could sustain any pressure. Most of it couldn't be touched at all. But Del found a small spot up near the knee that was fine and could be pushed on, and that was all he needed. While another spe-cialist worked on my ankle to keep it from warping downward and becoming permanently disfigured, Del fabricated an artificial foot that would fit around the existing foot and heel. "It was like we were building a keel for him so that when he walked forward it wouldn't be like he was walking on a peg," he says. What Del wound up with was a bit of a hybrid—a partial foot IDEO, or Intrepid Dynamic Exoskeletal Orthosis.

An IDEO is a customized, energy-storing, bracelike device that improves gait, stability, and function in limb prosthetics. The amazing thing about the carbon graphite device is that it provides feedback to the leg just like a normal foot would. The IDEO slipped under my heel and over the remnants of my left foot, and it had a strut that ran up the back of my leg and up to my knee, where it connected to the three-inch spot of good solid tissue Del had found. It was designed to integrate with my leg.

Meanwhile, John Ferguson fabricated a new socket that would attach to my right stump, and a customized, lightweight, carbon-fiber leg prosthetic that attached to the socket. A prosthetic foot rounded out the package. The big challenge was ensuring that the socket was as soundly attached to the stump as possible. John and Del used a traditional pin-locking system: a liner with a pin at the bottom of it was fitted to my stump, and that pin locked into the prosthetic socket, holding it in place. A simple button released it when I didn't need the prosthetic. They spent weeks refining both the IDEO and the right leg prosthetics, making sure everything was not only secure but also as painless as possible.

At the same time, a remarkable physical therapist at CFI named Raustin Harris was in charge of making me strong enough to handle my new hardware. A military brat whose father was in the Air Force, Raustin played high school and college football and admired the physical therapists who worked on his sore throwing shoulder (he was a quarterback). At first, he wanted to become a football coach, but soon concluded that physical therapists *are* coaches—they deal in movement, motivation, education, inspiration. While earning his doctorate in physical therapy, he secured a clinical rotation with the CFI's IDEO limb salvage program. By the age of twenty-six, he was named the physical therapist in charge of the entire program.

When I became Raustin's patient at CFI, I believed I'd accomplished quite a lot at BAMC and was walking fairly decently with the help of only a cane. Raustin's assessment, however, wasn't quite as rosy. "There was lots of stuff to work on," he says. "Range of motion, core strength, weak in the hips and glutes." He was right, of course: since the attack, I had lost some forty pounds, and for all the miracles the team at BAMC had worked, I simply wasn't as strong as I needed to be going forward.

Raustin set out to fix that. I met with him, as well as with Tony, Troy, and Marie, every single day so Raustin could check on my gait, see how my other injuries were progressing and put me through some blisteringly difficult workouts. He had me standing up, sitting down, balancing on one leg, bending, stretching, lifting, reaching, you name it. Lots of planks and overhead band work. If I had a full ninety minutes for our session, Raustin would lead me through four or five different exercises on my legs, four sets of at least fifteen reps each, moving from the hips to glutes to quads.

"I hammered those areas every day, and at the end of the workouts Ben was in agony," he says. "But he understood that these were the areas that would control his prosthetics."

Raustin also subjected me to a practice known as Blood Flow Restriction, or BFR, a process by which a tourniquet applied to the upper thigh cuts off circulation to the leg for the duration of a workout. This builds up lactic acid, which fatigues the muscles and fools them into thinking they are working at eighty percent of maximum strength, when in fact they are only working at thirty percent. "There are patients who come in who I can't ask to squat four hundred pounds," Raustin explains. "But with BFR, they can squat one hundred pounds while their glutes feel like they're lifting four hundred."

One side effect of BFR is that it temporarily turns your leg an uncomfortable shade of blue.

Another, as Raustin mentioned, is that it makes the workouts excruciatingly painful, particularly the third and fourth sets. But that part was okay with me. I never wanted to feel as if I'd been cheated out of a proper workout, and at the end of every session with every professional I'd ask, "Are you sure we accomplished everything we set out to do today?" With Raustin, I didn't have to ask that question. My ravaged muscles let me know we hadn't been the least bit cheated.

To my dismay, I didn't always get to have full ninety-minute sessions with Raustin. Along the way at CFI my many other nagging injuries needed attention. The skin on my left leg was not healing properly, which meant another skin graft. This time they took good skin from one of the only parts of me that hadn't yet been grafted from—my backside—and that was *exceedingly* painful. In the end I had skin taken from basically every part of my body except for my chest. I also had to slow down on my workouts to have some pins surgically removed from my left thumb. And I'd developed a deep and large blister across the back of my left ankle, which made walking all but impossible and wound up requiring a skin graft, too.

Still, my target departure date, July 23, was only a few weeks away. The progress I was making with my prosthetics convinced me I'd make it home for my fortieth birthday, and everyone at BAMC and CFI were rooting me on. "Ben's motivation became our motivation," says Raustin, the father of two young boys. "Get Ben home to his wife and kids."

In reality, my confidence had only lulled me into a false sense of security.

There was a problem with my left foot, specifically the remnants of the fifth metatarsal, the long bone that connects the ankle to the small toe. The problem required immediate surgery, and the surgery knocked me off my feet for the next two weeks. My progress screeched to a halt.

The dream of celebrating my birthday with my family disappeared.

TWENTY

YOU ARE THE MIRACLES HERE

The hallucinations mostly went away, but one of them was so vivid it has stayed with me ever since.

I was being wheeled from my room to get a CT scan, and as they rolled me down the hall, I felt like I was in Disneyland. Everything was animated and moving—walls, statues, potted plants—and when we passed through an atrium with trees and flowers I was sure I was in a rain forest.

Then I was in a room, and I saw the big CT scan machine, and as I was eased into it I was convinced it could go back through my life, all the way back to when I was a child, and reveal things to me about my past. It all felt very biblical, as if this were Judgment Day. Inside the CT scanner I suddenly started to believe that some very beautiful form of music had been taken away from me when I was young.

Because it had been taken away, I wasn't complete. In my mind, this beautiful music was the thing that made me whole. Not having it is why it took me so many years to finally connect with Alicia, with whom I was always fated to be. It was like we had somehow been torn apart when we were younger, all because I'd lost the music. When I found Alicia, I was given this magical music again, and finally I was whole again—my life had come together. The deprivation no longer mattered.

What was it that I'd been missing for so long? What had I been deprived of? I don't know, but for years I felt as if I wasn't so much living my life as watching other people live theirs. I was a spectator, on the outside, observing but not existing fully and freely in the moment. Then Alicia came along, and she gave me the key to unlock my real and actual life. Or perhaps she herself was the key.

It seemed to me that day that the CT scanner was God himself, taking me back and letting me see that I had everything I needed now.

• • •

I didn't make it home to be with my family on my fortieth birthday, and that was a temporary setback. As a consolation prize, Alicia made sure I had a little birthday celebration at Fisher House. She coordinated with an incredible social worker named Andrea Scott, who was my Case Manager at BAMC and handled so many different facets of my care: administrative issues, liaising with my family, helping with future plans, and on and on. Andrea was also someone I could talk to about anything. "We would sit together and have little conversations about his family and little things his girls had sent him," Andrea says. "Ben was so open about everything." It was Andrea who, among a hundred other meaningful accomplishments on my behalf, made sure I had a delicious chocolate sheet cake for my birthday party.

I received a second consolation gift for not making it home for my birthday: my mate Rick Findler and my childhood friend Cosimo Pandolfini flew in from London to celebrate with me in Texas.

Rick learned there was a rodeo happening in San Antonio that evening, and he decided I needed a proper night out. Jock drove us all there and dropped us off by the rodeo ring while he went to park the car. The minute he was gone, Cosimo cried out, "Beers!"

I was under strict orders not to consume any alcohol. But I hadn't had a beer in months, and anyway, how was I going to stop Rick and

Cosimo? They pushed me up a dirt track in my wheelchair as fast as they could, gravel shooting out behind us, until we reached the bar. Just as I was handed an ice-cold beer in a long-neck bottle and had taken my first swallow of the very best drink I'd had in months, a deep Scottish voice boomed out from behind me.

"Is that a beer, Benji?" Jock asked.

We were busted. I felt like a teenager trying to sneak my first beer.

"Mate, it's my fortieth birthday," I pleaded. "It's just a little beer."

"Just the one, then," Jock grumbled, and grabbed a beer himself.

Being in that bar with my mates felt like being back home. This was exactly what Rick and Cosimo and I would have done for my birthday even if I'd never been injured. We all shared a taste for spectacle and adventure. Rick and I, of course, had been together on the edges of civilization. Cosimo and I were the same way, and ten years earlier to the day we were sharing beers during a ten-thousand-mile car race through Iran and the Gobi desert to Mongolia. Hanging with these guys, drinking beers and having laughs, felt completely normal, and normal was all I wanted.

The rodeo was amazing. All these kid cowpokes jumping on the backs of rams, riders roping horses, bulls bucking the hats off fearless cowboys. About halfway through the show a man came over the intercom and said, "Ladies and gentlemen, we have a very special guest tonight," and he introduced me to the crowd. He explained how I'd been hit by a bomb in Ukraine and lost my friends there. For the rest of the show the locals came over and patted me on the shoulder and told me I was doing great and wished me luck. It was magical.

Yet it was also a bit unnerving, because I did not want all that attention focused on me. As I've said, I never wanted to be the story. For the rest of the show, I noticed people looking at me, and that felt strange. It was the beginning of my realization that, for the foreseeable future at least, people were going to stare at me wherever I went. Or people would learn about what happened to me and I'd have to share my story over and over. That was the way it was going to be, and I just had to get used to it. For me, normal would never be normal again.

• • •

At Fisher House I looked at a calendar and set a new departure date: August 29, my daughter Honor's birthday. No matter what, I resolved, I would be home by then. I even promised Honor over the phone that I would be there for her party. Alicia felt that I shouldn't have given Honor a set date, and so did Jock, but I did it anyway. There was still a lot of rehab and prosthetic fitting that needed to be done, and likely even a surgery or two, but I would not be deterred. I had missed one deadline; I wouldn't miss another.

Alicia and I had discussed the idea of her and the girls flying out to visit me in Texas sometime in July or August, but I told her it would be better if they just waited for me to get home. By then I was desperate to see my family, but having them there in the homestretch of my recovery would inevitably slow me down. And anyway, it was about a thousand degrees in Texas. Sometimes it felt even hotter than the Middle East. I promised Alicia and the children that I'd be home soon enough, and if I suffered any more setbacks, then we could schedule a visit.

The wonder of Fisher House was that it was a little community of its own. There were some patients who checked in and kept to themselves and rarely left their rooms, but for the most part everyone there was social. Like me, they valued the interaction. We were a bunch of broken people helping each other prepare to enter the real world again.

For me, being around people again, and being able to cook and eat meals together and sit around and share stories, was brilliant. I became especially friendly with a military veteran named James. James lived in Alaska with his wife and two young daughters, and they'd traveled to Colorado for a Wounded Warriors event. His wife was seven or so months pregnant, and they expected to be back home well before her due date. But her contractions began while they were still in Colorado, and because of her condition they could no longer fly home. They learned about Fisher House in San Antonio and drove there to wait out the pregnancy.

James was suffering from a very bad case of post-traumatic stress disorder, or PTSD. He'd been deployed to Afghanistan as part of a search-and-rescue unit, and his job was to chopper into battle zones and retrieve dead and wounded soldiers. "That's what we did all day, six or seven missions a day," James says. "You see things that are hard to forget."

James was there when the Taliban raided U.S. Camp Bastion in Afghanistan's Helmand Province, destroying eight aircraft and killing two Marines before being wiped out by U.S. forces. It was the worst loss of U.S. equipment in a single incident since the Vietnam War. James was supposed to come home after that, but he and fifteen other soldiers were stranded in Afghanistan without a flight home, so James wound up talking his way onto a C-17 for a five-day voyage back to Alaska.

He dealt with his PTSD as best he could and felt he had it under control—until 2015, when his best friend, who'd been deployed with him in Afghanistan, committed suicide. That's when the bottom fell out of his world. James submitted to two six-week, inpatient hospital stays to treat his PTSD, but nothing seemed to work. "I was hallucinating, not keeping track of time, losing myself, having angry outbursts, punching holes in Sheetrock," he says. "I simply couldn't function."

One day he returned home from work—except he hadn't been at work at all and had no idea how the day had passed. "Maybe I sat in my parked car all day, I didn't know," he says. He was holding his newborn daughter, Oakleigh, during a fireworks display on the Fourth of July, when he suddenly handed the infant to his wife and said, "I think I'm having a heart attack." It was actually a panic attack, one of many that followed.

James wasn't at Fisher House for treatment; he was just stranded there until his wife had the baby. We bonded quickly and spent a lot of time watching movies, playing chess, and just talking. We found we were able to be open with each other about how hard it was for us to reenter society after experiencing war. "A couple of times, we got really deep in the weeds," James says. "We both prided ourselves on being positive, but we acknowledged there were times when the bad thoughts crept in." James told me he was fine when he was around people, as he was at Fisher House. But when he was alone, the terrors returned. He warned me to prepare for those moments in the future, and he impressed on me that they could be far more dangerous than they seemed.

Our talks usually came back to the same question: *How do you deal with all the hard things you've seen?* There was no set answer for either of us.

James' stay at Fisher House helped him in a way he never expected. When he was part of a search-and-rescue team in Afghanistan, all he saw was soldiers with missing limbs and battered bodies. He would load them into his chopper and take them to a hospital and never see or hear from them again. Then, at Fisher House, he saw them again—patients arriving with missing limbs, broken and battered just like on the battle-field. Only now, he also got to watch them heal. "I'd seen human beings in their very worst state, and now I got to see them all patched up and playing basketball and laughing," he says. "For me, it was like coming full circle."

Similarly, James and his family helped me in a way I never saw coming. It had to do with his two lovely daughters, ages four and seven—pretty much the same ages as my two eldest girls. They, too, were stuck in Fisher House for several months, and their response was to turn it into their own personal playland. They were always running about and laughing and interacting with the patients, and when they saw me with their father they'd always run over and give me hugs and climb aboard my wheelchair.

Up until then, one of my biggest worries was how my three daughters would react to me in my new condition. How would they handle seeing me in a wheelchair with my "robot leg" exposed? How would *I* react to them? The day I played fetch with Huckleberry and got to hug him and hold him was my first step toward figuring out how to hold and hug my children when I eventually saw them in my new state. But now James' daughters took nearly all my fears away. It seemed like they didn't even notice my legs, and they didn't act the slightest bit weird around me.

"I knew Ben missed his kids and he just lit up when he was around the girls," James says. "He was happy to see they reacted the way they did."

During their stay, James took his family to a mall so the girls could visit a Lego store and build their own little Lego people. They picked out all the pieces they wanted, and they also picked out something for me.

"They came back with this little English-looking man in a Harry Potter sweater," James says, "and then they picked out a tiny pirate peg leg, a magnifying glass and an umbrella, and they made a Lego person for Ben."

When they presented me with my little British doppelgänger, I laughed harder than I had in months.

● ● ●

The metatarsal and ligament operation should have kept me in my wheelchair for several weeks, but I refused to be bedridden that long and Dr. Alderete agreed I could start walking just a few days afterward. We picked up where we'd left off, with the prosthetists fitting my new leg and me working hard to improve my gait.

Those sessions, though, were especially brutal. Every day I'd make it through ninety minutes at CFI with my team, walking every step as if it were perfectly fine, yet feeling intense pain firing through my foot with each landing. I had decided not to let anyone know, and at the end of the session I would walk round the corner and get out of sight before collapsing into the wheelchair Jock had waiting for me. Once again, I was afraid that if anyone saw how much it was hurting, we would have to slow down again. That was something I simply couldn't do.

The staff at CFI prepared me for my return to the real world in other ways, too. In some occupational therapy sessions, we'd lie on a bathroom floor pretending to fix a pipe under a sink. In others I'd practice crawling under beds to retrieve things. I even walked my buddy Huckleberry on a leash, so I could get ready for walking Bosco when I got home. Perhaps the most useful out-of-the-box therapy was preparing for the first time my three daughters saw me again. My great fear was that they would charge me and jump in my arms and send me flying. So we practiced holding heavy bags while kneeling, preparing me for the rush of little girls.

Every day I worked on my hand movement with my occupational therapist Meghan Lewis. She tried to make my fingers more flexible, improve my reflexes, and better my response time. We would play response games on a giant LED board, or on an iPad, testing my reaction times. The games could be fun, but afterward I noticed a slight mental slowdown.

Since then, I've found that it does take me just a bit longer than before the attack to react to things, to think of what to do, to analyze a situation, to find just the right words. It is not a very big gap, but I did suffer a traumatic brain injury and a frontal contusion, and that was something I had to keep monitoring. Quick thinking, of course, is the very nature of my job—making decisions on my feet, jumping on breaking stories, reacting to information pouring in. I planned to be highly attentive to all of my injuries, but I was especially keen to keep tracking of any improvements in my mind.

With ten days to go before my targeted departure date, everything was progressing well, and the intensity of the pain I'd felt lessened considerably. None of my doctors were all that happy that I'd imposed a kind of artificial deadline on them, and I think they all would have preferred I stay at Fisher House for at least another week or two. But they also understood my determination to get home, to see my family again, and they helped me race to my deadline in the best possible shape.

The partial IDEO on my left foot had been adjusted and readjusted and was working quite well. The prosthetic socket, leg, and foot on my right side were also just about there. I had learned how to carefully walk on my prosthetics, though I would need to walk with a cane and have a wheelchair handy. In terms of my journey to fully integrating the prosthetics in my life, I was only in the early stages of a long and challenging process. But with the prosthetics I could stand up, and I could walk, and most importantly, I could return to my family.

Somewhere around that two-week mark, the prosthetist Del Lipe had the idea to switch out the pin-locking socket that connected to my right leg prosthetic and replace it with something better—an elevated-vacuum socket. This was a battery-powered device that vacuum-sealed to my stump and theoretically provided a tighter, more comfortable fit. I agreed to give it a shot, knowing that if it didn't work, I could go back to my pin-lock socket.

Del made a new test socket prototype, and it fit on my stump beautifully. "A home run," Del says. "Worked great." He continued to fine-tune the socket until we were down to three days left. He brought it in for a final walk-through. I put it on and attached my prosthetic leg and foot, then got up and walked a single step.

The pain was *unbearable*. A searing pain shot up through my right leg that was impossible to hide. It hurt so much I literally could not walk another step in the new socket. It felt great just a day earlier. What went wrong? I tried not to feel too discouraged, but how else was I going to feel? How in the world was I going to leave in three days if I couldn't even walk a single step?

Del did what he always did—he took the socket and disappeared to his workroom. I don't think I slept more than an hour that night. The next day, Del was back with the same vacuum socket, only this time he'd removed the sleek, new liner sleeve he'd used between the socket and my stump. The new sleeve would not get torn up, as happened with the old one, but it was about a millimeter thicker, and that tiny millimeter was enough to cause me excruciating pain. Without the new sleeve, the socket vacuumed on and sat perfectly snug. Then I got up and took a step.

There was no pain. None at all. It felt great—better than great. It felt like part of my leg. I took several steps and was absolutely elated.

"I think you did it!" I yelled. "I think you bloody fixed it!"

The new liner had been the problem, and now the problem had been fixed. No one was more relieved than Del, except, of course, me.

• • •

Then it was time to go. The staff at CFI catered a huge barbecue meal as a going-away for me, and all my new friends gathered round and feasted on wings and ribs and slaw. I stood up for most of the party, hugging everyone and saying goodbye and trying not to cry. I also gave a little speech about how deeply grateful I was for all the care and friendship and love I had received. I said that I had loved every single day of my stay at CFI, and I meant it.

"I hope you all realize that you are the miracles here," I said to the doctors and nurses and therapists and attendants. "You give people back their lives. And you have given my life back to me."

Meghan, one of my occupational therapists, presented both Jock and me with white Stetson cowboy hats. All the staffers had signed the liner inside. I told her I was going to wear my cowboy hat home.

My final two days at Fisher House were deeply emotional. I had expected that, but what I hadn't expected was that I also felt quite scared. "The last five months have felt like I've been in a bubble," I said in one of my last video diary entries. Being on the cusp of leaving the bubble and going home, I said, "feels like a very strange place to be."

What was waiting for me when I finally rejoined the world? As well prepared as I thought I was, I also knew I had no way of knowing what would happen. I was determined to not be a burden to anyone, but what if I simply couldn't make it up a flight of stairs? Someone would have to help me then, and the thought of that filled me with apprehension. What if I couldn't even make it up the nine steps into the plane taking me back to London? If I had to, I told myself, I would crawl up step by step.

Most worrisome of all was the question of how Alicia and the girls and I would handle a new life that would be very different from the old one. I thought back to the first few times in the hospital when I looked down at my right leg and felt utterly surprised to see only a stump there. *What is that?* I'd think. I'd seen my full leg there for nearly forty years, and suddenly it wasn't there anymore. Suddenly I had a stump. Would Alicia and the children be just as surprised the first few times they saw me without my robot leg on? Would the girls be frightened of me?

The thought that they might be was more unbearable than any pain I'd experienced so far.

The uncertainty I felt in those final days reminded me of nothing so much as the dread of being in a war zone. It was the same sense of not being in control, of knowing that things will happen that you have no power to prevent. I reached for the same inner strength that got me through all those perilous situations, but even then, the uncertainty persisted. For the first time since the injury, I felt truly frightened.

A week or so earlier, Jock had driven me to a store so I could buy a pair of pants. I hadn't worn pants since I was in Ukraine, but I wanted to wear them for the first time the girls saw me. At the store Jock came into the changing room with me, and we struggled to figure out how to get them on me. I took my leg off and hopped around and got into position, all in this tiny space closed off by a small curtain and crowded with two grown men.

"No, not that way, Jock, move it here!" was a typical comment.

We could only guess what the other shoppers must have thought.

On my last day at Fisher House, I dressed in my new tan pants and a light blue button-down shirt. I wore my only fitting shoes: white sneakers on both my left partial prosthetic and my carbon-fiber right foot. My left hand was bandaged, but other than that I bore no scars or visible signs of having been injured. With my cane, I just looked like an ordinary fellow with bad knees.

I walked out of Fisher House with Jock pushing my wheelchair behind me, as he always did. A car was waiting there to take us to San Antonio International Airport, where a plane was waiting to fly us the five thousand miles to London. It was all happening now.

I was going home.

TWENTY-ONE

YELLOW JUMPSUIT

In London a special team came into our home to assess its suitability to house someone in a prosthetic or a wheelchair. Alicia watched as the men poked around narrow corners and frowned at sharp angles. There were no turning points for wheelchairs, no room for a chairlift, no bedroom on the ground floor. In the end they gave us a terrible grade. Alicia thought, *Well, it will have to do. And anyway, Benji is Benji. He'll figure it out.*

Alicia was as apprehensive as I was. Like me, she didn't know what to expect, and the perception of how bad something might be is inevitably far worse than the reality. We had always been an active, outdoorsy family: walks in the mornings, lots of sports and swimming, spirited strolls with Bosco. Now that was going to change. It is natural in situations like this to wish for things to return to the way they were. All you want is what you had before. But that wasn't realistic, nor was it even important. What truly mattered was that we would be together.

Fox News arranged for a driver to take Alicia and Rick to Farnborough Airport, outside London, where my plane would land. Fox also arranged for a plane to take Jock and me from San Antonio to London, and they sent Dr. Janette Nesheiwat, one of Fox's on-air doctors, to accompany me on the flight. We made it to London in only eight hours—the blink of any eye compared to my trip the other way in the C-17.

The plane landed at Farnborough and we taxied for a bit. I peered out the window to see if Alicia was there. In just a few minutes, her car pulled onto the tarmac and I saw someone pointing out the plane to her.

Then—there she was, on the plane, running down the aisle straight at me.

Before I could stand up, Alicia reached down and wrapped me in a hug and held on to me tightly, and I to her, as intense, overwhelming relief surged through me to finally be with her again. I felt the tears and I saw that Alicia was crying, too. I had promised her that I would make it home, and I did.

Before long we were both giggling and joking, a little shy around each other, I think, but also giddy with excitement. I walked down the seven steep airplane stairs on my own, gripping the side rail, and at the bottom an attendant handed me my black cane. Alicia joined me at the bottom and we walked together to the car. Rick, of course, shot video of the moment, and the footage shows Alicia and me smiling and laughing and simply touching each other on the arms, as if neither of us could quite believe the other was there.

There were so many questions Alicia and Rick wanted to ask me on the hour-long drive home, but at the same time we lapsed into occasional silences, as if there was nothing at all to say. With so much to talk about, where do you start? Back at the house, Alicia's parents were waiting with the girls, who had donned identical yellow floral party dresses. It had been a ritual of ours for the girls to wait for me to come home from work in the airy basement playroom, which opened onto a little courtyard. On the way in I would knock on the window, and the girls would race each other to be the one who let me in. They were waiting for me in the playroom now, beneath several big gold balloons that spelled *Welcome Home* and even bigger scarlet ones that spelled

Daddy. Croissants and orange juice and strawberries and cheeses were laid out on a table. As we pulled in front of our home, I felt butterflies in my stomach.

I stepped out of the car and walked slowly around a corner toward the door that led to the playroom. When I was outside, I knocked on the window as I'd always done, and I saw the girls spring to life. When I entered, Honor and Hero rushed me and cried out in joy. *Oh Daddy, you're home! We love you, Daddy, we love you so much!* Honor held on to me and would not let go. She clutched me around my legs, including the robot one, and wiped tears from her face. I had the thought: *I hope I don't fall over.*

I was overwhelmed. Perhaps even in shock. Here was my beautiful wife, and our beautiful children, and everything in the room was so bright and light and festive, so *perfect*, and Alicia's parents were crying as well, and I couldn't help but think of the journey I'd taken to get to this very room. I didn't know quite what to say, or even how to feel, it was all so monumental and powerful. I found that all I said, over and over, was:

I'm home again. I'm home again. I'm home again.

I sat on the sofa in the playroom and realized that Iris, our five-year-old who had greeted me when I came in, was now standing by herself in the back corner of the room, not quite watching as Honor and Hero and even Bosco jumped all over me on the sofa. Everyone else had formed this overexcited scrum around me the minute I entered, but Iris had chosen to keep back. It was clearly overwhelming for her, too, as if she couldn't make sense of all the emotions. She wouldn't even look at me, and instead just fiddled with her dress in the corner and swayed ever so slightly in our direction.

I had prepared for this moment. It was the moment I feared and dreaded most, but I had prepared for it. If Iris was afraid of me, that was okay, it wouldn't last. We'd both find a way to get over it. Don't overreact, just wait for all the excitement to die down. Alicia came over and scooped Iris up, and Iris whispered something in her ear, but I heard what she asked.

"Has he got Yellow Jumpsuit?"

The fuzzy-haired hedgehog. The one I'd sent her countless videos of. He was her favorite, him in his silly little jumpsuit, and she wondered if I'd brought him back. If I still had him. Or had he been left behind.

I reached down into my pocket and found him. I held him up, and Iris scrambled down from Alicia's hip and walked tentatively to the sofa. I handed Yellow Jumpsuit to her, and she held him and touched his hair and gave him a tiny hug. Then she sat down next to me on the sofa and leaned against me a bit, and she realized that Yellow Jumpsuit was home, and that was I home, too.

Then she hugged me and draped her arms around me.

In her sweet little voice, she said, "I love you, Daddy."

· · ·

I've had the same recurring dream for about the last fifteen years. It is World War II and I've escaped from a German prison camp. Now I'm being chased by the Germans along the side of a lake. I am desperately trying to avoid the gunfire coming from them, so I run around the lake, in a big circle, always just a few steps ahead of the Germans. Sometimes I'm running, sometimes I'm in a four-wheeler, sometimes I'm on a motorbike. If I keep moving, I'm okay. If I stop even for a second, I am dead.

The funny part about the dream is that I have never, ever *not* enjoyed having it. In fact, I love having it. When I wake up from it, I feel a real sense of accomplishment. I like that in the dream there is no time to rest, that I have to keep going as hard as I can every second in order to make it, and I even like that it never stops—it just keeps going. The dream varies from time to time: one night, I was cornered by the

Taliban, who found my hiding place and came in guns blazing, and I had to run across the rooftops and over the mountains in order to escape them.

Alicia was there when I woke up from that one, and when I described it to her, she said, "Oh my God, that's terrible." And I said, "No, Alicia, that was *great*."

Perhaps the dream is simply my mind reinterpreting my father's ordeal during World War II in a way that puts me in his place, desperately fleeing the enemy. Our experiences of war were very different, yet are somehow also linked, all the way to 2022, when I flew off to Ukraine just a few days after burying my father. He lost a great deal in World War II—his mother, aunts and uncles, a grandparent—yet he pushed on, kept going, and lived an extraordinary life. That inner strength was something I always admired and wanted to emulate, and now I'd have the chance to try to be as strong and resilient as he was. In a strange way, it was almost as if my father and I bonded most closely only after he was gone and I was on that airstrip in Poland, looking up at a Black Hawk the way he gazed at American airplanes dogfighting the Japanese in the sky. We shared a certain language of war, an understanding of its horrors, and that brought us closer together. And today, I feel that bond more vividly than ever—precisely when I need it the most.

Or perhaps the dream is my mind's way of letting me know I'll always be able to outpace the enemy. That everything I went through was worth it and everything I will go through will be worth it, too. I had the dream before I was injured, and back then it reflected the truth of what my life was like as a journalist—never resting, constantly running, staying one step ahead.

Now I suppose I am trying to outrun something else.

Most of the time, I feel like I am the same old Ben. Other times I realize I am someone new. It wasn't like I broke my arm or had appendicitis. My wounds will be with me forever. The question is, how do I rebuild my life around these new realities?

Sometimes it all feels very difficult. I have gotten so much better and faster with my prosthetics; maybe not quite running yet, but close, and certainly strolling at a more than decent clip. But I'm still only good on my legs for about twenty minutes at a time. I used to take Bosco for walks that lasted two hours. Now he gets shortchanged quite a lot. The other day I went with the girls to a climbing gym in London and sat nearby and watched them happily scale the walls. It was my first time ever as a father sitting on the sidelines while an activity was going on. That was hard. I know that someday I'll be able to get off the sidelines and get more involved, just not in quite the same way as before.

There are hard parts to every day. No longer can I just hop out of bed and get straight to it. My mornings are now devoted to a long ritual of assembly, as I put on my dressings and carefully reattach my prosthetics and otherwise prepare to be mobile. I take this ritual seriously, and if I am crisp and thorough about it, it sets a wonderful tone for the day. But sometimes it's just a hassle. Either way, it must be done.

Baths at the hospital were unpleasant and they remain the worst part of most days. Maneuvering in and out of a slick bathtub is never fun and falling to the ground is a regular occurrence. To get from the bed to the bathroom I have to mount a little scooter and scooch on over, or else I can lower myself to the ground and simply crawl there—though I will be having a special bathroom made for me to help me shower.

Through it all, the girls have been remarkable. They are not the least bit fazed by any of my odd rituals. In fact, they sometimes jostle with each other to see who will help me attach my legs. One time while they were trying to wrestle the leg from each other, they flung it and it bashed against my left leg, which immediately began to bleed heavily. It was the first time the girls had seen me bleeding since I'd been home, and they seemed a bit shocked. Alicia came by and gently ushered them away while I handled the bleeding.

My two elder daughters often have questions about the specifics of my injury. Alicia and I eventually told them I'd been hurt in a bomb attack, and after that Iris often told people that I'd been "bomb-shooted." The attack seemed to fascinate them more than frighten them. "Daddy, if the bomb hit here, how come it didn't take this hand off?" they'll ask, or, "Daddy, did you see your leg as it went away?" My answers are never too specific, but I don't lie to them, either. Alicia and I agreed early on that we would not try to shield the girls from everything having to do with the attack, and that includes not shielding them from me. When I am upstairs in my bedroom, I never lock the door, and if the girls wander in and see me without my leg or in some other state of partial disarray, then we deal with it, that's all. We don't ever want what happened to become something that needs to be covered up and never mentioned and ignored at all costs.

At the same time, neither I nor my family want what happened to me to be the prominent part of my identity, or our identity as a family. We want to just be who we are. The truth is, what happened to me has been much, much more of a gift than a horror. For instance, I hadn't sat down for dinner with Alicia and the girls for something like seven years straight. Now all I ever want to do is sit at the table with them and give them baths and put them to bed and read them stories and kiss them good night. Nothing—*nothing*—brings me more joy.

Not long ago I was in the living room with Iris when she stopped in front of me and put her arms out as if she wanted to be picked up. I'd been told not to do that, since I can't quite bend at the knees yet and leaning forward and gathering weight could cause me to topple over. But seeing Iris there with her arms outstretched, I just had to do it. I leaned against a wall, bent forward at the hips, and lifted her up as I prayed I wouldn't fall forward. I didn't fall, and I got to hold Iris and have her lay her head on my shoulder.

That moment, right there—*that* is the gift I've been given.

Alicia, of course, has been my hero. I have had to ask her to do things for me I never dreamed I'd have to ask her, and she has done them all with not a single word of protest or even a batted eyelid. She has embraced it all, and it has brought us even closer together. We both understand that it can only work if we are in it together, all five of us. We have become a real team now, stronger than ever, and anything that happens to me going forward will no longer be just about me. It will be about us.

When we got married, Alicia and I swore to be there for each other for better or worse, in sickness and in health. We've put that to the test and we've sailed right through.

• • •

I think a lot about the attack, and about Pierre and Sasha. Sometimes I replay the whole scene in my head. I imagine I'm back in that village, sitting on the ground, hurt, bleeding, trying to live, and in that instant, I suddenly realize that anything in life is possible—that we *can* get up when we get knocked down, and push forward and not be afraid.

What I don't like doing, however, is watching the footage Pierre shot leading up to the moment of the attack. I find it too hard to watch, and it brings the attack much closer to home than I like. The journalist in me should want to analyze the footage for any clues it might offer to what happened that day and investigate precisely who was responsible for the bombing and what weapons were used, something which is not yet clear—but that's still hard at the moment. The memories will come, and I will deal with them, but I don't need to make them any more vivid.

I also think back on how I was rescued and spirited to Poland. I think about all the things that could have gone wrong but instead went right—mainly because I was in the hands of such true professionals and extraordinary heroes. Sometimes I'd wonder why so much effort and energy was expended to rescue me. It was a message from Dave, one of the heroes who saved me, that provided me with an answer. "Pierre and Sasha's deaths were tragic, but not meaningless," Dave wrote. "In a conflict marked by propaganda, lies, corruption, and deception, they, with you, sought to bring to the light of truth the cause of right for history's witness. The role of reporters and information in this war is parallel with the role of the warfighter. Truth is the first casualty of war, but it survives when good prevails."

Dave, like me, sometimes can't quite believe the way things fell into place to get me home.

"The only reason I don't say that it was impossible," he explains, "is because, somehow, by the grace of God, it happened."

My friend Pierre pops back in my mind every single day. Sometimes it is the Pierre who was lying on the ground beside me, and when that happens, I work hard to summon the living Pierre. When I see photos of us together, I laugh and remember what he was like. Seeing Pierre with his bushy mustache and his goofy smile always makes me happy.

I remember being with Pierre in Afghanistan early in 2021, on the outskirts of Kabul. We'd been hearing the Taliban wouldn't enter the city, but we could see with our own eyes that they'd already gone in. So we had to report that the intelligence was wrong and the Taliban were already there. The precious little downtime we had in Afghanistan was the best. Pierre absolutely loved the terrain, and he loved the different tribes and people.

One day we came across some Afghanis racing horses straight up a very steep hill. We'd never seen anything like it. When the race ended, we saw two beautiful white horses and asked the mountaineers if they could let us ride for a bit. Pierre and I galloped into the peaceful part of the mountain, savoring the absolute silence, broken only by clopping hoofs. Far below us a war raged, but for about ninety minutes Pierre and I enjoyed a perfectly beautiful trot in the gorgeous Afghan mountains. We talked a bit, mostly about Afghanistan, and about how it was changing into a new country, a new world, and how the peace we were experiencing that very moment would soon be lost to the chaos of war.

So much goodness and beauty, we thought, *and soon it will be gone.*

When I am alone, I think about Pierre, and I believe with all my heart that he laid down his life to save me. I was in the back of the red car, in the middle seat—the death seat. I should have been the first person killed in the attack. Yet somehow I was the one who made it out alive. How? Why? Pierre jumped out of the car first, clearing the way for me to narrowly escape. He tried to protect me to the very end, warning me about the Russians, looking out for me. He was brave and selfless to his last breath. That day, he saved my life.

But every day that I knew him, he made me a better human. He taught me how to find the beauty in the ugliest places, as well as the goodness amid the worst of humanity. He fought even harder to make people's lives better than those who fought to destroy life. I think about Pierre every day and I hope he is still riding tall in his saddle, somewhere on a beautiful, untouched mountain.

• • •

I've spoken earlier about the duality I cultivated within me—the Ben who went away to cover wars, and the Ben who came back to London in search of a normal way to live. The challenge was always going to be bringing those two Bens together into one functional person. Meeting Alicia, taking a bureau job with Fox News, having children, moving toward anchoring—all of that was part of the process.

Then came the attack, which obliterated any distinction between my professional and personal selves. It was as if the bomb blew me into pieces—literally took me apart—before the heroes at BAMC and CFI reassembled those pieces and put me back together. But exactly who was the person who emerged from that reconstruction?

I can't say I spend a lot of time analyzing any psychological transformation I might have undergone. But what I can say, without any doubt, is that the person who is emerging from the bombing, from the more than twenty surgeries, from the continually painful rehab—the reconstituted *whole* Ben—is a better, stronger, and more joyful person than the one he used to be. Life is about moving, changing, doing new things, and I find there are more things for me to do, more challenges for me to embrace, now than ever before.

Every day I enjoy and cherish the simplest things: a ray of sunlight through the clouds, a lovely meal with my family, a piece of music. More than ever, I appreciate these fleeting little moments of life, and more than ever I understand that life and freedom are truly amazing, and to be cherished, and that we must fight to protect them.

However else I've been transformed, I now know for sure that I live in a world of good, a world where good will always triumph over evil, a world that requires we embrace every single wonder and hardship of being alive. I think of Bo, the courageous special operative who risked his life to save mine in Ukraine, and something he told me about what happened when his young son was diagnosed with cancer. "People just came out of the woodwork to help us," he said. "They didn't even ask what they could do, they just showed up at our door and got to work. It was amazing. Humanity is awesome." For this new clarity and positivity about life, I am forever grateful.

This book may have my name on it, but the story is really about all the people who came from around the world to find me, save me, and rebuild me. Who held my hand when I needed it held, who willed me on through the toughest of times. This book is about the community of courageous people who risk their own lives to help others, and about the opportunity we all have to join that community and be one of those people who help.

I am only one of many millions who have been touched by war, nearly all of whom have made bigger and braver sacrifices than I. As of this writing, nearly three hundred days into the war in Ukraine, the fighting continues, and the number of casualties keeps rising. Ukrainian troops heroically recaptured Kherson—the first town to fall to the Russians on March 2, 2022—but Putin's forces have not stopped shelling the area, and in just the last twenty-four hours three Ukrainians were killed there, and another seven were wounded. The war, it seems, will not be a short one.

What I've learned, however, is that fighting for what is good and meaningful is perhaps our highest calling in life. I may have a chance going forward to bring attention to the downtrodden everywhere, and I intend to seize that chance and strive to encourage the very best of humanity. Even now, during my recovery and rehabilitation, I am a participant in several war crimes investigations into Russia's attack on journalists in Ukraine. Sometimes I wonder if these trials will lead anywhere, or if any good will come from them, but, still, I am glad to be a part of them. At the very least, we must keep reminding the world of the atrocities of war.

I grew up believing in God, and, despite all the horrors I have seen and gone through, I still do. I know he was there with me in that forsaken village in Kyiv. I was on the scales, tipping back and forth between life and death, sucked out of my body, nothing but a hovering ghost, only to be pulled back in by the miraculous sound of my daughter's voice. I was given back to my wife and children. It wasn't my time yet.

All I can do is honor that gift by shining light into the blackness, and helping others find their way out.

And yet—it still calls to me.

I was at BAMC when I first had the thought that I could return to Ukraine in some capacity, maybe to interview President Zelenskyy, and maybe even sometime soon. I shared that thought with colleagues and was met with something like shock. Others, however, understood.

When Rick Findler came to see me at BAMC, he told me he was thinking about going to Ukraine himself. He wanted to see if my experience there had changed my view of war zones. He asked, "Benji, should I go?" and without hesitation I said, "Absolutely, go." I *still* didn't see any reason not to go in and get the story. Rick wound up not going, but he is still champing at the bit to be there. That pull, that calling, will always be strong for both of us. It never goes away.

I do hope I will be able to return to being a journalist in some way. Fox News has been absolutely brilliant at every step, sparing nothing to help me and my family, and I know they will save a spot for me somewhere, and I greatly appreciate that. Who knows, maybe I'll even be able to get out in the field and talk to people and find a story that way, back on the ground.

"Do I think Benji and I will step on a plane together one day and go somewhere to report something? Yes, I do," Rick says. "The drive we both have hasn't changed."

Yet while the pull remains, I cannot say it's a priority anywhere. The absolute iron will I had to get to the top of my profession by any means necessary isn't quite as intense anymore. For good reason. I am far too busy doing small, normal things.

The night I finally came home, after we put the children to bed, Alicia and I went to the bedroom and she saw me with my robot leg for the first time. She was curious about it and had questions. She wanted to see how it came off and on. It was all very casual, but it was also the beginning of a new chapter that we would write together. We'd gotten in and out of jams before, and here was another one and, boy, was this one a beauty.

But very shortly after that, we just went on with our lives. We resumed doing normal things. Breakfasts and baths and dinners and school affairs and tantrums and arguments and laughter and kisses. Life, nothing more, nothing less. We just went on.

That is all that matters. I made it home. I am back. Our lives continue. Everything I need or ever will need is here.

ACKNOWLEDGMENTS

I am indebted to so many people, but I'd like to start with a very special thank you to my wife, Alicia, and our daughters, Honor, Iris, and Hero. Alicia, you have always simply loved and supported me, and over the last difficult year you also saved me—many times. If I didn't have you and the girls pulling me through it all, I'm not sure what would have become of me. You have all blessed me beyond description and given me everything I could ever want. You are everything to me.

A heartfelt thank-you, also, to my larger family, including my siblings Barnaby, Andrew, Nonie, Peter and Michael, as well as Aunt Connie, and all my cousins who willed me on throughout. Alicia's parents, Kim and Scarlett, and her sisters, Imogen and Skye, along with Chris and Hugo, for rallying to our side when we needed you all the most. I am forever grateful for your love and care.

I very much want to remember my father, Roderick, and my mother, Jenny. Dad, you taught me the difference between right and wrong and showed me how to live a full and moral life. And Mama, you blessed me with your fierce spirit of adventure and curiosity, and you made me feel loved and protected. I love you both and I miss you every single day.

I want to thank my great friend and colleague Pierre Zakrzewski, who I believe gave his life to save my own. I will never know a better man than him. Nor will I ever forget Oleksandra "Sasha" Kuyshynova, who bravely sacrificed everything in service to her native Ukraine. The terrible truth of war reporting is that we can lose the best and brightest in an instant. But they will always live on within us.

Thank you to my fellow war correspondents and all the courageous journalists around the world—ours is a risky but vital mission, and the world needs you now more than ever. I am with you all in spirit, out there on the front lines of history. I owe so much to the many people with injuries similar to mine who have reached out and given me such great comfort and inspiration—I am proud of you, and keep fighting the fight.

I need to offer a very deep thank-you to the entire U.S. military— you rescued my father during World War II, and seventy-seven years later you rescued me. I could not be prouder of what America's armed forces accomplish every day, and what they represent to millions of people around the world. Your sacrifices and bravery are unmatched anywhere. A special thank-you to U.S. Secretary of Defense Lloyd Austin and U.S. Secretary of State Antony Blinken, and all the other government officials and employees who played a part in getting me home.

Thank you, as well, to the Ukrainian soldiers who were there to pull me to safety, and to Mykola Kravchenko and Serhiy Mashovets, two Ukrainian patriots who died in service to their country in the March 14 attack.

An endless thank-you to Sarah Verardo and everyone at Save Our Allies: your incredible commitment and expertise, and your devotion to the cause of helping those in dire need, quite literally saved my life. The team of heroes you helped assemble—Seaspray, Dave, Bo, Dr. Rich Jadick, and several others—beat the longest of odds, and risked their lives, to get me out of Ukraine. I owe you all my life.

I cannot say enough about all my friends and colleagues at Fox News, who sprang into action and stopped at nothing to bring me home. Thank you to Suzanne Scott, Jay Wallace, and Jennifer Griffin, who led the effort to rescue me, and to the Murdoch family for all their support. Thank you to Nicolle Campa, Dragan Petrovic, Bryan Boughton,

Maryan Jimenez, Tim Santhouse, Trey Yingst, Dudi Gamliel, Andrew Fone, Baz, Mal James, Greg Palkot, and everyone else on the Fox team. To every anchor, correspondent, producer, cameraman, and assistant who all reached out to will me on—thank you.

Thank you from the bottom of my heart to all the amazing medical professionals who quite literally put me back together. Thank you to Dr. Alicia Williams, my admitting physician and burn doctor at the remarkable Brooke Army Medical Center (BAMC), and to Dr. Joe Alderete, who pulled together a great team to stitch me up—among them, Dr. Casey Sabbag, Dr. Loftsgaarden, John Ferguson, Del Lipe, Kelly and Gil, as well as every nurse, and physio who was alongside me. Thank you to everyone at the Center for the Intrepid at BAMC, particularly Raustin, Troy, Tony, Marie, Carey, Meghan, Dr. Tiede, Jorge, and all the many wonderful nurses and physios and staffers who gave me back my life. A special thank-you to my case manager, Andrea, who helped us navigate the big and the small, whether dealing with endless paperwork, or finding a birthday cake—she did it all with a wonderful smile on her face. And thank you to everyone at Fisher House who willed me on, even the chess players who would never let me win— (thanks, John!). Thank you to all the Landstuhl doctors, and also to chief nursing officer Jody, who shepherded me and Alicia through those almost impossible early days.

And thank you to all the London doctors and physios who now look after me: Dr. Hettiaratchy, Dr. Collins, Dr. MacGreevy, and Dr. Ahmad, and Fazeela, as well as Sam, Helen, Allyson, Jack, and Dr. Philips at Remedy Healthcare. My UK case manager, Jason, has kept the whole show moving here, too. Thank you also to Nader and Elham, who graciously get me to wherever I need to be, and always with a smile on their face, and a story to tell.

Thank you, as well, to all the kind souls who swooped in to help Alicia and the children through those shaky early days—Alicia's friends Tash, Katie, Caroline, George, Martina, Eugenie, Joana, and all the

Queens Gate girls for making our children their children in the days that Alicia couldn't be there. All the mums from their respective schools, the girls' teachers and principal Mrs. Knollys, Mr. Fernandez, Miss Rafferty, Miss Coffey, Ms. McGregor, Ms. Hamdan, and the many others who stepped in and became even more like family to us. Their ballet school who made their time so incredible, and kept them so happy; Anna, Lindsey, Georgina, Eva, and Chloe and everyone at West London School of Dance, we thank you. Lor, our wonderful housekeeper, kept life as constant as it could be and has been part of our family for many years. Thank you.

To the many, many friends who have supported me throughout my life and particularly through this ordeal—thank you. Every day you remind me of how much support I have, how many people were willing me on, and how very lucky I am. A special thank-you to my friends who came to Texas, Cosimo Pandolfini, who has been my by my side for many an adventure, and Rick Findler, who braved the front lines with me and lifted my spirits when I was down. Thank you also to BJ and to Luke, who visited me, and brought me *Endurance*, a book about rescue and survival that truly inspired me.

So much of what happened could also not have been done without my great friend and agent Olivia Metzger. She has been guiding me and my career for many years, but during this she became family. Helping us, connecting us, guiding us, supporting us. I honestly think the world should be run by people as kind and intelligent as Olivia. Thank you also to Andrea, who has been there helping us all along as well—answering all the questions that I never could.

There is one person without whom this book would not be written, Alex Tresniowski. Alex brought this all together, listened patiently to every person and every story, brought out all the themes we wanted, then put it all together beautifully. This book is as much his as it is mine. Thank you also to Gail Ross for introducing us, and for all your help along the way.

I owe a great deal of thanks to HarperCollins, and to everyone there who has welcomed me and helped me tell my story, particularly Lisa Sharkey and Matt Harper—without you both, none of this could have happened the way it did. Thank you to the rest of the gang at HC—the copy editors, proofreaders, artists, sales and marketing teams, and all the others who played a part in bringing this book into being.

I also need to express my gratitude to the many, many people who I never met who have sent me letters wishing me well. Your encouragement and kindness toward me have been more meaningful than you'll ever know. And I want to thank all the people who have honored me by allowing me to tell their stories with the world, and all the fixers who made that possible. The people who let me into their homes, who trusted me with their deepest reflections, who accompanied me to the front lines, and who otherwise shared a piece of their lives in order to impact and inspire humanity.

Finally, I want to say a very special thank-you to Jock. You were there for me from the beginning and literally all the way through. You put your own life on hold for me and became my friend, my protector, my helper, my brother, my teacher. I could not have done what I did without you by my side. Thank you for everything you have given me— you mean the world to me.

ABOUT THE AUTHOR

BENJAMIN HALL joined Fox News Channel in 2015. A longtime war correspondent who has covered conflicts around the world, he has written for the *New York Times*, the *Sunday Times*, the BBC, the *Times* (London), Agence France Presse, the *Independent*, and *Esquire*. He lives with his wife and three daughters in London.